Acclaim for
Down Time: Great Writers on Diving

"This is real life experiences and observations by writers who know how to string two words together. A truly remarkable book (that) will no doubt remain a major work in the library of the oceans."
— *Scuba Diver* (Australia)

"This collection can hardly fail to catch the imagination of any diver. It's full of good writing and, as on an absorbing drift dive, you'll find you've been swept through to the end before you know it."
— *Diver* (UK)

"As NASA was quick to learn in space exploration, it is one thing to be able to explore outer space, and another to be able to verbalize one's impressions. The same holds true for underwater exploration, and *Down Time* accomplishes that feat admirably."
— *Long Island (NY) Advance*

"There is an overwhelming sense of the sensual and intellectual joys of breathing air underwater. This entertaining book is recommended to anyone who wants to see the world of diving rendered with elegance and originality."
— *DIVE* (UK)

"Not only are the authors mindful of the ocean's awesome power, but their voices also ring true with perspectives that come only from having been 'down there.' This singular anthology ... is a thorough take on the diver's world."
— *Aqua*

"Read this book for the writing. It is fresh, alive, amusing, touching, and at times frightening. Each author pulls you in a completely different direction, each story a distinct experience."
— AdventurousTraveler.com

"I found *Down Time* entertaining, educational (even for this veteran diver) and preeminently worthwhile for the discerning selection of its contributors. It is a bedside table book to browse and enjoy."
— Stan Waterman, underwater photographer and author

"As I turned every page I could feel the underwater world come alive. This is a must-buy for any diver or an excellent present for someone who isn't, and should be."
— DeeperBlue.net

"An absolutely fascinating collection of diving stories. This book is ideal for new and old divers alike."
— *Dive New Zealand*

"An eclectic, inspiring collection … providing insight to the underwater world and putting into words the wonderful experience of scuba diving. A refreshing approach indeed."
— About.com

"*Down Time* offers a wealth of viewpoints and voices, all centering on the experience of being 'down there.' "
— *Ocean Realm*

"We highly recommend this book to our readers and suggest you buy a copy for your dive buddy as well."
— OnScuba.com

DOWN TIME

GREAT WRITERS ON DIVING

EDITED BY
ED KITTRELL,
CASEY KITTRELL,
AND JIM KITTRELL

LOOK AWAY BOOKS

Published by
LOOK AWAY BOOKS
Austin, Texas

Publisher's Cataloging-in-Publication

Down time : great writers on diving / edited by Ed Kittrell, Casey
    Kittrell, and Jim Kittrell. -- 2nd ed.
        p. cm.
        Includes bibliographical references.
        LCCN 2001096159
        ISBN 0-9658344-4-1

        1. Deep diving--Literary collections. 2. Underwater exploration--
    Literary collections. 3. American literature--20th century.
    4. Underwater exploration. 5. Deep diving. I. Kittrell, Ed.
    II. Kittrell,Casey. III. Kittrell, Jim. IV. Title: Great writers on diving

    PS509.D44D69 2002   810.8'0355
                                        QBI01-701199

Printed in the United States of America

10 9 8 7 6 5 4 3 2 1

*For Grandma, who first brought
us down to the ocean...*

...and for Mom, who brought us back

"What shall it profit a man that he shall find again the pathway of the deep? What shall it profit him to be a diver, unless it be that there, as elsewhere, he may seek the proper balance of his human state?"

— *Philippe Diolé*

"Diving…is an active, physical form of meditation. It's so silent — you're like a thought."

— *Jerry Garcia*

CONTENTS

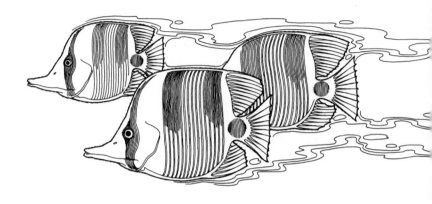

INTRODUCTION

It was one of our first boat trips to Grand Cayman's south side, and the divemaster was telling us about his passenger a month before. "He didn't *look* weird. On the way out, he was laughing and joking, like everybody else. But he was the last one in the water, and when we leveled off at a hundred feet, he just kept going down the wall. We tried to follow, but he went too deep too fast. He left a note in his dive bag. One of his fins washed up a week later."

Everyone who's been diving understands the impulse. Not the suicide part, but the urge to go deeper, stay longer. It's in our blood — like salt, like water, like the teeming bubbles of nitrogen that overpopulate our arteries.

Physics gives diving both its peril and its poignancy. Depth and time are absolutes. So from the first day of training, we learn that we must live and dive with limits — along with real, though minimal, risks. In the end, of course, that's what makes the scuba experience so acute. After all, doesn't the knowledge that time is short help focus the mind's eye on the immediate? And doesn't a little apprehension help us apprehend?

Danger, in fact, is a prime attraction for some. Stories from the '50s and '60s — including several selections here — often involve a lot of gin swigging, fish spearing, and male bonding. Over the years, as knowledge and the popularity of diving increased, fear (and testosterone) became less celebrated. Tens of thousands by now have experienced organized "shark dives" or other forms of orchestrated adventure. Defying death just ain't what it used to be.

A modern counterpart to the macho mentality might be trips to remote and exotic dive sites. Instead of sharks' jaws as souvenirs, today's trophies are log-book stamps from Sipadan, Palau, or the Seychelles. But bragging on the dive boat about virgin reefs often is as unsatisfying as recounting tales of terror, and for the same reason — sooner or later, someone will top you.

If not adventure, then what? For many, it's the chance to enter another world. Every dive *is* a little like a trip to a different planet. Gravity looses its grip; it's the closest counterpart to spacewalking. And the life forms are baroque beyond belief: There simply is no earthly analog for an octopus, nothing on land that looks like a flounder.

So we're entranced by the gap-toothed sneer of the barracuda, glinting like a dagger in the late afternoon light; the spotted moray jabbing from his hole like a cantankerous genie popping from his bottle. But we are interlopers in this other world. Despite the fossil facts linking us to aquatic ancestors, despite the genetic bequest that causes human fetuses to develop gills for a time in the womb, any conscious connection to our sea selves is long lost.

After eons on land, we have become an anomaly underwater. Even in places where the fish are familiar with us, we are nothing more than an occasional annoyance, a curiosity. Like the noisy neighbor who drops by unannounced, makes a spectacle of himself, and then leaves as suddenly as he came, we can't help sensing that life on the reef is an inside joke, and the joke's on us. We are, in the end, like guests at a party where everyone knows everyone else — except us.

And yet... Even limited by the laws of nature, even confounded by our clumsy attempts to communicate and comprehend, we find diving an immensely rewarding experience. Why? Perhaps it's because there are *no* limits to what diving teaches us about ourselves.

That is the theme underlying this anthology. The choices about what to include are necessarily personal. But we have tried to be representative of different styles, different eras, different attitudes. The selections span seven decades. The authors write about diving on reefs and in rivers, beneath the ice and under the earth, even in algae-glazed golf course ponds. And the range of equipment goes beyond traditional scuba and snorkel. One writer wears a glass helmet pumped full of air; another breathes by sucking from a plastic tube connected to a compressor on the surface.

Our roster of writers includes many familiar names. Clare Boothe Luce lyrically recounts her first reef dive in 1957. In a passage from a novel, Robert Stone evokes the suffocating sense of dread that can lodge in a diver's throat. Tim Cahill shares secrets from the set of an underwater epic filmed in Mexico. Years before his mega-selling *Jaws*, author Peter Benchley describes his first encounter with a real-live shark. Dave Barry confronts his fear of lobsters and other "unearthly biological contraptions."

The selections run the gamut. Some are comic. Some are serious. Some are just ripping good yarns. But despite the differences, all the authors — even the most macho or the most amusing — usually end up confronting the same thing: themselves. In poet Adrienne Rich's metaphor: "I came to explore the wreck...I came to see the damage that was done/and the treasures that prevail."

So Michael Crichton uses diving incidents to trigger discussions about the nature of wildness and risk-taking. The second-person narrator in James Hamilton-Paterson's short story realizes that his love of spear-fishing in the Philippines is driven partly by the need to reject his own childhood, his culture, his caste. Stephen Harrigan struggles not against his patrimony but against the "pedestrian imagination" that bars him from "truly perceiving the reef."

Conscious or subconscious, this search for something deeper is a part of why we dive. Once on a dank December evening, we walked into Westminster Abbey in London. We had come for the usual tourist reasons, to see the buried kings and the ancient stones. And they were there. But as we wandered in the winter twilight, something else happened.

From the center of the church came voices, keen and clear, braided together and rising like smoke toward the ceiling. The boys' choir was practicing for Christmas, hymns and harmonies seemingly as old as the abbey itself. And suddenly it was obvious: History isn't stones, it's songs. What resonates is not names and facts, but notes sung and heard over centuries. How many airs, how many eras had the old church shared with others like us? And how many of them had felt blessed, as we did, just to be there?

So it is with diving. We come for the usual tourist reasons, to see the sights. But sometimes, if we're lucky, something else happens. We stop memorizing dive tables and the names of fish; we look past the facts of physics and technology. Then the reef itself resonates, and we "hear" rhythms ages old, the way fish "hear" pressure waves of predators — and prey. It's only a moment, as brief as the bubbles that rise like smoke from our regulators. But it's an instant that reverberates across the years. Nothing is the same again.

Jacques Cousteau said it well: "Sometimes we are lucky enough to know that our lives have been changed, to discard the old, embrace the new and run headlong down an immutable course. It happened to me...when my eyes were opened on the sea."

It happens to the rest of us, too. In the end, we dive to explore not just the sea, but the self. And the adventure never ends.

Cayman Brac

WILLIAM BEEBE

From *Beneath Tropic Seas*, 1928

BROTHERING FISH

You are standing on a metal ladder in water up to your neck. Something round and heavy is slipped gently over your head, and a metal helmet rests upon your shoulders. Thus were the knights of old helmed by their squires for the grim business of war. Instead of a slotted vizor, however, you find two large frames of glass before your eyes. Turning your head you see emerald waves breaking upon the distant beach of ivory, backed by feathery palms waving in the sunlight against a sky of pure azure.

You wave good-by to your grinning friend at the pump, and slowly descend, climbing down step by step. For a brief space of time the palms and the beach show intermittently through waves which are now breaking over your very face. Then the world changes. There is no more harsh sunlight, but delicate blue-greens with a fluttering of shadows everywhere. Huge pink and orange growths rise on all sides — you know they are living corals, just as you know that the perfect clouds in the sky visible in the earliest light of dawn from Darjeeling are not clouds, but the snow peaks of the distant Himalayas. The first little people of this strange realm greet you — a quartet of swimming rainbows — four, gorgeously tinted fish who rush up and peer in at you. You reach out for them, and they vanish.

Now your feet touch ground and you walk slowly about on the cleanest white sand in the world. An ostrich feather of a sea-plume as tall as yourself sweeps against you; it is royal purple and might well be some weird fern from Mars. On a mound of sand you gently seat yourself, sand-colored crabs and small fish skittering just out of the way. You lean against a fret-work of purest marble while at your elbow is a rounded table of lapis lazuli on which are blossoming three flowers — flowers unearthly and which lean toward you of their own free will. Their petals are resplendent in hues of gold and malachite, and are fluted and fringed like some rare and unknown orchid. You reach forward to pluck one, and, faster than the eye can follow, the blossoms disappear beneath the fur of lapis velvet from which they seemed to sprout.

Dozens of fishes, all strange, all graceful and beautiful, play about you, nibbling at the coral, rushing toward the sponge which you have lifted from its place, hoping for some disturbed tidbit. When you sit quietly they gather closer, and peer in through the glass at you again and again. Their absurd mouths forever open and close, and if you are a good lip-reader you cannot fail to decipher the syllables which seem to issue in watery waves. They say, "Oh! Oh! Brother! Brother! Oh! Oh!" And you answer them in kind, speaking from the safe, dry, airy room of your helmet. They are so friendly, so curious, so utterly unlike the nervous, useless-lived inmates of our aquariums.

Your attention swings from wonders to marvels and back again. You begin to say things to yourself, gasps of surprise, inarticulate sounds of awe, you are troubled with a terrible sense of loss that (as the case may be) twenty, thirty, or fifty years of your life have passed and gone without your knowing of the ease of entry into this new world. Are you under water? There is no sense of wetness, the air you breathe is, if anything, better than that in the motor-boat rocking overhead. You hold up your hand and see little washerwoman's wrinkles on the soles of your fingers and you realize you are where you are. A great blue enameled fish glides past, then suddenly stands straight upon his head and mumbles something; a skein of fairy lace drifts against your helmet; to your friends in the boat it is merely a school of jelly-fish.

Only a moment has passed since you left the world overhead, or was it many hours? A gentle tug comes along the hose and you resent this reminder of an existence which you had almost forgotten. But you rise and half walk, half float to the swaying ladder, and regretfully mount it.

You find that you have been down forty minutes and another impatient adventurer is waiting to take your place. You had planned to tell the others all about it, but you suddenly find yourself wordless. You exclaim something bromidic which sounds like Marvelous! Great! Wonderful! then relapse futilely into silence and look helplessly into the distance where the emerald waves still break and the palms wave as if fairyland had not intervened in your life since you saw them last.

All I ask of each reader is this — Don't die without having borrowed, stolen, purchased, or made a helmet of sorts, to glimpse for yourself this new world. Books, aquaria, and glass-bottomed boats are, to such an experience, only what a time-table is to an actual tour, or what a dried, dusty bit of coral in the what-not of the best parlor is to this unsuspected realm of gorgeous life and color existing with us today on the self-same planet Earth.

GUY GILPATRIC

From *The Compleat Goggler*, 1938

MEROU THE BONEHEAD

As inward love breeds outward talk,
The hound some praise, and some the hawk;
Some, better pleased with private sport,
Use tennis; some a mistress court:
But these delights I neither wish,
Nor envy, while I freely fish.
— *The Compleat Angler*

or nearly three hundred years after Izaak Walton wrote his masterly treatise on angling, the world was content to accept him as final authority on the art, science, and mystery of catching fish. From time to time false prophets arose with patent hooks and chemical and electrical contrivances for knocking fish cold in wholesale quantities, while during the War the French infantry perfected an ingenious technique of chucking hand grenades into the Moselle River, thereby blasting many a gasping and disillusioned mud-gubbin out into the adjacent vineyards, and at the same time altering the course of the historic stream considerably. But all such devices of science, though effective, were flagrantly unsportsmanlike and therefore anathema to true amateurs of the rod and reel. However inefficient the old painstaking method, it was better, because fairer, than the new. Olde Izaak Walton, it seemed, had said the last word.

Then, suddenly, there came strange rumors. Somebody, somewhere, had evolved a radical and super-sportsmanlike manner of fishing — or, at least, so he claimed. His name (it was whispered by Seminole guides, Canuck gaffers, Highland gillies, and Negro boatmen) was olde Guyzaak Gilpatric. His method, they said, was called goggle fishing. Here is the dope on it.

First, because so many fish go through life handicapped by names like scrod, chub, guppy, and squid, I must explain that goggle fishing doesn't mean fishing for goggles, because goggles aren't fish. Goggle fishing is fishing with watertight eye-glasses and a spear — going down like McGinty to the bottom of the sea and scragging the wary denizens of the deep on their own home grounds. It is a sport so full of special tricks and dodges that I was minded to entitle this volume *The Sport of Kinks* until better judgment prevailed.

The first thing you need, to be a successful goggle fisher, is a body of good clear water. Personally I use the Mediterranean Sea and there is still plenty of room in it, but parts of the Atlantic, the Pacific, the Mexican Gulf, and the Caribbean will do just as well, and I know of many lakes and streams which would provide grand goggling. Next you need a pair of watertight goggles. I made my first pair myself from an old pair of flying goggles, plugging up the ventilating holes with putty and painting over it. The ones I now use were built for sponge and pearl diving.

In goggle fishing, the spear is thrust like a sword and is never thrown, for you cannot throw a spear much farther under water than you can throw a motorbus on land. The spear being of necessity fairly short, you will be wondering how it is possible to approach within striking range of a fish. The answer is partly skill but mostly the fact that a fish is less suspicious of a man swimming under water, right in its own element, than of men or boats floating on the surface. I discovered this characteristic quite by accident, shortly after I began swimming with goggles and before I had any thought of spearing fish. My idea, originally, was merely to study the submarine scenery and vegetation, which in the clear warm water of this Riviera region I believed would be worth seeing. Accordingly, one day, I shoved off from shore on an innocent sight-seeing trip. I had ridden in the glass-bottomed boats of Catalina and Bermuda and used waterscape boxes in the Gulf of Mexico, but I was unprepared for the breathtaking sensation of free flight which swimming with goggles gave me. It wasn't at all like flying in a plane, where you are conscious of being borne by something tangible; there was a nightmare quality to this sensation as in a dream of falling, and in that instant I knew how Icarus felt when his wings melted off. I jerked my head out of water and looked around to reassure myself. The bottom was fifteen feet below me, now, but every pebble and blade of grass was distinct as though there were only air between. The light was a soft bluish-green — even, restful, and somehow wholly appropriate to the aching silence which lay upon those gently waving meadows and fields of flowers. On the pinnacle of a rock like a little mountain I saw a dwarf palm tree. I swam down to study it. I touched its trunk and — zip! — the feathery foliage vanished as quickly as the flame of a blown candle. I came up for air, a portion of which I used in vowing to get the explanation of this flummery. I swam along on the surface until I found another palm tree. This one I sneaked up on (or rather, down to) stealthily. I reached forward, touched the leaves and — they weren't! But this time it hadn't fooled me. The trunk had simply sucked the leaves inside itself. If my finger had been an anchovy or other small fish, it might have been sucked in with them, there to be consumed for the nourishment of the confounded plant. I have since learned that this was the *Spirographis Spallanzanii,* not a plant at all, but an animal; but I decided right then and there that it is as foolhardy to go picking flowers on the sea bottom as it is in front of the cop in a public park.

Soaring on my way above hills and valleys upon which grew blossoms snowy white and flaming red, I came to a great submerged rock from one side of which projected a wide shelf. I could see small fish flashing in and out along its edges, and went down to have a look at them. The underside of the shelf, though only ten or twelve feet below the surface, was fifty feet above the bottom. It was heavily grown with weeds. Anchovies and sardines — thousands of them — were swimming around eating this foliage. But — I rubbed my goggles — they were swimming on their backs! Had I discovered a new species? At first I couldn't believe what I saw; then a larger fish happened along and he, too, was swimming on his back. I dove right under the ledge, where it was dark and cold, and shooed the whole crowd out. As soon as they left the shadow and saw the sunlight above them, they turned right side up and went their ways like any self-respecting fish. Now those fish did not have to turn on their backs in order to eat weeds on the ceiling, for fish can eat in any reasonable position as well as in several which I might call scandalous. No, those fish were not aware that they were on their backs. They thought that the ceiling was the floor; they didn't know up from down, being in practically the same fix as the oldtime aviators who, lacking instruments for flying in clouds and fog, used to lose all sense of direction and turn upside down without realizing it until loose objects, such as bottles, commenced falling upwards out of the cockpit. My discovery that sardines and anchovies can swim on their backs is fraught with significance and I have no doubt that after the publication of this book I will be the recipient of appropriate decorations and degrees from scientific organizations the world over.

Feeling pretty pleased with myself, I swam around to the other side of the rock. This face of it went down sheer until its base was lost in deep blue gloom. I had the sensation of flying in the chasm of a New York street. Below me I saw vague forms moving — fish, they were, and whoppers. I watched them for a long time as they lazed about in stately grace or poised in rumination, fearing that my slightest move would startle them. But presently a couple came up to within fifteen feet of me and seemed to be giving me the once-over. I thought I'd return the compliment. Swimming down as close to them as I dared, I hovered in suspense which they didn't seem to share. They were big fat dorades; I was so close that I could see the gold bands on their blue foreheads but I didn't hope that they'd let me come closer. I needed air and started upward. Suddenly, I found myself staring into the eyes of what looked like a German U-boat — a three-foot loup in a fine state of indignation, his dorsal fin jutting up like the bristles of a bulldog. Without stopping to think, I cut loose my right and pasted him square on the jaw. I heard a whirring sound like that of wings as Mr. Loup departed under forced draught.

I came to the surface, gulped some air, and pondered on the sorry state to which I had fallen in being unable to knock out a three-foot fish. No use kidding myself, that blow wouldn't have bruised a stewed oyster. My knuckles were bleeding but this merely meant I'd scratched them on the little needles along the edge of his gill. I filled my lungs, swam down a way and indulged in some expert mental shadow boxing. I soon found the trouble. Being full of air and therefore lighter than water, my punches simply pushed me backward, and the harder I walloped, the faster I shoved myself away from what I was aiming to hit. Also, I was using a lot of energy in resisting my tendency to float up to the surface. I blew out my air, sank down further, and uncorked a couple of rights and lefts. Now, I felt that my blows really had a little steam behind them. My body being heavier than water, my punches had something to react against.

I was feeling pretty tired, and I noticed that the skin on my fingers was shrivelled from being in the water too long. As I swam toward the beach, I thought of what I'd learned — namely, that some fish are not afraid of swimmers, and that to exert power under water you have to empty your lungs. It occurred to me that in these discoveries might lie the basis of a new sport.

It was along toward the end of October and the days were pulling in pretty short. Sometimes the storm clouds would stack up on the mountains to the west of us and swallow the sun by four in the afternoon. Our front yard, the Mediterranean Sea, was as full of fish as ever and so clear that you could see bottom in sixty feet, but with the diminishing sunlight, its greens and blues and purples had taken on a grayish tinge and it was turning colder every day. All summer long we'd had priceless sport. For month after month, with water temperatures of between seventy degrees and eighty degrees, we goggled for six hours a day; and more than once, in August, we had worked the beach and harbor of Sainte Maxime for eight hours straight. We had learned things about fish and their habits which certainly no fisherman and perhaps no scientist had ever known; we had observed submarine phenomena which we couldn't explain ourselves and which were so strange that we hesitated to mention them to outsiders lest they stroke their chins and murmur "Oh, yair?"

Around the ends of the rocky capes of Antibes, Ferrat, and Roux, on the reefs beyond the Lerin Islands and at the foot of the red rock cliffs where the Esterel Mountains go into the sea, we had looked down upon scenes of grandeur beyond the dry land's grandest and had seen no billboards. But now, if we goggled for only half-an-hour, diving down fifteen or twenty feet or following the fish into the rock grottoes which the sun never penetrates, the cold knotted us up until we couldn't have speared a crate of dried codfish with a mile of picket fence. All along the Riviera, from Le Lavandou to Menton, people were complaining about the unmuffled speedboat motors when what they really heard was the chattering of goggle fishers' teeth.

November 1 dawned a rotten day, with a high layer of clouds moving eastward and another scudding oppositely just above the sea. Ducks, geese, and herons were going over in bunches headed for Egypt, proving that ducks, geese, and herons do not believe all they read about the Riviera's winter climate. But at ten o'clock, faithful to our daily tryst, the Antibes Local of the Gogglers' Guild convened with spears on the wave-pounded beach, and a solemn lot we were. Our number included a Russian, two Frenchmen, an Irishman, and myself, so that all we needed to make a comic dialect story was somebody named Levinstein. But we didn't feel like comic stories, for any of us could see with half a goggle that our sport was finished for the season.

There was a long silence while we viewed the desolate scene.

"Well, what shall we do?" asked somebody.

"What is there left to do?" snarled somebody else.

"I know!" I said, brightly. "Let's go fishing!"

For a moment they stood as men stunned; then —

"Fishing?" inquired an incredulous voice. " — Fishing? You mean — fishing?"

"Yes, fishing. With hooks and lines and bait and boat. Regular old-fashioned fishing."

Well, the sheer novelty of the stunt swept them off their feet, and so an hour later we were bobbing at anchor just west of the tip of Cap d'Antibes. We dropped our lines over the side and waited for something to happen. For a long time nothing did happen. It was a frightful bore. Even when we started pulling in a few fair-sized ones our tackle kept getting tangled in our yawns. Once a man has goggled — once he has hunted his fish, stalked it, pursued it in its own element and finally speared it or lost it as he or the fish was the smarter — the conventional flummery of hooks and lines and rods and reels is merely so much near beer.

By noon I'd had enough — and at noon, precisely, the sun came out. "Madam Chairman and beloved lodge sisters," I said, "I'm going overboard for a final hack at it." I peeled off, put on goggles and knife belt, took my five-pronged spear and slid over the gunwale into the (br-r-rh!) water. I swam toward the Cape, which at that point goes down from the surface in sheer walls like the facades of Florentine palaces. At some places the depth was thirty or forty feet; at others I could not see bottom at all and everything below was the dark velvety blue of February evening sky. A school of black mullets like a flock of crows passed under me. I saw a rock as big as a church swinging back and forth, back and forth; I lifted my face out of water to keep from feeling dizzy and to remind myself that I and not the rock was see-sawing in the swell. And when I put my face under again I saw Merou the Bonehead.

I didn't recognize him, at first. I only knew that the biggest fish I'd encountered to date was lying on a rock ledge twenty feet below me. I blew out my air and sank toward him. Before I was halfway down I realized that even if I speared him I'd have a tough time bringing him up. I stayed where I was, watching him. He returned the scrutiny with an eye the size of a horse's. His pectoral fins barely stirring, he moved majestically along the ledge and as a beam of sunlight struck him I saw that he was a merou. I swam up to the surface and back to the boat with the news.

Now the merou is a fish rarely landed in this part of the Mediterranean. They have a pair of them in the Oceanographical Museum of Monaco — their largest living specimens — who have been ogling the tourists through the plate glass side of a tank for over twenty-five years. Dr. Oxner, the aquarium director, does not know how old this piscatorial Darby and Joan were when caught, nor can he say with any certainty which is Joan and which Darby. This is due to the merous' confusing habit of changing sex from time to time, so that, in meeting one socially, a person doesn't know whether to take off his hat and hand her an orchid or to slap him on the back and ask about the missus.

Well, we sat in the boat and discussed the merou problem while the wind from the snow-capped Alpes blew the clouds across the sun again and I developed a fine case of three-way shivers. All we knew about the merou was that he was a very athletic and very nasty fish and that, having speared him, you should not grab him by the throat lest he crush your fingers in his edged and armored gills. Or maybe hers. At length we decided to row to within fifty yards of the rocks, put a rope around me and my spear and try our luck. When I yanked on the line the people in the boat would yank me and (we hoped) the merou up to the surface; meanwhile I would be giving him appropriate treatment with my knife.

I went over the side again — and have you ever noticed how much colder cold water is the second time? It was awkward, swimming with the line around me; my feet kept getting tangled in it. The merou was still on his ledge but he had moved a little way along it to a spot where he could watch the proceedings better. He wasn't in the least afraid of me as I started down but as soon as he spotted the rope curling and snaking in the water, he ducked back into a crevice out of sight. Evidently, some time in his career, he'd had an unfortunate experience with a line with a hook at the end of it and he wasn't intending to fall for that gag again.

No, the rope wouldn't do. I went up for air, cast it off and called to the boat to stand by. I now planned to dive, plant the spear in him and then let go of it, hoping that once wounded he wouldn't be able to swim far. When he had tired himself by thrashing around I could go down again, do a little knife work on him and eventually bring him to the surface. Soon I saw the great brown snout come out of the crack — cautiously. I was about to dive when it bobbed in again. I lay on the surface and watched and shivered and cursed and shivered and watched for fifteen minutes. Yes, and shivered. Suddenly, further along the crack, I saw his whole head. I beckoned the boat to come closer; then, blowing out all my air to enable me to sink fast, deep and with minimum effort and water disturbance, I went for him. Just as I came within range — say four feet — he started back into the crevice. I couldn't see his body, only his head, and I knew I would have to hit him quickly and hard. "Alright, Sir or Madam, as the case may be!" I said. "How's — THIS?"

I let him have it smack on the dome. There was a frightful ruction, a brown flash and — Merou was gone!

All five spear teeth had struck him at once. The shock of the blow through the spear handle made my elbow tingle as though I'd hit a rock. Each of those teeth was needle-pointed and razor edged. But as far as I had seen or felt, not a single one of them had gone more than skin deep into Merou. Merou the Bonehead!

Well, the season was over, but though some of us had brought in well over a hundred fish, it ended on a sour note for me. It was easy enough to blame the loss of Merou on the cold water; perhaps, in August, I could have pasted him harder than I had done in November; and surely, if I hadn't had to strike him on the head, I would at least have put a dent in him. But still, I felt that something was wrong. I suspected my spear.

That spear, hand forged and highly tempered, had brought in some pretty big fish. With it I had landed an octopus measuring six feet seven inches across the tentacles, which is somewhat larger than the *octopus vulgaris* is supposed to grow. But it should have gone into that merou — and it hadn't. Why not? The answer came from India.

A Britisher just back from Benares was telling us how simple the *fakirs'* tricks are when you stop to figure them out. The famous couch of nails, for instance, is simply so chuckfull of nails that the holy man's weight, distributed over the points of all of them, does not bear down hard enough on any one point to puncture the skin. "But," said our friend, "I offered any number of the filthy brutes seventy-five rupees to sit on a single nail and there wasn't a sportsman in the lot." Right then and there we saw the trouble with our five-toothed spears. The force of the blow was divided among all the teeth and distributed over too great an area of the fish. What we needed was a spear with a single point in which the full force could concentrate.

For weeks, then, as the word went forth and good gogglers got together, the marble tops of cafe tables throughout the Alpes Maritimes were covered with pencilled designs for single-toothed harpoons. We went over to Monaco and studied the late Prince Albert's collection of native spears, as well as the various harpoons which he used on his expeditions. We whittled wooden models of harpoon heads and jabbed oranges and loaves of bread with them to study the nature of the wounds. At last we figured out a design which looked good to all of us. This was a steel shaft three-eighths of an inch square and forty inches long with a forged triangular head and a hinged barb. The barb would close tight against the shaft while entering the fish but would swing out at right angles at the slightest opposite pull, thus preventing the fish's escape. This entire gadget screwed into a tubular socket which accommodated the wooden handle, the handle varying in length to suit the individual owner. My own harpoon, when finished, was six feet long and weighed about two pounds. It was a mean weapon. The only trouble was, we didn't know whether we could hit anything with it. Our five-toothed spears had given us a margin of error of almost six inches, but with our new harpoons every shot had to be a bull's-eye.

By the middle of summer we began to realize that certain individual fish spend their time in fixed neighborhoods and that others, like some migratory birds, come back to the same spot at the same time year after year. We had known all along that many rock fish, such as the sargue and the serre, are confirmed stay-at-homes and we had come to know a number of them by their first names, but it surprised us to meet a giant linte for the third successive August in a little cove where no other linte is ever seen. At least three of us saw and recognized him and we believed that he recognized us. Then there was a big old loup who lived in a hole in the base of the jetty of the Port Mallet; as a rule loups are nomads, but this fellow didn't move twenty yards in seven months.

Thinking of this and talking it over with the others made me wonder if Merou — Merou the Bonehead, the only merou any of us had seen thus far — was not one of these confirmed home bodies. Certainly he'd known all the ins and outs of that crevice as though he'd lived there a long time. The rock ledge outside it was a comfortable front porch for him to loll around on, there were plenty of octopus for him to snag and all in all, if I had been a merou, I couldn't have asked for a nicer set-up myself.

The more we discussed it the more likely it seemed that we'd find him still in business — a year older, a little bigger but, we hoped, with arteries and skull no harder.

On September 28, in calm, warm water and bright sunshine, four of us went out to look for him. Because I remembered the bottom from the year before (somehow a goggle fisher acquires the knack of finding his way by the bottom, unerringly, and rarely uses landmarks) I had no difficulty in leading the caravan to the proper territory. And there on his ledge, look-ing up at us with his horsy eye, lay Merou the Bonehead, exactly as I'd first seen him eleven months before!

I suppose I should have gone down and mingled with him at once. I could see his whole body and I believe I could have scragged him then and there. But a merou is not to be taken lightly, and at least two of our number had legitimate scientific reasons for wanting to see such a grand specimen at large. The grand specimen, however, had legitimate scientific reasons for getting to hell out of there, and he did so with a single caudal flip which took him into the crevice and out of sight. It was apparent that he didn't care for crowds.

Now by all rules of goggling, this merou was my own personal fish; and so, with the gesture of a matador ordering his *peons* from the ring and hoping to God that they won't take it seriously, I waved my companions away and prepared myself to settle the thing, man to Merou. They swam away twenty yards or so and lay with their faces under water to witness the drama of life and death which all of us felt would shortly unfold.

As for myself I floated with spear couched and knife loosened in its sheath, ready to sink down and deal the lethal blow. He didn't come out. I lay there for a long, long time — so long that I studied his old homestead in detail, even noting that the seaweed on his ledge — a species of white flower very like the gardenia of dry land — had a foot-wide path worn through it by the friction of his belly.

He stuck his head out exactly where I knew he would. I went down, just as I had planned and hoped and dreamed and known I'd go down. I drew back my arm, sighted along the spear, uncorked my soul and — SMACK!

There was a frightful ruction, a brown flash and — Merou the Bonehead was gone! When I came to the surface I found that the steel shaft of my harpoon was bent two inches out of line.

Excalibur had failed us!

Thus ended the goggling for another season.

JACQUES COUSTEAU

From *The Silent World*, 1953

A STATE OF TRANSPORT

One morning in June, 1943, I went to the railway station at Bandol on the French Riviera and received a wooden case expressed from Paris. In it was a new and promising device, the result of years of struggle and dreams, an automatic compressed-air diving lung conceived by Émile Gagnan and myself. I rushed it to Villa Barry where my diving comrades, Philippe Tailliez and Frédéric Dumas, waited. No children ever opened a Christmas present with more excitement than ours when we unpacked the first "aqualung." If it worked, diving could be revolutionized.

We found an assembly of three moderate-sized cylinders of compressed air, linked to an air regulator the size of an alarm clock. From the regulator there extended two tubes, joining on a mouthpiece. With this equipment harnessed to the back, a watertight glass mask over the eyes and nose, and rubber foot fins, we intended to make unencumbered flights in the depths of the sea.

We hurried to a sheltered cove which would conceal our activity from curious bathers and Italian occupation troops. I checked the air pressure. The bottles contained air condensed to one hundred and fifty times atmospheric pressure. It was difficult to contain my excitement and discuss calmly the plan of the first dive. Dumas, the best goggle diver in France, would stay on shore keeping warm and rested, ready to dive to my aid, if necessary. My wife, Simone, would swim out on the surface with a snorkel breathing tube and watch me through her submerged mask. If she signaled anything had gone wrong, Dumas could dive to me in seconds. "Didi," as he was known on the Riviera, could skin dive to sixty feet.

My friends harnessed the three-cylinder block on my back with the regulator riding at the nape of my neck and the hoses looped over my head. I spat on the inside of my shatterproof glass mask and rinsed it in the surf, so that mist would not form inside. I molded the soft rubber flanges of the mask tightly over forehead and cheekbones. I fitted the mouthpiece under my lips and gripped the nodules between my teeth. A vent the size of a paper clip was to pass my inhalations and exhalations beneath the sea. Staggering under the fifty-pound apparatus, I walked with a Charlie Chaplin waddle into the sea.

I looked into the sea with the same sense of trespass that I have felt on every dive. A modest canyon opened below, full of dark green weeds, black sea urchins and small flowerlike white algae. Fingerlings browsed in the scene. The sand sloped down into a clear blue infinity. The sun struck so brightly I had to squint. My arms hanging at my sides, I kicked the fins languidly and traveled down, gaining speed, watching the beach reeling past. I stopped kicking and the momentum carried me on a fabulous glide. When I stopped, I slowly emptied my lungs and held my breath. The diminished volume of my body decreased the lifting force of water, and I sank dreamily down. I inhaled a great chestful and retained it. I rose toward the surface.

My human lungs had a new role to play, that of a sensitive ballasting system. I took normal breaths in a slow rhythm, bowed my head and swam smoothly down to thirty feet. I felt no increasing water pressure, which at that depth is twice that of the surface. The aqualung automatically fed me increased compressed air to meet the new pressure layer. Through the fragile human lung linings this counter-pressure was being transmitted to the blood stream and instantly spread throughout the incompressible body.

My brain received no subjective news of the pressure. I was at ease, except for a pain in the middle ear and sinus cavities. I swallowed as one does in a landing airplane to open my Eustachian tubes and healed the pain.

I reached the bottom in a state of transport. A school of silvery sars (goat bream), round and flat as saucers, swam in a rocky chaos. I looked up and saw the surface shining like a defective mirror. In the center of the looking glass was the trim silhouette of Simone, reduced to a doll. I waved.

The doll waved at me.

I became fascinated with my exhalations. The bubbles swelled on the way up through lighter pressure layers, but were peculiarly flattened like mushroom caps by their eager push against the medium. I conceived the importance bubbles were to have for us in the dives to come. As long as air boiled on the surface all was well below. If the bubbles disappeared there would be anxiety, emergency measures, despair. They roared out of the regulator and kept me company. I felt less alone.

I swam across the rocks and compared myself favorably with the sars. To swim fishlike, horizontally, was the logical method in a medium eight hundred times denser than air. To halt and hang attached to nothing, no lines or air pipe to the surface, was a dream. At night I had often had visions of flying by extending my arms as wings. Now I flew without wings. (Since that first aqualung flight, I have never had a dream of flying.)

I thought of the helmet diver arriving where I was on his ponderous boots and struggling to walk a few yards, obsessed with his umbilici and his head imprisoned in copper. On skin dives I had seen him leaning dangerously forward to make a step, clamped in heavier pressure at the ankles than the head, a cripple in an alien land. From this day forward we would swim across miles of country no man had known, free and level, with our flesh feeling what the fish scales know.

I experimented with all possible maneuvers of the aqualung — loops, somersaults and barrel rolls. I stood upside down on one finger and burst out laughing, a shrill distorted laugh. Nothing I did altered the automatic rhythm of air. Delivered from gravity and buoyancy I flew around in space.

Fifteen minutes had passed since I left the little cove. The regulator lisped in a steady cadence in the ten-fathom layer and I could spend an hour there on my air supply. I determined to stay as long as I could stand the chill. Here were tantalizing crevices we had been obliged to pass fleetingly before. I swam inch-by-inch into a dark narrow tunnel, scraping my chest on the floor and ringing the air tanks on the ceiling. In such situations a man is of two minds. One urges him on toward mystery and the other reminds him that he is a creature with good sense that can keep him alive, if he will use it. I bounced against the ceiling. I'd used one-third of my air and was getting lighter. My brain complained that this foolishness might sever my air hoses. I turned over and hung on my back.

The roof of the cave was thronged with lobsters. They stood there like great flies on a ceiling. Their heads and antennae were pointed toward the cave entrance. I breathed lesser lungsful to keep my chest from touching them. Above water was occupied, ill-fed France. I thought of the hundreds of calories a diver loses in cold water. I selected a pair of one-pound lobsters and carefully plucked them from the roof, without touching their stinging spines. I carried them toward the surface.

Simone had been floating, watching my bubbles wherever I went. She swam down toward me. I handed her the lobsters and went down again as she surfaced. She came up under a rock which bore a torpid Provencal citizen with a fishing pole. He saw a blonde girl emerge from the combers with lobsters wriggling in her hands. She said, "Could you please watch these for me?" and put them on the rock. The fisherman dropped his pole.

Simone made five more surface dives to take lobsters from me and carry them to the rock. I surfaced in the cove, out of the fisherman's sight. Simone claimed her lobster swarm. She said, "Keep one for yourself, *monsieur*. They are very easy to catch if you do as I did."

CLARE BOOTHE LUCE

From *Sports Illustrated* magazine,
September 16, 1957

THE REEF AND ITS TREASURE

Methought I saw a thousand fearful wrecks,
Ten thousand men that fishes gnawed upon,
Wedges of gold, great anchors, heaps of pearl,
Inestimable stones, unvalued jewels,
All scattered in the bottom of the sea.
   — *Shakespeare*

I was in Bermuda sixteen days. Fourteen of them ranged from drizzly and bad to torrential and foul. They were not days on which an experienced and prudent instructor like Park Breck would take a rank amateur diver into the open sea. We continued to make shallow dives in the coves from sheltered beaches. I learned to clear my mask under water, to make the proper underwater signals, to judge how many weights I needed in order to sink or rise without fighting the water. I saw little interesting. I picked up a shell or two deep from the bottom. And once I saw an angelfish lurking in a dark cave. In the murky waters he looked like a sunset seen through smog. He didn't count.

Meanwhile, Park Breck and Jeanne, his attractive blond wife and partner, generously sought to divert me, and at the same time maintain my interest in diving. They asked me to parties with their fellow Bermuda divers and their wives.

There were the Teddy Tuckers; the Ted Goslings; the Henry Whites; the Freddy Hamiltons; Peter Stackpole (who was doing an underwater movie documentary about treasure diving) and his wife; and the Mendel Petersons. Mr. Peterson, curator of naval history for the Smithsonian Institution, was in Bermuda studying the underwater artifacts brought up by the Bermuda divers, especially those brought up by Teddy Tucker, the thirty-three-year-old diver who, it seemed, had done more "bottom time" than any diver of his age in the West. Divers all, they welcomed me warmly.

"So you've joined the Flipper Fraternity?" somebody said.

"I suppose, at my age, I am mad even to try."

Mr. Peterson then said, "The best diver I ever knew was a California woman seventy-three years old."

(Nice people, divers.)

Someone else commented, "Oh, everybody's diving; lung-diving is the fastest-growing sport in the world. I saw in the *Times* today, it's a thirty-million-dollar business."

Breck said, "It would grow a lot faster if they'd make equipment easier for instructors to handle and safer for amateurs."

"Then you'd have every tourist in the island out on the reefs. In the end, they'd be plastering underwater signs in every lagoon: 'Use Breck's Polyps Paste for your ginger-coral itch.'"

"'Do you get the bends? Use Tucker's Little Decompression Pill.'"

Divers are as generous with their talk as they are with their energies. In the moist Bermuda evenings, I listened to diver talk.

Talk about equipment: some liked hard fins, others softer. Some liked the Squale mask, others the Pinnochio. Some swore by Cousteau's scuba, others by the Scott Hydro-Pak. Teddy Tucker, the treasure diver, went down without any flippers, breathing from a tube that stretched all the way back to an air compressor unit on the boat. But *he* worked for hours on end at the bottom. They all agreed on only one thing: no matter what kind of equipment you use, don't use it after late evenings and many drinks. And most of them were off smoking.

They talked: about how many hundreds (or thousands) of dives they had made. And about what ill fortune they or their comrades had suffered on them: about how eardrums had cracked and bled beneath the pressure (especially when you forgot to equalize); and how a man's sinuses could swiftly plug up at certain depths; about how it felt to have sharks smell your knees, or to have your breathing tubes get tangled in the rigging of new wrecks; and how nitrogen narcosis, called the rapture of the depths, can make a man so drunk he can throw away his mouthpiece thinking himself Neptune, only to join the God of the Sea and his wrack forever.

And everybody talked of wrecks.

"There are more wrecks lying on the Bermuda barrier reef than in any other area in the world."

They showed me their diving treasures, while the Smithsonian man beamed with antiquarian joy: artifacts they had plucked from the ocean floor, all encrusted thickly with centuries of sea lime. There were ancient pewter porringers, long-barreled clay smoking pipes, breech-loading swivel guns, jugs, breastplates, sword hilts and scabbards, a pair of dividers like those Amerigo Vespucci used in discovering the New World.

Each one talked about "my wreck." That was the next one he intended to dive on. He described it minutely, hinting at the significant signs of real treasure that he would find there; but he jealously concealed its exact location.

"There's gold in them thar wrecks..." "Teddy Tucker hasn't found it all..."

Then Teddy Tucker showed me his treasure: the greatest underwater bonanza found in western waters in this century. He had made the discovery at a depth of only twenty-five feet, in the remains of a Spanish wreck off the coral reefs. He spread the golden pieces before me, but not as a miser spreads his gold. He displayed them as a champion displays his trophies, a soldier shows his medals to good friends. There were a sixteenth century bishop's pectoral cross of purest gold, studded with seven sea-green, sea-smooth emeralds; pearl earrings; and a fist-heavy ingot of mellow Spanish gold with romantic markings, "Pinto" and "Don Hernandez."

I held the pieces one by one in my hand. I admired them, but I admired more the courage and patience of the man who had found them. Myself, all the treasure I wanted to find was a golden angelfish.

You never enjoy the world aright, till the sea itself floweth in your veins...
— *Traherne*

At last, the sunny days came. Captain Taylor took us six miles out to the divers' Promised Land: the barrier reefs. We dived at the northeast point of the breakers; off the reef where the *Elda* wreck lies; and seven miles out to sea in the North Rock area, by the old beacon light, inside the barrier. In these areas we made four dives. Which was which, and where was what I saw there? As memory often merges the events of scattered days of joy into "the happy time," so now I merge my memories of diving off the reefs into one long dive.

As I remember this long dive, I see myself hauling my heavy tank-burdened body over the side of the *Wally III* and backing down the ladder. I am eager now to shed my weight under the sparkling waters. Happily, I let go. Splash, and down a few feet. I wait for my flippers to be thrown over the side. I tug them on, level off on my face, and look down.

There, twenty feet below, lies the liquid blue jungle of the barrier reef. The world of madrepores and polyps, where everything is endlessly living and endlessly dying to make the fretted vaults and cloistered crannies of the reefs, of rose coral, star coral and brain coral, coral with antlers and horns, coral formed like tree stumps, anemones and sponges; and crustaceans, worms and fishes... And there in the midst of this wild calm jungle, lying ten feet deeper, I see a lovely sandy cave.

Along its walls the waving purple fronds of the sea's fans beckon me in... I glide down to the cave slowly, at a gentle plane. I can see a hundred feet in every direction. As far as I can see, the colors are Gauguin's and Cézanne's and Seurat's. Beyond, the dark blue-green sea belongs to Dufy and Chagall. I'm almost on the cave. I throw back my head and my flippers' tips touch the shining floor. I feel like a bird lighting on a bough. I sink to the bottom of the cave and, lolling, look up at the even feathers of bubbles which fly up from my neck, expanding as they go into shining silver mushrooms, little pearly parachutes, seeking the far sun. Overhead, the bottom of a rowboat is a liquid yellow plate, and on the distant surface, the shadowy silhouette of the *Wally III* is a salver of spinach jade. Circling high, thirty feet above me, looking like little frogs, are a pair of skin-divers with spears. They drift slowly along on top of the waters searching out snappers and rockfishes below.

I look around. Park is there. He is pointing a camera in a plastic case at me. His body is the color of polished amber, his short hair is a dandelion going to seed. Jeanne is there, on her knees, head down, fingering through the creamy sand. It flows like gauze through her fingers. Her hair is floating straight above her, a restless golden halo. She looks up, as I sink beside her, and her eyes are smiling aquamarines.

She sees something and slides away, beckoning me to follow. We glide to the crannied wall, sink on our elbows and peer under a coral ledge. We see two crimson enameled wires and peer deeper and see an elegant lobster, rich with eggs made of old red Chinese lacquer. Jeanne tickles its antennae and it draws into its dark palace with mandarin dignity. She wishes to tease it more. I don't. I have only an hour to explore my enchanted liquid acre. Only an hour to find an angelfish...

I drift up the crenelated sides of the cave. I begin to see they are deliciously full of mysterious holes. A delicate, slightly open mouth pokes out of one of them. I flipper slowly over to the hole and stop. It is the white beak of a rainbow parrot fish. I see his body, the length of my forearm. It is all purple and red and gold. I swoon softly closer. We eye one another. I, in what delight can he know?

Oh, small squamulose miracle, do you know what we say on the land above? "Imitation is the sincerest form of flattery." These blue fins I wear are for your sake. This monastic silence I keep is in order to share yours.

Gently I reach out, hoping he will let me scratch his beak. He withdraws, flicks around, shoots out another hole and, squittering delicately, hovers in the clear water ahead. I pursue. He moves and hovers again. We repeat our little ballet.

Three little sergeant majors, gold with black stripes, draw across my chase. They tipple at me. I bubble at them. *Delighted to meet you, young gentlemen.* They pass, and I glide, like a gondola, among waving gorgonians, in and out of madreporic crevices. I am careful to skirt the ginger coral — the poison ivy of the sea. I am cautious with my hands and knees lest they be punctured by the waving black needles of the giant sea urchins, like pincushions in their coral waterpots.

Now I see another parrot fish nibbling on the rocks in the distance. I cruise toward him, among the sea plumes and antler coral. I stop. Down behind a mauve sea fan I see a childhood friend, a starfish. I float down and pick it up and carry it to Jeanne, as a child on the beach carries a shell to his mother. Jeanne sees my delight. She takes it, caresses it knowingly and lets it float away.

I float away, too.

I no longer think whether I am cold or tired, or down too far, or breathing right. I no longer struggle against gravity. How can one struggle against what does not seem to exist? I am living in the sea, outside myself. All but my eyes, which are seeking that angelfish...

Park taps me on the arm, points. Jeanne is examining something on the reef. We swoop down. Park makes a sign of a pistol pointing. Jeanne crawls along the pale pink and green lime-encrusted thing he is pointing at, and I crawl with her. I do not know that I am looking at the barrel of an ancient Spanish cannon from a wreck come to grief in the days of the conquistadors. I swim away. I prefer the great bonito that I see in the distance.

The bonito is a quarter of the size of me, and much prettier. Park follows with his camera, resigned to my disinterest in artifacts.

Park points again. I see two lean, gaunt, steely fish, two and three feet long, swimming toward us. Barracuda. I stop and hover. They do, too. They tipple and show their ugly teeth. I flipper and push my ugly mouthpiece in their direction. *Plug-uglies, that's what you are. Git!* They flick away.

Near a tiny waterpot, I meet a little fish, no larger than the palm of my hand. He charges my mask furiously. It is a demoiselle fish, spunkily guarding his coral *garconnière*, where his mistress lies sleeping. *If the demoiselles could talk they would talk like sharks, surely.*

Now I see a shimmering cloud moving toward me. It is a large school of small fry, curtaining a spear diver who searches the waters below, his long steel spear glinting in the blue. I swim deliberately through it. The cloud shatters into a million soft glassy splinters all around my body, and reforms into a silver curtain in my wake. I turn to Park, laughing with glee. My mouth opens. Water rushes past my mouthpiece. I experience a moment of terror. I spit out the water through the tube, breathe slowly, spiral, and drop to the floor of the cave, and rest.

How long have I been here? I do not know. Time, under water, is not a mechanical thing. It is organic. You judge it by the strength and slant of the light, the warmth of your blood, the rhythm of your breathing. But for dark and cold, and weariness and lack of air, you might stay there forever and call it a minute.

In the cave, I have a sudden visitor. It is a man-fish. He shoots across the sandy floor pulled by a small yellow submarine half the size of his body. It is Pete Stackpole, who has joined us in his Link underwater scooter. He rollicks around in the cave like a dolphin, shoots away, comes back, and lets go of the power-diver. It drops to the sand. Park, Jeanne, Pete, and I huddle around it. Pete explains by signs how to use it. Park wafts Pete his camera, and he and Jeanne take turns with the scooter. They disappear and reappear out of the dim green where visibility stops. *It must be my turn now.* When Jeanne comes by again, I flipper hard and take the handles from her. I press the switch and am away, sweeping over cranny and cave, shearing through sea plumes and grasses. They break into brown clouds as I reap them. I see fish torpedo away from me as I come toward them. *I can't find an angelfish this way.*

I whoosh back, gripping my mouthpiece which loosens in the wash of the scooter's propeller. I drop the scooter when I pass over the cave. It sinks to the bottom like a sodden banana. I feel freer — and fishier — without it. I resume my whimsical game of floating tag: with silver breams, with a platter-shaped, navy-blue doctorfish, with gray snappers and chub, with a pink and black Spanish hogfish and a speckled redhind. I encounter a pair of brown pipefish. They have seahorse heads, but their bodies are straightened in a stiff horizontal. I wait for them to race by me into the stretch. Unexpectedly, they become a medium's trumpets: they fly backward.

Now I notice with delight that a large rockfish weighing about thirty pounds is swimming in a friendly fashion at our flippers' tips. I test his friendship. I spurt away. He spurts after me.

Suddenly my rockfish friend whooshes away, toward a rock ledge. Too late. Overhead a skin-diver has been stalking him. The skin-diver comes down in a long powerful diagonal. His steel spear speeds through the water. My friend is impaled and is carried struggling and bleeding to the top.

I am angry. I breathe harder. I lie on a rock to rest.

I know about the feeding cycle. Little fish eat plankton, bigger fish eat the little fish. Why should I care if man then eats the big ones? Have not many fish eaten man down here? I remember Teddy Tucker's gold and emerald pectoral cross... They have even dined on bishops.

I go cruising again in the gorgonian forest. And then — there, in a perforation of the coral maze, I find *my* treasure. I find the jewel of the lapidary sea, the rarest gem of ray serene the bright and fathomed caves of ocean bear. He is as large as two of my fingers. His body is all lapis lazuli; his brow is sprinkled with turquoise. He glows all over. I don't move, for I know now that a teasing movement will drive him away. Oh, to be a Saint Francis of Assisi among the Fish! Poor Saint Francis, born out of time, never to have met Brother Jewel Fish and Sister Sea Fan at their own level! What canticles you would have sung to them! What holy converse held with them about their Maker!

The jewel fish sinks, forever, from my eye. Never from my mind. I slide away. I still hope to see an angelfish, a heart-shaped angelfish, a Fra Angelico angelfish, a Queen of the Angelfish, in all her sunlit glory.

I see a shark instead. Out there where the waters grow dim, the ugly gray squaloid form is cruising toward us. My finger shoots like a rifle barrel, pointing it out to Park. Pete sees it, too, and flippers hard toward it. Park snaps its picture. Breathlessly watching, I sink to the floor of the reef. Park swings his camera toward my face to catch my expression. Then he swims after Pete. The shark disappears in the gloom. Overhead the spear divers are still floating and stalking. I remember that the blood of wounded fish sometimes attracts sharks. So does Park. He thumbs everyone up. Only Saint Francis would feel completely safe down here. The day is ended.

You never enjoy the world aright, till the sea itself floweth in your veins...
— Traherne

I sit alone in the stern of the *Wally III* and look back to the jagged reef. Gentle waves kiss its rough lips. The sea around grows wider and the reefs disappear. A flying fish shoots out of the azure veil that conceals their beauty. Foolish fish to flirt with gravity! Oh happy mortal who has for an hour eluded it!

I had indeed rejoiced and delighted, "as do misers in gold and kings in sceptres," in God's Little Underwater Acre.

PETER BENCHLEY

From *Holiday* magazine, August 1969

"I KNOW WHAT I'M DOING HERE, I THINK"

My breath came in with a noisy, rattling whoosh, then stumbled out in liquid bursts. My movements were slow and unsure, my balance nonexistent. Through a blue haze I saw curious faces staring at me — like the student audience at a momentous operation. Or maybe an autopsy.

I closed my eyes and slipped backwards, tripping over my elongated feet. I landed on my back with a resonant bong!, then looked up to see the irate visage of my instructor behind his faceplate. He motioned for me to stop horsing around and get back to work. Levity, I was reminded, has no place in the business of learning to scuba dive — especially not at the bottom of the eighteen-foot-deep practice pool, with about five minutes of air left in your tank. The instructor waved the onlookers away from the windows, and we recommenced the arduous routine of removing all our equipment and putting it on again.

For almost all of recorded history, man has been trying to re-acclimatize himself to the water environment enjoyed by his ancestors before evolution deprived them of their gills. Perhaps there is an element of chemical or emotional atavism involved—after all, blood is chemically quite similar to sea water. But whatever the impulse may be, as far back as 360 B.C. Aristotle was writing about divers who worked under water by breathing from metal containers of air, while a fifteenth century Italian, whose neighbors must have branded him an eccentric, spent his days off with his face submerged into a horse's leather feed bag filled with water.

As recently as thirty years ago man was still a clumsy stranger to the water. In 1941 it was a hot item of gossip that a nutty actor named Errol Flynn was spearing fish underwater. And then, in 1943, Jacques-Yves Cousteau bettered all known breathing devices with his aqualung and mankind was on its way back to the sea.

I have spent most of my life in and on the water, but never had ventured under it. Oh, sure, a little snorkeling here and there, to ten or fifteen feet or so, but not with the freedom of actually breathing beneath the surface. So when I was given the chance to go to scuba school (SCUBA, by the way, stands for Self-Contained Underwater Breathing Apparatus), I figured it would be a lark: a few minutes learning how to operate the equipment, then a week of dashing around the reefs.

And thus perish the illusions of the indolent. In the next ten days, I was to discover that to become a competent diver (competence in this sense meaning the ability to keep yourself alive and reasonably healthy underwater) requires a long, involved course that is as taxing mentally as physically. A good diver must be an amateur physiologist, chemist, ichthyologist, oceanographer, physicist, and mathematician, as well as being cool-headed, robust, instinctively quick, and possessed of a good physique.

There are diving schools all over the world, offering varying qualities of instruction. Some — the ones that will take your word for past experience and then remind you not to hold your breath while ascending — sell you a ticket to suicide. Others provide a full thirty-hour course and eventual certification by NAUI, the National Association of Underwater Instructors.

Few are as well-equipped as the Underwater Explorers Club in Freeport, Grand Bahama. The club ($40 to join, $10 yearly dues for off-islanders) has a regular pool, a deep practice tank, a clutch of expert instructors, half a dozen diving boats and — only a mile or two offshore — some of the best reefs in the hemisphere.

The general manager of the club is a tall, sinewy, forty-four-year-old ex-Marine and ex-pro-football halfback named Dave Woodward, who wears a goatee and pumps pills and sera into himself to stave off allergies that could ruin his diving life. He has been teaching diving for eighteen years.

"For a long time, diving was taught by the fear technique," said Woodward as he explained the need for protracted lessons. "Instructors would say, 'This is what's going to happen to you' — not might happen or could happen, but *will* happen. I made a survey of all the people I'd taught in my first two years and found I'd scared hell out of ninety-five percent of them; only five percent were still diving. We still run into people who are terrified to dive.

"Nowadays, the instructional emphasis is on teaching the diver, on making sure he's totally familiar with his equipment, on giving him a broad background to cope with any situation that might arise, and on showing him his own personal capabilities and limitations. It is very important that a diver knows just what he can and can't do. We don't encourage over-confidence; we try to erase fear and replace it with apprehension. A diver should always be apprehensive in new territory or a new situation. The ones who aren't are the ones who don't survive."

The thirty-hour course consists of sixteen hours of classroom work, and for two days I sat before a blackboard and took notes. Medical monstrosities like spontaneous pneumothorax and mediastinal emphysema were bounced off my skull, and I was crammed with facts and statistics about pressurization and the absorption rate of nitrogen into fatty tissue of which I have my share.

The life support mechanism of scuba gear is a tank containing 71.2 cubic feet of air compressed to about 2,150 pounds per square inch. Sea level air pressure — referred to as 1 a.t.m. (atmosphere) — is 14.7 p.s.i. (pounds per square inch). Underwater, atmospheric pressure increases at a rate of .445 p.s.i. per foot of descent, so at thirty-three feet the pressure is 29.4 p.s.i., or plus 1 a.t.m. The subsequent increase is steady — another atmosphere for every thirty-three feet. The deeper you go, the more air you consume. Again the rate is steady.

Presuming that a diver uses reliable equipment and is not attacked by some predatory beast, he has few worries while submerged. The problems come with ascension. The cardinal rule for divers is: never hold your breath on the way up, even from a depth of only four or six feet.

Air that has been compressed will, when the pressure is released, expand. If you take a good lungful of air and then rocket to the surface without exhaling, the air in your lungs, finding no way out of your mouth will expand and rupture a lung's air sacs, sending bubbles into the blood stream. The bubbles will cause a neat little problem called aeroembolism — a circulation blockage in the heart, spinal cord or brain — that will most likely kill you.

There are of course, other problems — such as the notorious bends, the crippling and potentially fatal affliction that occurs when a diver stays at a certain depth far too long and neglects to decompress by ascending in slow stages to allow the nitrogen in his blood to dissipate.

All of these problems, Woodward said as he led me — weak-kneed and stammering — to the practice pool, can be avoided by care and common sense.

He explained the equipment to me.

Most, like the mask, fins, and snorkel, were familiar. But the tank and regulator, which governs the air flow into your mouth, were new. There are safety precautions to be taken with the tank. It should be laid prone: if a tank should fall over, and the valve at the top crack off, the tank will depart like a missile. Careless folks have watched helplessly as their tanks shot through several concrete walls.

We spent several hours checking me out with the equipment in the deep pool — removing the mask, putting it back on, and clearing it by pressing on the face plate and blowing through the nose; pulling off the tank and laying it in my lap; discarding the mouthpiece, relocating it, clearing it (by exhaling into it), and breathing again.

Finally Woodward conceded that I could probably essay a shallow dive on the reef (escorted by him) without killing myself. We had discussed a maneuver called "buddy breathing" — if you run out of air, you share your associate's air, two breaths at a time (a very basic reason for never diving alone) — but Woodward preferred to wear two mouthpieces on his regulator.

"Buddy breathing is fine with an expert," he said, "but I've tried it with a panicky student, and he wouldn't give the mouthpiece back to me."

He began to don his gear before we left the dock, and the process continued until we entered the water. Fully attired, he looked like a combination of Batman and an electronics salesman. On his back were the tank and a regulator with three hoses protruding — two mouthpieces and a gauge to tell him precisely how much air was left in his tank.

He also wore mask, fins, a weight belt, and an inflatable vest with a tiny auxiliary tank of air. On his arms were a watch, a thermometer, a depth gauge, a light meter, and an underwater camera; on his legs a decompression meter (to tell him if he needed to decompress and if so, how much and at what depths), a snorkel, and a knife, the latter not so much to fend off predators as to deal with a constant problem in busy waters — monofilament nylon fishing line, discarded or lost from passing boats, which can ensnare a diver and trap him underwater. From a quick calculation based on the prices I had noted in the club's supply shop, I determined that Woodward was sporting about $1,000 worth of hardware.

When we arrived at the reef, Woodward easily slipped his tank over his head and down onto his back while I groveled in the bilge, trying to struggle into my harness. He demonstrated a suitable entry into the water — called a "back roll" — and after he had departed with a splash, I checked and double checked my equipment and positioned myself on the gunwale.

I grasped my mask fore and aft, took a deep breath and gracefully arched over backwards into the water. It was a perfect descent, except for the fact that I had forgotten to locate — let alone insert — my mouthpiece. I scrambled to the surface, found the hose, bit down hard on the rubber, and lurched back down.

The water was only twelve or fifteen feet deep, and in the bright sunlight the coral shone — beige elkhorns that spread majestically along the bottom, purple seafans as intricate as snowflakes, and mustard-colored fire coral, which I had been warned against. It is covered with a toxic film that burns if you touch it.

I breathed easily — though too fast I was later told — and glided through the forest of coral and sponges. Schools of small fish fed off the rocks and swam unafraid, around my face. The only sound was my own respiration—purr, gurgle, purr, gurgle, like a man breathing his last in an iron lung.

That afternoon Woodward said I might not be a menace to navigation in slightly deeper water, and we went out further on the reef, to where the water was eighty feet deep. I wasn't going to go all the way down but was to swim with Woodward at twenty-five or thirty feet so that the photographer could take pictures from below of us in silhouette against the sun. When we were fully costumed I plopped myself on the gunwale and asked Woodward if I should proceed.

"No," he said. "Let's go by the book. I'll go first. In case there's a fish of any size down there, I have time to scare him away before some jumpy girl sees him and panics. We haven't got any jumpy girls on board, but I like to keep up the precaution. Maybe it's silly. We don't see sharks around here more than once in a hundred dives."

We swam back and forth over the anchor line for a few minutes, and the photographer shot some pictures. Suddenly Woodward pointed off to his left. Just on the edge of the underwater horizon, circling slowly in the blue gloom, was a shark. Swell. I should have this kind of luck in roulette, hitting hundred-to-one shots.

Woodward turned to me, raised his eyebrows, and made the "Okay" sign with his thumb and finger in a circle. Was I okay?

I looked back at him and, for lack of a suitable signal, shrugged and rolled my eyes. I thought of the rules the textbooks dictate for dealing with sharks: "Keep sharks in your vision at all times with your back by rocks or growth. Exit on bottom into shore if possible." Sorry, Teach. The bottom was sixty feet below. There were no rocks or growth handy. Should I have carried a Handi-Pak of instant growth?

"A circling shark is up to something," says the book, "but will not necessarily attack." Not necessarily.

A man attacked by a shark, I extrapolated, may well die. But not necessarily. A man killed by a shark may well go to heaven. But not necessarily. The shark moved still closer. Woodward and the photographer left me under the boat and advanced toward him. Since I had the convenient excuse that my air was running low, I stayed put. (The book: "Try not to get into a situation where you have to surface when a shark is around. It presents your back and legs to him unprotected.") I thought for a moment that those two brave souls were offering themselves to the leviathan so I could escape.

Fat chance. Woodward whipped out his light meter; and he and the photographer began snapping flash pictures as the shark circled. I climbed out of the water and into the boat, surveying the engine to see if I could drive the boat alone back to the dock, where I knew I'd have to convey sad tidings to two families.

A moment later, they popped into the boat. "Let's change tanks and get back down before the sun goes lower," said Woodward.

"Terrific. And what," I asked, "do we do about *him?*"

"He's gone," he said. He turned to the photographer. "You know, it was kind of curious that he circled for so long." They flung themselves back into the water. After a quick, private supplication, I followed them.

When at last we were safely ashore, I admitted that the experience had given me some pause. (The word "terror," I thought, might have been appropriate in less blasé company.)

"Was that your first shark?" said Woodward. "Well, you've lost your virginity. It's all downhill from here."

I dressed and headed straight for the bar at the club. Not only did I need sustenance, but I thought the shark tale might be worth telling over a friendly grog.

"You saw a shark?" said Kurt Amsler, a bearded-young Swiss who is the club's photographer. "Wonderful. They're back. I can now get some good pictures." He seemed, as did the others at the bar, to be totally unafraid of sharks. Their main fear was that the Grand Bahama reef would acquire the reputation of being dangerous and thereby discourage divers.

"Ninety-nine times out of a hundred," said one of the instructors, "sharks will leave you alone." And the hundredth time? He smiled. "That's the breaks. But I've never heard of it happening around here."

Woodward came in as I was guessing that the shark had been about eight feet long and about fifty feet away. He laughed. "It was five or six feet long," he said, "and it got to within twenty feet of us. Water distortion makes everything seem a quarter or a third bigger than it is."

Compensating for the distortion of the water was just one of the environmental confusions that I found besetting me. It takes considerable practice for a land mammal to orient himself underwater in a strange area. I found that I could determine direction if I noticed on submerging which way the waves were running. From beneath the water, surface wave motion is still visible — presuming that you're not down ninety or a hundred feet and that the day is windy enough to whip up waves.

It was all too easy to become entranced with soaring in the coral canyons, chasing fish, swooping over hills and across sand plains, until I lost all sense of geography. (I kept feeling that my lumbering flight should be accompanied by a nice schmaltzy melody — say, a Mantovani rendition of *Greensleeves.)* If I couldn't find the boat from underwater, I'd have to surface — consuming energy and air — re-orient myself, then plunge down again.

If, as happened once or twice, I would accidentally lose sight of the rest of the divers — and despite the clarity of the water, straying for thirty yards would do the trick — I would rest on the bottom for a moment and stare at the surface, imagining the thousands (millions! billions!) of gallons of water pressing down on me. I would feel caught at once in the grips of claustrophobia and agoraphobia. The water was hemming me in, but at the same time I was alone on a vast open plain.

At the outer edge of the deep reef begins the Grand Bahama Ledge — a precipitous drop to twelve hundred or so feet. After four or five days of diving in the eighty-ninety-foot area, I was scheduled to make a dive to the edge of the ledge; about 150 feet down.

Woodward issued me double tanks, to ensure that I would have enough air for the fifteen minute dive. He also gave me the jacket to a wetsuit. A few days earlier, when we had first dived to eighty feet, Woodward had read the bottom temperature as eighty-one degrees and had suggested that I wear the jacket. I had kissed it off; I was used to Massachusetts water, I said, and that was a lot colder than eighty-one degrees.

"You don't know how fast body heat vanishes," he insisted. "Swimming is one thing: you're in and out of the water. But you try to exist for fifteen minutes in eighty-one-degree water and you'll be freezing." I was. So since then I'd worn a jacket.

It was made of foam neoprene and fit snugly against the skin. A small amount of water could enter the jacket, and it was warmed immediately to body temperature. I was able to dive for half an hour or more at eighty feet without feeling chilly.

Before we left the dock Woodward took us back to the classroom for a briefing. According to the Navy decompression tables, a dive of fifteen minutes at 150 feet necessitated decompression of three minutes at ten feet. Adding an extra safety margin, Woodward scheduled us for a two-minute stop at twenty feet and a seven-minute stop at ten. Four decompression bottles (extra tanks) would be hung over the side of the boat in case anyone ran out of air during a stop.

He warned us against nitrogen narcosis, the drunkenness caused by depths greater than a hundred feet. (The peril is also known as Martini's Law: every fifty feet of depth is supposed to have the same effect as one Martini.) A diver loses coordination, feels dizzy, and tends to do stupid things — like continue to descend or (the classic) offer his mouthpiece to a passing fish. If we felt at all dizzy we were to stop, grab something solid, and hold on until the feeling passed. If it didn't, we could ascend fifteen or twenty feet, and it would.

When we arrived at the spot where Woodward wanted to anchor the boat, we found ourselves in eight-foot seas. We could have made the dive, for below the surface waves are of little importance. They might perhaps have made for a hairy return to the boat — trying to grab the bouncing diving platform after hanging onto a swaying anchor line.

But the current was another matter. It was running onshore at about a knot and a half. Theoretically, one should always dive up-current of the boat, so that if he exhausts himself, he can drift back to safety. At the ledge, however, diving up-current would mean diving over nothing — twelve hundred feet of water. Woodward aborted the dive. "It's too much for safety," he said. "Let's go feed some grouper."

Every diving resort tries to cultivate an area on the reef where fish will come to feed out of divers' hands. It's a frustrating project, for spearfishermen who hear of such an area flock there and pick off the easy prey, who are conditioned to believe that man does nothing worse than offer food.

Woodward's groupers were still chary of humans because of a massacre that had taken place two weeks earlier. Of the original group of nine, only three were left, and one bore an ugly spear wound in his side. We hung by a massive piece of brain coral and tried to lure the groupers to us with succulent pieces of conch. The yellowtail and angelfish were less shy. They swarmed around us and ate from our fingers. One black angel-fish hovered directly in front of my mask — four or five inches away — displaying interest in nothing but my ears, one or the other of which he would lunge for at brief intervals. Woodward had warned me about this ear-fetishism; a fish bite can spoil the look of a lobe and take several weeks to heal.

By the next day, our last at the club, I was completely confident in the water. I was still breathing too fast and using my hands too much, but I felt there was nothing, save, perhaps, the appearance of another shark or two, that I couldn't cope with without panicking.

In the morning we dove in the sixty-five-seventy-five-foot area for about forty minutes. We left the water at exactly 12:30. We were scheduled to make another dive — to eighty feet — at 3:30. The instructor took his Navy tables to lunch with him and concluded that we could stay down nearly twenty minutes without having to decompress.

As I departed the diving platform, I checked my reserve valve to make sure it hadn't been released. If it had, there would be no warning that I was running out of air. It was fine.

For ten or fifteen minutes we gamboled about on the bottom, chasing fish and taking pictures. I was studying some minute creature when suddenly a shape flew past my mask. I turned to see an octopus scuttle under a rock just before a large grouper banged his nose in pursuit. There were three guides with us, and one reached under the rock, grabbed the octopus and slapped it across another guide's chest. The octopus clung to him as if she were the shortest girl in the class dancing a waltz with the basketball captain.

I noticed then that my air was getting low, but I was loath to pull my reserve valve, knowing I'd have to surface immediately and miss all the action.

The guide managed to pry the octopus off himself, and he caught his tormentor and planted the tentacles directly on his mask. Clearly terrified, the octopus kept shooting globules of viscous "'ink"— wondering, I had no doubt, how he had ever wandered into this nest of lunatics.

Finally I knew I had to pull my reserve ring, for l was all but out of air. The sensation was like holding an empty glass to your mouth and trying to draw a breath. I had no idea where I was, but I was sure I could surface and swim to the boat.

I pulled the ring. Nothing. I pulled again. It was all the way down, all right, but there just wasn't any air coming through the mouthpiece. Something was wrong with the regulator. Or maybe I had knocked the reserve valve open against a piece of coral.

I looked around desperately. The pack leader, Bob Farrilly, was signaling that it was time to go up, and he didn't see me. On the surface, the vague shadow of the boat bobbed in and out of my vision. I had a flash thought of something Woodward had said earlier: "In eighteen years of teaching I've never seen an air embolism or a drowning. I suppose the odds will catch up with me, but God! I hope not." Well, chief, here's number one.

About forty feet away another of the guides was frantically motioning me to go up. Our time was over. A few more minutes at this depth and we'd have to decompress. I drew my finger across my throat, the signal that I was out of air and he began to swim toward me, holding out his auxiliary mouthpiece. Farrilly, still further away, noticed the commotion and started toward me. I floated where I was, feeling the pulse pounding in my temples wondering if I had the guts to try a free ascent. If done properly it poses no problem: a diver had recently made a free ascent from 100 feet. If done improperly — you exhale too quickly — you pass out.

Then the mouthpiece was there. I forgot an elementary rule — to clear it — and I gulped four or five thousand gallons of water. But the mouthpiece was lodged firmly and as I gagged and choked, the regulator cleared. I made a feeble "okay" sign and, clutching my savior, started for the surface. From below, I was told, we made a weird pair — a couple of creatures mating in a cloud of bubbles.

I struggled onto the diving platform, gasping and glassy-eyed, like Dante's man "who with panting breath has escaped from the deep sea to the shore, turns to the dangerous water and gazes." So much for being a cocky diver, I thought as we chugged ashore. Just a few minutes learning the equipment — right? — and then go diving on the reef.

When we had tied up for the night, I remembered a textbook platitude that had been pumped into me during those long hours of classroom work: "Remember — a good diving course is preferable to an impressive funeral."

From *Go to the Widow-Maker*, a novel, 1967

HIS CAPITAL M MANHOOD

"We know this area underwater like you know your backyard at home," Bonham said, like a pat spiel for nervous clients, from the helm as he peered out through the opened windshield. Ali had done all the casting off and they were now moving out into the bay channel, past the luxury hotels close on the right and so different from the dirty commercial docks and warehouses stretching around the curve of the bay behind them. The sun poured down on them making a strong light in the cockpit, and equally strong shade under the little roof where Bonham stood. It glinted off the water at them like steel points. The air had freshened noticeably already. "That's the Yacht Club over there," Bonham rumbled as he swung the boat away from it.

"Where are we going?" Grant asked. He knew the Yacht Club, had been there with his "mistress" and her husband, but he looked at the eighteen or twenty small sailing boats and launches tied fore and aft and swinging between their rows of mooring buoys. From the Yacht Club veranda someone waved at them gaily. Bonham's helper Ali waved back. Grant did not. Four days of training with Bonham had materially increased his sense of the dangers involved in diving, and the gay waver at the Yacht Club — who apparently thought they were going off on some kind of a happy sea picnic — had suddenly increased his irate nervousness and given him a gloomy sense of isolation.

"I'm takin' you out to one of the coral reefs," Bonham answered him from the wheel.

"How deep will it be?"

"Ten feet to sixty feet: ten feet at the top of the reef, sixty at the bottom on the sand. Be just right for your first dive, and it's the prettiest reef this side the island."

That had to be a lie. Ocho Rios was supposed — "Are there any fish?"

"Hell, yes! Lots of them."

"Any sharks?"

"Sure. Sometimes. If we're lucky." The Navy tender, quite small as Navy ships go, now loomed up ahead of them in the deep main channel, appearing so huge from this close up that it filled the sky and threatened to fall on them. Bonham swung the boat slightly to pass it close by on his port side and increased his throttle. They were now out in the open bay. Bonham suddenly began to whistle merrily, if offkey, as if just being out on the water, headed for a dive, made him a different, happier man.

On the other hand, Grant was finding it impossible to put into words exactly how he felt, but which was mainly — if it must be said in one word without nuance — cowardly. He did not want to go on. He would give anything he possessed, not to. He had worked and planned for this, had dreamed of it — and for quite a long time. Now he realized that if Bonham's engine suddenly failed, he would not be disappointed. He hoped it would fail. He would be more than glad to wait at least until tomorrow. Or longer, if it required repairs. And that was pretty cowardly. It was even pusillanimous. But he was too proud to say this, admit it out loud. "I was a little surprised at you taking me out so soon," he essayed, finally. "Especially after — you know — after what happened yesterday."

Bonham's bloodthirsty smile passed up over his huge face. "Oh, that happens to everybody. At least once. Usually more." Again as if he were eerily looking right into Grant's mind, he suddenly pulled from the drawer immediately in front of the wheel a half-full bottle of Beefeater's gin (one of the two which Grant had bought yesterday), looked at it, and motioned with it to Grant. "Want a snort? No, you handled that very well yesterday I thought."

Grant took the bottle. Of course that eerie understanding undoubtedly came from so frequently handling people who reacted exactly like himself. But Grant hated to think he reacted like everybody else. Yesterday, which was supposed to have been his graduation day, during what was in fact supposed to be his graduation exam, he had made a serious booboo on the bottom of the pool. The result was that he had taken in a quick fullsucking breath of water instead of air from the tubes of the aqualung and, strangling and in total panic, had dropped everything and swum up blindly and choking to the surface, clawing mindlessly. While he clung to the pooledge desperately, strangling and whooping in terror to get air down his locked throat, Bonham standing just above him spraddlelegged in his sloppy faded trunks had thrown back his head and roared with laughter — a reaction which Grant when he finally could breathe again, though he grinned, found, if manly, nevertheless rather insensitive. Grant had always had this terrible fear of strangling, of not being able to get air. Also, whenever he looked up from the pooledge, all he could see were those two huge oaktree legs disappearing into the gaping legholes of Bonham's trunks, within which he could see the shabby, raveled, somewhat ill-fitting edge of Bonham's old jockstrap revealing a crescent-shaped section of hairy balls, all of which he found embarrassing and distasteful.

The exercise he was attempting was not one he had not done before. He had already done it twice that same day, successfully. It consisted of diving to the bottom of the pool fully geared, divesting oneself of flippers, weight belt, mask and lung in that order and swimming back up; that was the first half. The second (after a few deep breaths) was to swim back down, nearly blind, because maskless, find the lung and clear it of water and then, once one was able to breathe through it again, redon all the other gear and come up. Now, all this would be comparatively easy if one had attached to one's tubes a mouthpiece with 'non-return valves' which did not let water get into the tubes; but Bonham insisted implacably that all his pupils complete this exercise with the old-fashioned open mouthpiece so that, to clear the lung, you had to hold it in a certain way with the air-intake tube up and the exhaust tube down. And then you had to exhale sharply all your precious air to blow the water out. That particular time Grant, hurrying, apparently had held the damned thing wrong, with the exhaust tube up, and instead of the quick relieving flow of air into empty lungs, he had sucked down water.

Standing in the boat cockpit, holding the gin bottle in his hand and looking at the familiar Tower-of-London-Watchman label, Grant could feel all over again the rush of water into his throat, his throat itself locking, the blind rush upward, and then the long drawnout process while hanging on the pooledge of trying to get a tiny bit of air down into those heaving lungs whose heaving only locked his throat up tighter. Uncapping the bottle, he took a big swallow of the straight gin and waited for it to hit his stomach and spread out, warm and soothing. When he finally got his breath back yesterday, he had insisted on going back down and doing it again, right away, because he knew the principle from springboard diving that when you crack up on a dive, don't wait: go right back while your back or your belly is still stinging and do it again before time and imagination can make you even more afraid. Bonham had apparently admired him for that, and the second time he had done it perfectly, but that did not relieve his memory of the strangling terror.

Later, of course, Bonham had told him it happened because he hurried, that if he had tested it with just a little suction till he found water, he could have swum back up with his lungs empty: he had plenty of time. But for Grant it had required every last ounce of will he had each time to exhale into that tube down there. How could he have that much more control? Time, Bonham said; practice. And panic, *panic*, was the biggest danger, enemy, the *only* danger that there was in diving.

Luckily, Grant thought, last night he had not told his mistress or her husband about the little accident — now that they were going out. But then they did not even know that they were going out. Almost furtively, he glanced up again at the villa where they were up on the hill and still visible even from here, and once again that black-draped, mantilla-ed, half-hidden-faced image standing on the church steps pointing swam over him. Sometimes he positively hated her guts. Politely wiping the neck of the bottle with the palm of his hand in the time-honored gesture of all bottle drinkers, he passed the gin back to Bonham at the wheel, grateful for the warming.

"Look!" Bonham rumbled, rather sharply. "You ain't gonna have to take your lung off down there out here. Only the mask, like I told you. Outside of that we're just gonna swim around and look. I got this new camera case I wanta try out for a friend. So I'll take some pictures of you." It was a clear bribe. And as such, angered Grant a little. He didn't need bribes to do it, or anything. Bonham slugged down a healthy dollop of the gin himself, and then, after a hesitation, as if he were not sure he ought to do this in front of Grant, wiped the bottleneck and passed it over to Ali — who bobbing and grinning took a drink himself and wiped the neck and capped it.

Grant did not fail to note the hesitation, or its meaning, but he did not say anything — about that, or about Bonham's rather sharp remark. He was, actually, after having looked up at the villa, at the moment much more interested in and concerned with himself. Why was he doing this? Reality? To find reality? Search out and rediscover a reality which all these past six or eight years and two plays he had felt was beginning to be missing from his life and from his work? Yes; a reality, yes. Because without his work he was nothing. A nothing. And work was vitality, vitality and energy, and — manhood. So go ahead and say the rest of it. Yes, reality; but also to search out and rediscover his Manhood. His Capital M Manhood, which along with reality and his work he was also losing. Yes, all that; and also to get rid at least for a while in a genteel way of his aging mistress, the black figure on the church steps, whom he had once loved, but whom now he both loved in a strange way and did not love at all, equally and simultaneously, and whom he considered at least partially responsible for the loss of reality (and Manhood) that he suffered. Maybe he considered her, probably he considered her, *totally* responsible for the loss. But in the end he had not gotten away from her at all, because she had invited herself to come with him, along with her husband. Actually it was she who had found Al Bonham for him! She had come on down ahead, while he was in New York, had looked up and had waiting for him a diving teacher she considered reputable.

And in the interim, during his "business" trip to New York with his newest, his latest play, something else had happened. Grant had met a girl.

Big Al suddenly swung the wheel hard right, and the little boat made a sharp turn to starboard and headed off in that direction. They were far out on the open bay now. Directly ahead a mile away was the jet airstrip, one of three on the island, almost touching the blacktop road that ran along the water's edge. "It's right off the end of the airstrip, this reef," Bonham said. "Bout half a mile out. I got two or three reference points I line up to hit it exact." As violently as he had made the turn, which Grant considered strangely unnecessarily violent, he suddenly cut throttle and Grant grabbed the gunwale to keep from falling forward, as did Ali. For three or four minutes Bonham jockeyed the boat backward and forward, peering down over the side. "There she is," he said. "My special spot."

Grant too looked over the side. Below him in the bluegreen water yellow and brown color-patches swirled and quivered under the water's wash. Just beside these, and as if he were standing shoetips to the edge of a vertical high cliff, he could now and then as the sea flattened catch a glimpse of clear sand far below, dark-green colored through the surface. The sun hot on his back, Grant felt cold at the thought of being immersed in water which was not in a bathtub and whose lack of heat could not be controlled. "Let's get you dressed out," Bonham rumbled from just behind him, and began hauling tanks and gear around as if none of it weighed anything.

As he had before, Grant noticed that Bonham dropped his bad grammar whenever he was giving instructions. Now he kept up a running comment of instruction while the two of them, he and Ali, got the neophyte ready. Flippers first, then the mask spat upon rubbed till it squeaked rinsed and resting on his forehead, rubber wet shirt, weightbelt trimmed to exactly the right weight by Bonham, finally the tank his arms through the shoulder straps crotch strap attached to the weight belt. Grant simply sat, like an electrocutionee he thought, and let himself be handled. The running comment of instruction had to do with clearing his ears and equalizing the pressure in them as he and Bonham went on down, and with what Bonham wanted him to do with his mask, which was to remove it when they reached the bottom of the anchorline, put it back on full of water, and clear it. Grant was to go first, swim forward to the anchorline, descend it ten or twelve feet, and wait for Bonham. Then last, the mask lowered over his eyes and nose, the mouthpiece stuffed into his mouth, and he was falling backward onto the tank on his back while faces and boat wheeled out of sight to be replaced by nothing but bright blue sky, what was he doing here? Then the water closed over him, blinding him.

Still holding the mask to his face with both hands in the approved manner to keep the fall from dislodging it, Grant rolled over quickly but he still could see nothing. He was now lying on the surface. Masses of bubbles formed by the air he had carried under with him rose all around him, blinding him even more effectively than a driving rainstorm would have done up in the air. He waited, vulnerable, what seemed endlessly but was really only seconds. Then, miraculously, everything cleared as the bubbles rose on past him, and he could see. See at least as well as he could on land. Maybe more. Because to his congenital mild myopia everything looked closer. It was supposed to. Snell's Law. (n Sin a = n' Sin a'). Oh, he'd studied all the books — and for years. But this was different. Below him the yellow and brown patches were now clearly delineated fields of yellow and brown coral but in amongst these, invisible from the boat, were smaller patches of almost every color and color combination imaginable. It was breathtaking. And, as far as he could tell, there was nothing dangerous visible.

Tentatively, cautiously, for the first time since he'd gone under, Grant let out a little air and took a tiny breath. By God, it worked! He became aware of the surface swell rolling him and banging the tank against his back. Bending double he dove down to where there was no swell as Bonham had told him, and swam slowly forward along the boat's big shadow above him, toward the slanting anchorline. In the strange silence he could hear odd poppings and crackling. With each intake of breath the regulator at the back of his neck sang eerily and gonglike, and with each exhale he could hear the flubbering rush of bubbles from it. Everything, all problems, all plans, all worries, "mistress," her husband, new girl, the new play, sometimes even consciousness of Self itself, seemed to have been swept from his mind by the intensity of the tasting of this new experience, and new world.

At the anchorline, after he managed awkwardly to grab it, he pulled himself down deeper hand over hand until his ears began really to hurt, and then stopped. As Bonham had shown him, he put thumb and fore-finger into the hollows in the mask's bottom and pinched his nose shut, and blew. One ear opened up immediately with a loud squeak, but he had to try a second and a third time before he could get the other one completely opened. Then he pulled himself a little deeper, feeling the pressure start to build again, and stopped again. Wrapping his legs around the line, he peered at the diving watch Bonham had sold him and set its outside bezel dial with the zero point over the minute hand. Then he peered at the huge handsome depth gauge beside it which Bonham had also sold him and saw that he was eighteen feet down. On his right arm the enormous Automatic Decompression Meter which Bonham had sold him still read zero; its nitrogen-absorption-measuring needle had not yet even started to move. And so there he hung, having let go with his legs and grabbed the line with a hand, looking around. If Marty Gabel and Herman Levin could only see him now! His nervousness had left him, and he felt a kind of cautious rapture.

To his right and left coral hills forty and fifty feet high stretched away in minor mountain ranges into bluegreen invisibility. Directly in front of him at the foot of the deep end of these rounded ranges, a pure white sea of virgin sand sloped away ever so gently out toward deep water. In between the coral hills he could see down into channels — glaciers; rivers — of sand which debouched onto the vast sand plain. In these channels, varieties of brightly colored fish poked their noses into holes in the coral, or rowed themselves gently along with their pectoral fins like small boats with oars. None of them seemed to be concerned with bothering any of the others, and Grant relaxed even more.

Then, in the corner of his mask which acted like a horse's blinders and cut his field of vision, he caught a flash of silver. Turning his head he saw through the plate of glass a barracuda which appeared to be at least four feet long. It was about twenty feet away. Slowly it swam out of sight beyond his mask and Grant turned again. This process went on until Grant realized the fish was circling him. Regularly, staring at him with its one big eye, it opened and closed its enormous mouth, exposing its dagger teeth, as if flexing its jaws preparatory to taking a bite of Grant. This was its method of breathing of course, he knew, but it didn't look nice just the same. Grant had read that in cases like this you were supposed to swim straight at them as if you intended to take a bite of them whereupon they would turn and flee and run away, but he did not feel very much like trying this. Besides, he was not supposed to leave the anchorline. On the other hand he felt he ought not just sit here and let the fish have all the initiative. But before he could make up his mind to do something, and if so then what, another figure swam into his mask's field of vision, further complicating matters till Grant realized what it was.

It was Bonham. Looking like some antennaed stranger from another world, which in a way he was, he swam down on a long slant behind the barracuda, leisurely beating the water with his flippers, his left arm with its hand holding the camera case stretched back at rest along his thigh, his right arm extended out straight before him holding the four-foot speargun. In the green water-air he was gravityless and beautiful, and Grant would have given anything to be like him. As he came on down getting closer, he stopped kicking and, hunching his shoulders in a strange way as if to make himself heavier, coasted down. Just as Grant saw his forearm tightening to squeeze the trigger, the barracuda gave an enormous flirt of its tail and simply disappeared. It didn't go away; it just simply was no longer there, or anywhere visible, with an unbelievable speed if you hadn't seen it. Bonham looked after it, shrugged, and swam on to the line.

There was a great paternalism, protectiveness, about Bonham underwater. He looked Grant over carefully, turning him about and inspecting his gear, then with a violent hand motion downward swam on down the line toward the bottom. Grant followed, his nervousness returning. Twice he had to stop on the line to clear his ears and he suddenly noticed that Bonham apparently did not have to do this at all. On the bottom, like some huge calm great-bellied Buddha, Bonham seated himself crosslegged on the sand, took off his mask, blinked blindly, then put it back on and blew the water out of it by tilting his head to one side and holding the upper side of the mask. Then he motioned for Grant to do the same, as he had, upstairs, warned him that he would.

Grant had done this in the various pools, but down here (his depth gauge Bonham had sold him now read fifty-nine feet) he found it was more scary. It was all that water above you. Kneeling on the sand, he forced himself with the greatest reluctance to reach up and pull off his own mask. When he did, he immediately went blind. The salt water burned his eyes and the insides of his nose. He found himself gasping for breath. Bonham was now only one great blur to him. He made himself breathe deeply several times, and blinked. Then he put the mask back on and cleared it. Not as adept as Bonham, he had to blow several times to get all the water out. But when he looked at Bonham, the big man was nodding happily and holding up his thumb and forefinger in the old circle salute for "okay." Then he motioned for Grant to come and went swimming off six or eight feet above the sand. Grant followed, his eyes still smarting. He was ridiculously pleased. At the moment he felt very much the son to Bonham's massive paternalism. This did not irritate him. Instead, it gave him reassurance.

Bonham proceeded to point out the various corals. They were all very beautiful and interesting to look at — in a slimy, repugnant sort of way — but you could only look at coral so long without getting bored. Apparently fully aware of this, Bonham — after pointing out a number of varieties (including two which he warned Grant not to touch by wringing a hand and shaking it as if stung) — chose the exact moment of Grant's increasing restlessness to show him something else. At the end of the coral hillock they had been exploring he swam over to Grant and motioned for him to follow. He led him straight down over the steep side of the hillock to the sand channel bottom (here Grant's depth gauge Bonham had sold him read 63 feet), and there he pointed out two large caves. It was apparently true that Bonham knew this area like Grant knew his backyard. It was also apparent that he was conducting his tour and displaying his treasures one by one with the dramatic sense of a veteran entrepreneur.

To Grant the caves were both exciting and frightening. The one on the left of the sand channel went back in under the coral hill they had just swum over; way back in there some hole running clear to the top of the coral allowed a shaft of sunlight to penetrate all the way to the bottom, illuminating greenly some strange coral shapes growing on the sand;

outside, its entrance was huge, not a real cave mouth at all, but more an overhang that ran almost the entire length of the side of the hillock. From under this overhang Grant carefully stayed away, as he looked. By contrast, Bonham had already swum on in. Turning his head, he motioned Grant to follow. Biting hard on the two rubber tits of the mouthpiece between his teeth, tightening his lips over the whole, Grant descended a little and entered. Scared as he was, it was magnificently beautiful in there. The ceiling was only fifteen or twenty feet from the sand floor, much lower than it had looked from outside. Several good-sized tunnels showing sunlight at their ends led off from it and looked safe for exploring. But Bonham was already swimming back out, motioning him to follow.

The other cave, across the channel, was really no more than a fissure, running maybe thirty feet up an almost perpendicular dead-coral cliff, hardly wide enough to admit a man, and it was to this one now that Bonham led him.

Gesturing Grant to follow, the big man swam up the fissure to a point that appeared slightly wider than the rest, snaked himself through, and disappeared. When Grant followed, he found he had to turn his shoulders sideways to enter. When he did, his tank banged alarmingly on the rock behind him. He remembered reading stories of fellows who had cut their air intake hoses on sharp coral, and who had barely got out alive by luck, superior experience, and by keeping their heads. Trying to keep his air intake hose (without being able to see it) somewhere near the center of the cleft, Grant pulled himself along with his hands on the sucky, unpleasantly viscid living corals growing here. But when he was in far enough that he could no longer bend his knees to flutter his feet, the panicky breathlessness, the sensation of being unable to breathe, to get enough air, which panic brings, and which he knew from before, hit him debilitatively. Stopping, he forced himself to breathe deeply but it didn't help. Suddenly his instinct was to throw off everything and run for the surface blindly, even though covered by coral rock, get to anywhere where there was air. Instead, he reached out with his hands and pulled himself further in, trying to keep his movements slow and liquid, unviolent, though by now he didn't care whether the coral cut him or not.

Actually, he had only been inches away from freedom. The last pull with his arms brought him head and shoulders almost to his waist out into the open. One breast stroke with his arms and he was free, swimming almost forty feet above the bottom. Bonham, who Grant now realized had been directly in front of him watching and ready to help, had already rolled over head down and like an airplane in a full dive was swimming straight down toward the bottom, his flippers beating leisurely and slow, his arms holding camera and gun extended backward along his thighs to streamline. For a moment Grant was seriously angry at him, for taking such a chance with him on his first dive. Still breathing deeply, though slower and slower now as his heart and adrenal glands got back to normal, Grant watched in a kind of witless stupor as Bonham got smaller and smaller and smaller. A few feet above the bottom the big man leveled off over a huge coral toadstool and rolled over face up, and slowly sank to a crosslegged sitting position on it, his head back looking up, for all the world like some great, oneeyed humanoid alien frog from Alpha Centauri or somewhere. Still looking up, he motioned for Grant to come on down. Still staring, still breathing deeply from his fright in the narrow entrance, Grant suddenly realized with a start which brought him back out of his post-panic stupor that he was lying here all stretched out forty feet up in the *air* from this other man, relaxed, his arms out over his head like a man in a bed. Because it really could have been air. *Seemed* like air. The green-tinted water was crystal clear here inside, and Bonham by seating himself on the toadstool had avoided stirring up any sand clouds as they had done outside. For the first time with any real physical appreciation, Grant realized how delicious it was to be totally without gravity like one of the great planing birds; he could go up, he could go down, he could stay right where he was; in the strange spiritual excitement of it, his fear left him completely. Feeling ridiculous again because of his recent panic there, he glanced once at the narrow entrance fissure, then rolled over head down using exactly (though slower) the same body movements he once used to do a full-twisting half gainer, and corkscrewed gently down — relishing the leisurely control — into a vertical dive, his hands and arms straight back along his thighs palms up, his fins beating lazy and slow, as he had seen Bonham do. Only once did he have to clear his ears, and he did it now without pausing. Below him Bonham got larger and larger. Then, duplicating Bonham's maneuver, he rolled over onto his back, exhaled and sank into a sitting position on the giant toadstool beside him, his knees clasped up to his chin. Unable to speak, or even to grin, he gesticulated wildly and waggled his eyebrows to show his enthusiasm. The big man nodded vigorously, then touching him gently, pointed upward, sweeping his arm across the view like a man unveiling a painting. For the first time since he had entered, Grant looked up.

What he saw very nearly took away the breath he had just regained. He was in an immense cavern at least sixty feet high. Apparently the bottom here inside was ten or so feet lower than the sand channel bottom outside. From where he sat at one end the other was almost lost in a hazy near-invisibility. In the dim ceiling a dozen holes allowed clusters of greenish sunrays to strike at varying angles across the interior until they shattered against the sand bottom or rock walls. Each beam wherever it struck against bottom or walls revealed weird outlandish coral sculptures. It was more than breathtaking, it was like having stumbled upon some alien cathedral on some other planet, which some otherworld race with their incomprehensible architecture and alien sculpture had ages past built, decorated, and dedicated to their unknowable God. Grant was suddenly frightened again, not physically this time, but spiritually. For a moment he forgot he was diving underwater in an aqualung. Was that some four-headed Great Saint whom they worshipped, there on the side wall? Was that seventy-eyed monster, all head and almost no body, resting on the sand floor, the Great Being Himself? And as always, when he found himself alone in an empty church — as he had when a boy, as he had when visiting the great churches and cathedrals of Europe and found one or another of them deserted — Grant felt himself beginning to get an erection in the dim stillness. Was it the privacy? Was it the quiet? Or was it the highceilinged dimness? Or was it maybe the nearness of God? The nearness of Unknowable? Embarrassed, he shifted away sideways, afraid Bonham might notice what was happening inside his tight, scanty bikini, and the feeling began to subside. Anyway he knew one thing for certain. One day while he was here in Ganado Bay he was going to come out here alone — come alone if he had to rent a *row*boat and aqualung from

Bonham's competitor — make a dive down here alone, strip off this damned bikini, swim around this cave stark naked with his erection, then sit on this toadstool and masturbate, come like a fury, and watch his milky semen swirl and mingle with the green water which itself swirled about his body with every tiniest movement.

Maybe he'd hire a nondiving native to handle the boat for him. The very secrecy of it, the native up there working the boat and him down here masturbating, made it a tinglingly exciting prospect. But, was this not a too-ambitious project for a neophyte diver just starting out: jerking off underwater? Well, he would find out. The idea of masturbating made him think of his new girl in New York. She, it had turned out, had loved that.

Bonham touched him gently again, on the shoulder, and Grant started guiltily. When he looked over, the other was motioning upward with one hand and beckoning with the other. When Grant asked "Why?" by shrugging up his shoulders and spreading out his hands, Big Al pointed to his watch. Looking at his own Grant saw they had been under thirty-two minutes, and could hardly believe it. And it reminded him of something else. During his last few breaths it had seemed to Grant that it was getting slightly harder to breathe each time, but the difference was so slight he had thought he was imagining it. Now he tried again and found it was distinctly harder to suck air from the lung. His neophyte's nervousness returned to him suddenly. But neither man had yet pulled his reserve valve. Grabbing his mouthpiece with one hand and pointing to his tank with the other, Grant made a heaving motion with his chest as if trying to breathe. Bonham nodded. But then he followed the nod by fanning his hands back and forth across each other in a gesture of "Take it easy; don't worry." Gesturing Grant to follow, and without pulling his reserve, he took off from the toadstool with a little leap upward like a bird.

But it was more like a foot-winged Mercury than a bird, Grant thought as he followed. He was no longer nervous. Underwater at least, he now trusted Bonham completely. Forgotten was the momentary anger at Bonham's having taken him through the narrow fissure.

Ahead of him Big Al swam upward on a long diagonal straight across the length of the green cathedral. He did not turn off to the right toward the fissure. Grant assumed, rightly, that there was another entrance —

which made him feel good, because he had no liking for the fissure. As he rose on the long diagonal, the air in his tank expanded as the pressure lessened and it became easier to breathe and he understood why Bonham had motioned him not to worry. Only if they had had to descend again into greater pressure, he remembered now from the books, would they have needed their reserve valves. Grant remembered to exhale frequently as he rose to avoid air embolism and when, as he swam, he looked at his Automatic Decompression Meter Bonham had sold him it showed there was no need to worry about decompression. So they were leaving, or — rather — returning.

Ten yards ahead of him Bonham swam into and then out of some of the slanting rays of sunlight which crossed the cave, strangely bright and glowing when he was in one, almost invisible when he was in the darker water in between. Grant could not resist pausing and turning for a look back. He felt a curious sad tranquillity, toward all inevitability, because he had to leave. But when he looked, he found he was already forty-five or fifty feet above the bottom and the toadstool was no longer visible from here. With a second's tingling excitement in his groin he knew now more than ever that, eventually, he would come back here and descend into that invisibility and sitting on that same toadstool looking up, masturbate himself. Play with himself, he added, in the jargon of his parents. Then he swam on.

Ahead of him Bonham had turned the corner into an alcove-cum-tunnel almost at the ceiling of the cavern and was waiting for him. Ahead at the end of it was sunlight, and together in this more than comfortably wide space they swam toward it, then through it and back into the world.

But the dive was still not over. Emotionally, it was, perhaps; but they still had to get back to the boat. Bonham did not even bother to surface and look around but (he really did know this area like his backyard) struck off and over the coral hillock they had just left the insides of, and which came to within less than ten feet of the surface. Grant could not see boat or anchorline ahead, but Bonham was obviously heading straight for them. Below them as they swam were the tangled, trashy staghorn-coral beds — the brown ones, their hunks of old fishing line caught here and there, rusting beercans in the low spots — which marked the hillock's crest. But now after the cave all that was boring. It was hard to believe they had been inside this hill, and that it was damned near entirely hollow. Grant's sadness at leaving it — out here in the sunlit, brightly coral-studded, open water — was slowly turning into a wild kind of elation. Above him the surface was only a few feet away, and every now and then — as in some silvered but unsolid mirror — he could see himself or Bonham, grossly distorted, reflected back from the underside of it as it moved. His air, without his pulling of the reserve lever but getting harder and harder to draw, lasted just exactly to the side of the boat. At the boat he had a bad moment when, trying to shuck out of his tank straps and pass the lung up to Ali, he went under gulping seawater and almost choked; but then he was over the side and in the boat safe from sharks, barracuda, Portuguese men-o'-war, the bends, air embolism, busted ear-drums, and mechanical lung failure. Why the hell had Bonham tried to make it seem so hard? His elation continued to grow.

Behind him Bonham handed up his own lung easily and smoothly, moved his bulk smoothly up the little ladder and over the side and, dripping wet, started the motor. Ali ran forward to haul in the anchor. Before Grant could get himself out of Ali's clinging wet shirt Bonham had sold him, the diver and his helper were headed back to shore full throttle like two men going home from the office, Bonham at the wheel and Ali dismantling the lungs. In the west the sun was still quite a few yards above the big mountain that jutted out into the sea.

DAVE BARRY

From *Tropic* magazine, February 19, 1989

BLUB STORY: A VERY DEEP EXPERIENCE

I'm swimming about twenty feet below the surface of the Atlantic, a major ocean. I'm a little nervous about this. For many years my philosophy has been that if God had wanted us to be beneath the surface of the ocean, He would never have put eels down there.

But I'm not panicking. That's the first thing you learn in scuba class: Don't panic! Just DON'T DO IT! Even if a giant eel comes right up and wraps around your neck and presses its face against your mask and opens its mouth and shows you its 874,000,000,000,000 needle-sharp teeth, you must remain COMPLETELY CALM so you'll remember your training and take appropriate action, which in this case I suppose would be to poop in your wet suit. I don't know for certain, because in my training we haven't gotten to the section on eels.

Also, I am just now realizing, we haven't covered the procedure for what to do if a large tentacle featuring suckers the size of catchers' mitts comes snorking out and grabs your leg and starts hauling you into a vast, dark, hidden underwater cave whose denizens have little if any respect for the Bill of Rights.

Also there is the whole issue of shar... of sha... of sh...

There could be s—ks down here, somewhere.

But so far, all the marine life has appeared to be harmless. Mostly it has consisted of what I would describe, using precise ichthyological terminology, as "medium fish," many of which are swimming right up and giving me dopey fish looks, which basically translate to the following statement: "Food?" That's what fish do all the time — they swim around going: "Food?" You can almost see the little question marks over their heads. The only other thought they seem capable of is: "Yikes!" Fish are not known for their SAT scores. This may be why they tend to do their thinking in large groups. You'll see a squadron of them coming toward you, their molecule-size brains working away on the problem ("Food?" "Food?" "Food?" "Food?"); and then you suddenly move your arm, triggering a Nuclear Fish Reaction ("Yikes!" "Yikes!" "Yikes!" "Yikes!") and FWOOOSSHH they're outta there, trailing a stream of exclamation marks.

This is a lot of fun to watch, because many of the fish are spectacularly, psychedelically beautiful. I'm sure there are all kinds of practical reasons for their coloration, but I don't want to know what these reasons are. I like to think that whoever designed marine life was thinking of it as basically an entertainment medium. That would explain some of the things down there, some of the unearthly biological *contraptions* you see hanging out in the nooks and crannies of the reef or contraptioning along the bottom on a ridiculous number of arms and legs with all kinds of feelers and pincers and eyeballs sticking out randomly on the ends of stalks.

It is a comical place, the sea.

So anyway, I'm swimming along the reef, with my nervousness gradually being replaced by a sort of high — a combination of fascination and amusement — when suddenly I hear my scuba instructor, Ray Lang, make the following statement: "Brnoogle." Everything anybody says through an air regulator underwater sounds like "brnoogle," which can mean: "Hi!" Or: "Isn't this fun?" Or: "I'm having a coronary seizure!" So generally people communicate with hand signs.

When I look at Lang, he's pointing excitedly off to my right, so I turn and see a large ray, which looks sort of like a giant underwater bat. This is a major test of my ability to not panic. The only other time I've been in this kind of situation was in 1970 in the Virgin Islands, when I was snorkeling with a friend named Buzz behind a small, crowded dinghy, and a ray swam directly underneath us. I have never seen a missile launched from a submarine, but I can't imagine that it leaves the water at a higher velocity than Buzz and I attained as we vaulted, arms and legs flailing, into the lower atmosphere, creating a minor hazard for commercial aircraft before finally landing in the dinghy, which nearly sank.

And that was a smallish ray, compared to this one. This ray has enough square footage to qualify as a voting district. And it is very close, swooping along, flapping its enormous wings and going: "Food?" Instantly I wish that I had brought my *Miami Herald* identification card (which is laminated and would work underwater) so I could identify myself as a journalist. As it is, I have no choice but to strike what I believe to be a fairly inedible pose.

But the ray pays no attention to me. It just cruises by, very casual, very nonthreatening, a ray taking care of ray business. And as it passes by, I find myself, without really thinking about it, trying to *follow* it — me, a weenie of legendary stature when it comes to dealing with the Animal Kingdom; a person who has on more than one occasion fled in desperate, armpit-soaking fear from *chickens* — here I am, flippering through the blue-green Semi-Deep in pursuit of this nightmare-inducing *thing*.

Swimming next to me, Lang points toward the surface, up above the ray. I look, and there, silhouetted against the surface, is a large school of: barracuda. Yes! The ones with the teeth! In person! They're long and lean, looking very alert, all pointing in the same direction, as if awaiting orders from their commanding officer. ("OK, men. Today we're going to swim around and eat.")

But for some reason, the barracuda don't seem scary, any more than the ray does. For some reason, *none* of this seems scary. Even the idea of maybe encountering a smallish s—k doesn't seem altogether bad. It's beginning to dawn on me that all the fish and eels and crabs and shrimps and planktons who live and work down here are just too *busy* to be thinking about me. I'm a traveler from another dimension, not really a part of their already event-filled world, not programmed one way or another — food or yikes — into their instinct circuits. They have important matters to attend to, and they don't care whether I watch or not.

And so I watch.

Before I took lessons, virtually everything I knew about scuba — aside from the fact that it stands for "self-contained underwater breathing apparatus" — came from the syndicated television series *Sea Hunt.* This was a very popular half-hour adventure show that ran from 1958 through 1961 and starred Lloyd Bridges as Mike Nelson, "free-lance undersea investigator."

There were 156 episodes of *Sea Hunt,* but they all merge together in my mind into one basic plot, namely: Mike Nelson is swimming around, conducting a free-lance underwater investigation, when suddenly a bad guy swims up behind him and *cuts his air hose.* Mike always acted surprised about this, which was pretty funny because in fact he got his air hose cut about as often as the average person burps. You'd think it would have eventually dawned on him that for whatever reason — possibly related to the Gulf Stream — the waters around his boat were *teeming* with air-hose cutters, but old Mike never seemed to catch on.

So the climax of *Sea Hunt* was always an exciting underwater fight (accompanied by dramatic underwater horn music) in which Mike, his bubbles shooting all over the place, would struggle to get some air into his lungs and subdue the bad guy and get back to the surface and head over to the air-hose store, where he probably got a volume discount. *Sea Hunt* was great entertainment, but it did not leave you with the concepts of "scuba" and "safety" firmly cemented together in your mind.

The truth is, however, that scuba diving, especially at the relatively shallow depths recommended for recreational divers, is quite safe. Bad things can happen, but not nearly as many as can happen in a truly dangerous environment, such as the Palmetto Expressway. And virtually nothing bad is likely to happen unless you go out of your way to help it. So far, I'm pleased to report, I have not had my air hose cut one single time. I did have one terrifying Lobster Encounter (which I'll describe in harrowing detail later, when I feel you're ready to handle the emotional strain), but fortunately I was able to handle the situation through a combination of a) not panicking and b) letting go of the lobster. But I probably never would have thought of this without proper scuba training.

The training I got was the standard course authorized by the Professional Association of Diving Instructors, or PADI. If you want to get into scuba diving, you should take an authorized course. For one thing, you'll learn many useful tips that will help to make your dive as enjoyable and fatality-free as possible. For another thing, if you don't have a card certifying that you've been properly trained, reputable dive shops will not rent you equipment or fill your tanks with air, which, as you can imagine, comes in very handy in the aquatic environment.

The guy who trained me, Ray Lang, thirty-nine, knows a lot about the aquatic environment. This is ironic because he was born and raised in Wichita, Kansas, a locale you very rarely see featured on Jacques Cousteau underwater specials ("Henri excitedly gestures to Pierre that he has found a piece of the sunken tractor"). But in his early twenties he became obsessed with scuba diving and moved with his wife, Teresa, to South Florida, where they eventually opened a small chain of dive shops called Divers Den.

Lang's true passion, however, is competitive free-dive spearfishing, a moderately insane sport in which you wear only a mask and flippers — no air tank — and, holding your breath for two minutes or more, dive down as far as 100 feet, trying to locate, stalk, and spear the largest possible fish without blacking out from oxygen deprivation and maybe getting hauled back to the surface, but maybe not, which has been known to happen. Lang and two other men won the 1988 national team free-dive spearfishing championship; he also holds world spearfishing records for six species of fish, including three species of s—ks.

Lang has dived all over the world and had some fairly remarkable experiences, which he describes in a flat, Midwestern-style twang, often employing unconventional but surprisingly useful words such as "motate," as in:

"...so I look up, and I see I'm about to swim directly into this *large* tiger shark, has to be fifteen feet, and I think, whoa, time to motate out of here, so..."

Or:

"...so I figure, how hard can it be to catch one of these things? So I grab it, and I'm trying to motate on out of there, but it gets one tentacle wrapped around a rock, and now it has hold of *me*, and I mean those things can develop some *suction*, so I'm thinking, whoa..."

I should stress here that this type of anecdote does NOT form the basis of the diving-course curriculum. When you take the course, you start out with some classroom sessions wherein you learn basic diving theory, including a lot of information concerning how Pressure relates to Volume. This is of course exactly the kind of thing that put you to sleep in high school, but you find yourself paying very close attention in scuba class, once you realize that the volume they're talking about is the air in your own personal lungs, and that if you take a deep breath from your tank at a depth of, say, forty feet, and then, while holding your breath, you shoot, missile-style, to the surface, your little air sacs could start exploding like defective condoms, a situation which, as Lang put it, can be "very fatal."

Fortunately, there is a very simple preventive measure: All you have to do is *keep breathing*. That's it. You'd think there would be no way you could forget it. But it turns out that's the biggest danger you face underwater — not eels or s—ks, but the failure to perform an act so simple and natural that you have presumably been doing it on a routine basis since early childhood. Yet it was stressed so heavily in scuba training that I found myself writing it repeatedly in my notes, as if were some kind of radical new science breakthrough. "IMPORTANT TO KEEP BREATHING," I would write. And: "NEVER STOP BREATHING!"

The highlight of the classroom training, for me, was when we learned about the equipment (or, as we scuba veterans say, the "gear"). Your basic diving outfit is a mask and flippers, plus the breathing apparatus, which you can rent. But there are all kinds of other neat gear objects you can get, the neatest one, as far as I'm concerned, being: a knife. All my life I've wanted an excuse to wear a knife, and here I have found a sport where it is actually *encouraged*. "Diving knives are practical tools," states the PADI course manual, "providing you with a means to measure, pry, dig, cut, and pound under water." But the REAL advantage, which the manual fails to note, is that you can wear your knife *strapped to your leg.*

There's something about striding around with a knife strapped to your leg that makes you feel exceedingly James Bondlike. If you can keep a little secret, I will confess to you that right at this very moment, as I write these words, I have my knife strapped on. Just in case somebody comes along and, for example, tries to cut my word processor cord. As Ray Lang put it, during one of his colorful diving anecdotes: "You never can tell when the inevitable is gonna happen."

Speaking of the inevitable, there comes a time in your scuba training when you leave the classroom and get into some actual water, usually in the form of a swimming pool. This is where I encountered my first major diving challenge, namely, putting on the wet suit. The wet suit does an excellent job of protecting you and keeping you warm even in cold water, but putting it on for the first time is like trying to get into a giant foundation garment that has been possessed by an evil spirit. You wind up lying idiotically on your back, legs in the air, tugging and straining at this malevolent piece of rubber, fearful that if you let go, it will leap to its invisible feet and start dancing around you, laughing silently and making invisible but unmistakable hand gestures.

My first scuba experience was equally exciting. Lang and I were standing in about five feet of water, and all he wanted me to do was kneel on the bottom. That was it. So, bearing firmly in mind the Two First Rules of Scuba Diving — Don't Panic and Never Stop Breathing — I put my air regulator in my mouth, ducked my head under water and immediately, with a natural effortlessness that suggested I had been doing these things all my life, I (1) panicked and (2) stopped breathing. My feet started inexplicably drifting upward of their own accord, my mask started filling with water, I started choking and flailing my arms ineffectually around and the lone thought I could summon into my brain was: "Yikes!"

So I thrashed my way back to the surface, a failure. If you want to feel like a complete dweezil, the best way I know to accomplish this is to stand in front of a guy who has swum down into the depths with no air tank and speared a ten-foot hammerhead, and explain to this guy why you seem to be unable to accomplish the mission of kneeling on the bottom of a swimming pool in five feet of water.

But Lang, who's used to this, was patient, and before long I was motating around the pool like a regular frogperson, making all kinds of astounding underwater discoveries. When you consider that approximately 0.000000000003 percent of our planet is covered with swimming pools, it's shocking how little we really know what goes on beneath the surface of these mysterious bodies of water. It turns out that there's a whole world down there: cracks, leaves, the occasional dead worm, and — for those with the courage and skill to challenge the deep end — a drain.

In between my ground breaking exploration, Lang had me practice various skills, such as removing my mask and air regulator underwater, then getting them back into place. This is not difficult if you simply remember what you were taught, although at first your instinct is to yell, "Time out!" and make all the water go away while you get yourself straightened out, which of course would not be a practical solution if you were fifty feet down.

Another skill I learned, I'm pleased to note, is "buddy breathing," which is when two divers share one air tank because one of them has run out of air or had his hose cut. I had no trouble with this skill because I had seen it so many times on *Sea Hunt.* As Lang and I swam along the pool bottom, passing the regulator back and forth, I could almost hear dramatic horn music.

But the true drama came the day I dove in the ocean. We went to the John Pennekamp State Park/Key Largo National Marine Sanctuary complex, which is one of the world's most popular dive sites because of its spectacular and accessible reefs. These are made up of several jillion living and deceased creatures called "polyps," whom we might think of collectively as nature's own enormous halftime marching band because of their ability to form themselves into amazing formations. The reefs, and almost all the life forms that thrive on and around them, are protected by strict laws, as Lang explained to me in detail before we went out.

"You may not spear or possess any snook," he informed me. Frankly this had never crossed my mind, but I wrote it down anyway, because the last thing you'd want to do is to wind up in prison and have the other inmates ask what you were in for, and you'd have to answer: "snook possession."

Lang said I could take a lobster if I found one big enough, but I figured there was no chance of this. I hate lobsters. As far as I'm concerned, lobsters are large underwater insects. I don't like to be in the same *restaurant* with them. Unfortunately, I failed to mention this to Lang.

(Sound of horn music starting to play quietly but dramatically in the backgroud.)

I will spare you a gushy description of the dive itself, except to say that when you finally see what goes on underwater, you realize that you've been missing the whole *point* of the ocean. Staying on the surface all the time is like going to the circus and staring at the outside of the tent. At first Lang had me practicing my scuba skills, but after that I basically just motated along, very relaxed, grooving on the scenery, the fish, the comical marine contraptions. Even the giant ray, even the barracuda, merely served to heighten my enjoyment. The whole thing was going perfectly.

A little *too* perfectly.

(The horn music gets louder.)

OK. So I'm swimming along, and suddenly Lang gestures for me to swim down to where he's crouched in the sand, next to a coral ledge. He is pointing to something, but I can't see what it is. Suddenly his hand flashes out.

(Very loud music now.)

And now Lang is thrusting something into my hand, and it is, as you have deduced, the dreaded Big Bug of the Deep. And I am *holding* it. And it is gesturing violently with all 758 legs, clearly conveying the underwater message: "HEY! Let GO, dammit!!" Which of course I do. Instantly the lobster motates at very high velocity in reverse gear back under the ledge, causing bnoogles of chagrin to erupt from various watching divers, who were hoping to *eat* it.

Perverts.

That was the only upsetting thing that happened. Although I did see an eel. This happened near the end of the last dive; I was following Lang back to the boat, and as he went by a cave, he casually gestured for me to look inside. I did, and there, maybe ten feet away, was Mr. Moray.

I looked at Lang, and held my arms way apart, the international diver gesture for, "Hey! This is a BIG eel! Right?"

Lang shrugged, the international gesture for, "Nah." Maybe six feet, he told me later. Nothing to gesture home about.

But I am here to tell you that this is one bad-looking creature. You could barely see his body — just his whitish head, hanging there, mouth open, a grinning skull floating in the gloom. Not that *I*, personally, was nervous. It takes more than a moray to scare a man who has made a lobster back down.

Now Lang is drifting in front of me. He makes a circle with his thumb and forefinger, the sign for, "OK?"

I make the OK sign back. But that isn't enough, not for what I'm feeling — the adrenaline, the elation, the high. This is *way* more than merely OK.

"Bnoogle," I inform him. It comes from the heart.

WAYNE GROVER

From *Sea Frontiers* magazine,
January/February 1989

DOLPHINS

I was on my second dive of the morning, working my way north along the reef off Palm Beach, Florida at about twenty meters depth. Visibility was in the moderate range, perhaps twelve meters. A steady north current pushed me along with little need for exertion on my part, except to move laterally to investigate reef overhangs that might harbor a large grouper.

I had been down about ten minutes when I heard a distinct clicking noise. It grew louder, and I stopped and looked around, unsure of what caused it. Then from upcurrent to the north, three shapes came into sight at the limit of my visibility. The clicking noise filled the water now, and I could feel it against my eardrums.

From the deep east side of the reef, I saw the three shapes coming toward me. Within a second, they were with me — three bottlenose dolphins. But then I saw something that bothered me deeply.

There were two large dolphins and a smaller one swimming close together. The two larger ones were on each side of the smaller one, which was a baby about 1.2 meters long. Wrapped around the tail of the baby dolphin were many meters of heavy monofilament fishing line, trailing well behind its tail.

The three dolphins circled me rapidly, slightly higher than my position about 1.5 meters from the sea bottom. As they did, I saw that the shaft of a large fishing hook was embedded about thirty-six centimeters ahead of the baby dolphin's tail fluke. The monofilament line was wrapped around the baby's body several times, and it had cut deeply into the tail fluke area, actually being embedded under the skin near the base. The embedded hook was the source of the meters of trailing line.

My first reaction was one of wonder. I have been diving in most of the world's seas for thirty years and had never before had a dolphin or porpoise come near me in the water. My second thought was pity for the baby, probably in pain and frightened.

As I watched in wonder, the three dolphins slowed down and nearly stopped quite close to me. I could clearly see that the large hook had gone deeply into the flesh of the little creature with the perpetual grin.

I reached out to touch the dolphin nearest me, and the three shot away only to return in seconds and stop again. They looked at me with a steady gaze, and I looked back in awe, absolutely thrilled with this close encounter.

Again I reached out and again they moved away, but only a meter or so this time. Then the larger dolphins started making clicking noises and, with the baby between them, slowly swam around me. Whether it was my imagination or a logical deduction, I suddenly felt that I was being asked for help. I settled on the bottom very slowly and sat motionless, thinking what I perceived were calm, loving thoughts directed at the dolphins.

For perhaps three minutes, I sat there breathing slowly, watching the three watch me.

The clicking increased, then stopped altogether. The three dolphins then moved very cautiously toward me, with their tails barely moving up and down. The large ones closed in on the baby from either side until they were touching it with their pectoral flippers. They settled the baby to the seafloor right in front of me, still holding it from each side. I thought I knew what they wanted.

I reached out to touch the baby, but it shot away, trailing the fishing line behind. The two larger dolphins immediately swam away to join the baby.

Again they shouldered the baby to place it right in front of me. This time I very gently reached over to stroke the little one's head with my gloved hand, stopped, removed the glove, and ran my hand from right behind its blowhole to the dorsal fin. The baby's eyes rolled up to watch my every move as I did it again.

On the third gentle stroke, I slipped my hand over the dorsal fin and down to the embedded hook in the tapering last third of the body. I could see that the hook had torn the delicate skin for about two centimeters, where the little dolphin had originally been snagged before breaking loose. The flesh was raw and slightly bloody.

I decided I would get the hook out but knew it would be hard to hold the little creature still enough to do it. I had with me only a fairly sharp, large diving knife, which seemed too big for delicate surgery, but I had no options. I knew I had to try because I thought the baby would die from infection or get snagged and drown.

Suddenly, the three dolphins all clicked together and left, climbing up out of visibility. Within a minute they were back, right where they had started. I realized they had to surface to breathe, so I had to work fast.

I tried unwinding the fishing line from around the narrow part of the baby dolphin's body at the tail shaft, or caudal peduncle, but it seemed to cause the animal pain, and it moved away from me. One of the other dolphins then literally pushed the baby back to me with its snout.

Again I tried to work the line loose, but it was too tangled. I took out my knife and very gently started cutting the line where it was hanging loosely away from the body. Bit by bit, piece by piece, I removed what I could.

The baby wriggled and made high-pitched noises but stayed by me. I pulled some of the embedded line from the flesh, which brought another series of noises and caused some blood to flow out and drift downcurrent. The blood, although red, seemed green in the depth, and I worried about sharks trailing the injured baby.

I was able to unwind the line, piece by piece, until I had all of it free from the tail except for a short piece still attached to the hook shaft.

I knew the next part would be painful to the baby, but I hoped it would stay while I tried to cut out the shaft. I touched the shaft, and the baby jumped and trembled under my hand and tried to leave. I held the baby in place by grabbing its dorsal fin and pushing its body back down to the bottom.

For a few moments, I held the baby dolphin there, trying again to hold onto the hook shaft. Again the baby tried to get away. Then the two larger dolphins, hovering about 1.5 meters away, started clicking again; the noise calmed the baby.

I gently applied pressure on the hook back toward the rip in front of it, but I could feel it was tightly caught. I knew that to sink the heavy bladed knife into the wound would cause more damage, but there was nothing else I could do.

I held the knife between my fingers like a pencil, with about seven centimeters of the blade exposed, and started slowly working it into the wound where the shaft had disappeared into the baby's flesh. The little dolphin shook and cried a series of high-pitched noises, but I held it down with my left hand and my left leg which I placed over its head just behind the blowhole.

I tried not to hurt the baby dolphin, but the hook did not move, and I realized that to get it out would require a deep cut into the flesh. I pointed the knife straight into the tear and slipped it in. Once committed, I held the baby tightly and worked the knife until I felt it hit the upturned part of the hook with the barb.

The baby was vocalizing, the large dolphins were clicking, and I was breathing faster as I struggled to get the hook out. I ran two fingers into the wound, down along the hook shaft until I found the barb. I then started wriggling the hook, pulling it up and away from the cut. It came free in my hand, and I extracted it!

Blood flowed freely in the current, and I pushed down hard on the wound with my hand and held it closed. I do not know how much time elapsed while I held the baby dolphin there trying to slow the blood flow. I had not thought about my air pressure. In fact, I had not thought about myself at all during the entire episode.

After a time, the bleeding slowed and seemed to stop; there was just a little trickling between my fingers closed over the wound. I took my hand off the dolphin and let it up. Slightly buoyant, the young animal rose about thirty centimeters from the bottom and just hung there, stabilizing its position with its pectoral fins.

The smaller of the two other dolphins then came right up to the baby and looked at the slightly bleeding wound. The larger one swam away upcurrent. Then, rapidly, the largest dolphin reappeared and clicked rapidly, again pulsating my eardrums with the strength of its sonar.

The baby and the other dolphin swam over to meet the largest one, which immediately looked over the wound area. Then they all swam in a large circle around me, clicking loudly.

The largest dolphin came to me, stopped at eye level, and looked into my eyes behind the mask. For a brief moment, we looked deeply into each other's eyes, and then the dolphin nudged me with its snout, pushing me slightly back.

I had the distinct impression that we were communicating but, even as I thought it, my logical mind tried to dissuade me, saying it was imagined.

Then the three dolphins were gone. Without a sound, they rapidly climbed upward toward the surface, leaving me alone again.

I looked at my air gauge. I had 1,100 pounds left, so I continued my dive, feeling an almost dreamlike quality for the remaining time I was down.

As I surfaced and rejoined my diving companions in our dive boat, I felt too awed to share what I had just experienced. It was a precious experience, and to share it would have detracted from the lingering feeling of the beautiful companionship I had shared for a few minutes with three creatures from the sea.

I have often thought about this close encounter since that dive, and many nights I lie awake feeling that same sense of communication with the dolphins that I felt down in the sea.

Again my logical mind says, "It can't be; it's only wishful thinking," but still I feel they are out there someplace, thinking about me too.

CARSTEN STROUD

From *Reader's Digest* magazine,
November 1979

THE DOLPHIN AND THE SHARK

Along the windward shore of the popular resort island of Cozumel off Mexico's Yucatan Peninsula, my wife Linda and I discovered a small, reef-bound lagoon. It was isolated, reachable only by Jeep on a spine-cracking road through jungle palms, but it was ideal for scuba diving. A rocky spur ran down the beach at the northern edge, curving out into the sea for almost 300 yards. It stopped at a deep-water trench that had been cut away by a rapid tidal flow, leaving a sea gate about ten yards wide. The circle was completed by a ragged chain of limestone rocks. The area contained by this natural breakwater was close to 400 yards across, and reached a depth of fifty feet. Beyond the reef, the waves boomed and crashed, but within, all was calm.

At least on the surface; underneath, the lagoon was filled with the bizarre flora and fauna of tropical oceans. Most of the larger predators — the barracuda and sharks — were kept out by the sea walls. This pool was teeming with life. In it, we became completely involved in the visual and spiritual delight of tropical diving.

At three o'clock on the afternoon of March 18, we were finning along in thirty feet of water just inside the mouth of the lagoon. A few minutes before, I had been pulled through the sea gate by the tide. Linda, always a cool head in a crisis, had braced herself in a seam and dragged me back in. The whole action hadn't taken thirty seconds, but I had blown a fair amount of air in my fright, and my lungs were still laboring.

People are less alert after such an incident, so neither Linda nor I realized what was happening when a large, dark shape hurtled by us, putting out a pressure wave strong enough to send us spinning. Linda's mask came off. My mind screamed *Shark!* as I fumbled for the shark billy I always carry. Then I spotted Linda swimming toward me, mask back in place. At that moment a smaller form rocketed through the sea gate.

Instinctively, Linda and I lined up back to back, scanning the waters above, behind and beneath for whatever it was that had buzzed us. Forty yards away, swimming in a tight, agitated circle, were a bottle-nosed dolphin and her pup. We could hear their high-pitched chattering squeals through the water and, when the pup turned, we saw a cut which was trailing a dark mist just back of the blowhole.

I wondered why the pair had strayed so far from their school, and then a slow chill gathered around the back of my neck. Linda and I moved closer to each other, and I pulled her to the bottom of the lagoon. Somewhere nearby, and closing fast, there must be a shark.

In the taut seconds that followed, local marine life slowed into a profound silence. Just beyond the sea gate, something was moving up the incline of the sea floor — a dark flicker of sinuous motion. My breath stopped, and a vein began to pound in my right temple. Suddenly, a twelve-foot-long tiger shark weighing perhaps 500 pounds cruised through the gate, head moving from side to side as he sensed the waters. A school of pilot fish clustered around his flanks, and we could make out his markings, dirty brown on top, with faint shadowy stripes, a notched dorsal and a gray-white belly. As he passed by, no more than twenty feet away, one black eye tracked us. His jaws were open slightly, his gills were distended and his tail fin was stroking; his nostrils stirred with the blood scent of the wounded dolphin pup.

If the shark ran true to form, concentrating on his bleeding prey, we might be able to bottom-crawl to the shallows and — with luck — get out of the water safely.

I hooked into Linda's weight belt (she would guide us while I watched the rear), and we began moving slowly along the bottom. We covered 100 yards without seeing either the shark or the dolphins. Another twenty... no sign, no movement, no sound anywhere. Where was he? What was he doing?

Something moved to our right. I snapped my head around and saw a thick, black shadow rippling over the sandy bottom. Flipping over on my back, I got my shark billy up barely in time to plant the spikes in the shark's gills. He was on top of us, massive jaws pushed open, jagged rows of triangular teeth inches from my face. With a hideous snaking twist he drove us down into a small trench.

I heard a muffled snap as his jaws closed down on the water in front of my faceplate. They sprang open, and he snapped again and again at my chest, shredding my gear, held off by the flexing shaft of the shark billy, his sheer brute force driving it into the rocks at the base of the trench. Linda twisted underneath me, and sank her blade into the shark's throat. Blood began to darken the water. I heard a splitting crack, and the handle of the shark billy gave way. The tiger turned above me, jaws opening, and then something struck him heavily in the side, knocking him away from us.

Blood and sand swirled around us as we lay in the trench. Linda, her eyes wild behind her faceplate, put her hand out and ran it tentatively over my chest, unable to believe that I hadn't been bitten. My wet suit was in tatters, my flotation vest had been chewed away, but I was all right.

The tiger was within ten yards, circling without rhythm, shudders rippling down his flanks as he jerked his head and bit at the water. Whatever had delivered that ferocious blow, knocking him away from the trench, had saved our lives — for the moment.

Then he turned to come in again — one obscene killing machine, jaws gaping between cold eyes. He got to within fifteen feet of us when, with blurring speed, the female dolphin shot in from the right. She struck him with terrible force near his pectoral fin. A huge black bubble burst out of the shark's mouth, and he swerved to strike at his assailant. He was certainly hurting, but how badly it was impossible to guess.

The shark was now less than six feet away in the murk, rolling on his side to pursue the dolphin. We seized the moment to try to get into clear water again. While we were kicking out of the blood and wrack, expecting the tiger's bull-like snout to explode out of the mist in front of us, I ran out of air. I pulled the reserve rod and gave Linda the throat-cutting sign to let her know that I was now on emergency air. It might last three minutes.

Suddenly, the dolphin pup skimmed over us, taking this chance to run for the open sea. It flew past with eyes wide and beak shut tight, and was gone. With the pup safe, the mother might run for it. That would leave us roughly seventy yards from the beach, with the wounded tiger shark about fifty feet away. As we knelt in the sand, he turned and headed for us again, passing overhead, looking like some lighter-than-air craft and trailing a steady stream of blood from his gills.

Out of the corner of my eye I saw the dolphin, swimming some distance to our right, moving roughly parallel and making a clicking with her blow-hole. The shark was at the edge of the shallows, between us and land. He stopped his erratic turns, and began to swim quickly along the shoreline; then he gave a violent twist of his muscular torso and hurled himself away from the beach, right at us. I kicked up and away from Linda, holding out the splintered shaft of the shark billy. I think I had some idea of wedging it into his jaws. When he was within six feet of me, I struck out — and hit nothing. In less than a second the tiger had covered the distance separating us, dipped underneath me and cut straight out for the gap in the sea wall. Within seconds he was out of sight. The dolphin circled us and flashed out to sea in the wake of the tiger shark.

For some seconds, Linda and I hung suspended in the water, minds blank. Then we blew out hard and kicked for the surface. When our heads broke into the air, we were ten yards from shore. Wordlessly, we swam to the shallows, staggered up the beach and collapsed on a rock facing the ocean. I was vaguely aware that the vein pounding in my temple was slowing its beat. Linda burst out in a short laugh, and showed me her watch. It was 3:10 p.m. The entire episode had lasted less than ten minutes.

That evening, we went down to the beach in front of our hotel room and tried to make some sense out of what had happened. Why the shark decided to attack us instead of his chosen prey, we can't imagine. I wouldn't care to speculate on why a shark does anything; I doubt they know themselves. I think that the mother dolphin took advantage of the shark's interest in us to try to eliminate the danger to herself and her pup. Linda sees it differently. She thinks the dolphin fought for us — that in the midst of all the cruelties of nature, there is room for kindness as well.

DENNIS RYAN

From *Bahamas:*
In A White Coming On, 1981

DEATH'S ACUTE ANGLE

As we kick through the shallows,
the troughs and shoals stir
with the synchronized movements of innocent pilchards.
Like quicksilver,
they engulf us within their light,
hug our hollows,
protected from lunging lane snappers.
But a growing spot
— that peculiar inclination of a head —
excites them into frenzy
and we become part of the headlong rush,
arms and legs flailing out against
death's acute angle: barracuda
sleek skull and keen teeth foremost,
ripping the school with indiscriminate ease.

HANS HASS

From *Manta: Under the Red Sea with Spear and Camera*, 1953

THE FIRST SHARKS

I glided down without further ado. I found myself in what appeared to be an oriental city full of temples, that had sunk beneath the waves, its ruins overgrown with creeping plants of a hundred hues. Castles of coral, thirty and thirty-five feet high, towered up, their battlements gorgeously adorned with numbers of small turrets. Among them precipitous defiles wound like streets through the rock. The amazing color of this vision was due to the extraordinarily rich growth of leather corals, spreading every-where like a primitive forest of luxuriant vegetation. Unlike the rock corals, these had not developed from a chalk foundation, and their polyps had not six, but eight tentacles, which were, moreover, feathered. They opened out like thousands and thousands of little stars, pulsated rhythmically, and drew in their tiny heads as I approached.

Brownish-yellow catkins grew everywhere, resembling clumps of pulpy bracken. The delicately blooming sprigs of prickly Alcyonaria branched out in every direction, glimmering with lilac or reddish hues. Grayish-blue Xenia corals grew out of beds of orange-tinted and deep-black dermoid Alcyonaria, with delicate polyps bearing diminutive violet and reddish-purple stars.

Among the many fishes that fluttered like insects and birds among the ruins of this sunken city two big dark groupers took a special interest in my arrival. They pursed their thick, puffy lips inquisitively in my direction and stared gloomily at me with their goggle eyes. But in spite of these signs of friendly attention they kept well out of the way of my harpoon, though resplendent yellow angelfish came dancing right up to me and took their time to look me over.

The streets of the coral city led obliquely downward and ended in a precipice falling almost vertically into the depths. When I reached this point in the jungle of coral, twenty or thirty blue-black fish ascended from the depths. Their shape and the double quill of their tails indicated a close relationship to the green rhinoceros fish, though their heads were horn-less. I gave them the name of "boobyfish," for they were really exceptionally silly. They swam, with frank curiosity, right up to the gleaming point of the harpoon, examined it with the greatest assurance, turned this way and that around it, and brought their little snouts close to the sharp tip as if they meant to use it as a flute.

I soon made up my mind and ran the point of the harpoon through the body of the first one. The point came free, the fish wriggled frantically on the harpoon, and I was dragged behind the shaft through the corals. The strength of the creature was amazing. After it had described, at lightning speed, a number of figures of eight, the wire that attached the point to the short length of cord on the shaft of the harpoon broke. The fish vanished in a side alley.

The other members of the shoal surrounded me in the greatest excite-ment. If I had still had a point on my harpoon I should have been able to send it through any of them I chose. But that excellent point of mine was gone now, unfortunately. I had to come to the surface and fetch another.

The entire sea bed had risen in revolt. Small fishes, as though attracted by a magnet, had fled to the shelter of the gaily colored vegetation of the rocks; but they now reappeared and spread out till all the rocks seemed to increase in size. No fewer than three large and four small spiny-rayed perch had risen from the depths and were staring inquisitively up at me as they flapped their fins. A moray eel stuck its ugly head out of a hole. An enormous, angular fish came spiraling diagonally upward toward me with irresolute movements. I kept a sharp lookout in all directions, in case a shark, too, might turn up. But except for a few mackerel that arrived full tilt, in the guise of camp followers, and also made me the center of a merry-go-round, the fishy tumult had now subsided again.

Bill was quite surprised to see me return to the boat so quickly.

"Anything wrong?" he called.

"Oh, no. Quite the contrary!" I cried back breathlessly. I waved the broken wire at him and told him what had happened.

As the wire attached to the other points was also by this time a bit old and rather rusty, I swung myself into the boat and tied on some new wire. In addition, I fastened a double line to the shaft this time, by way of reinforcement. Those blue fish were not going to get away from me again if I could help it.

They were, in fact, on the spot once more when I descended. But their attitude was now distinctly less enterprising. The change may have been partly due to the "panic-creating material" which, when a fish is injured, is distributed through the water from its skin, gradually spreads, and warns other members of the species that danger threatens in the neighborhood.

I decided to swim a bit deeper into the abyss, till I reached undisturbed regions again. The growth of coral was just as fantastic down there. Several fish past which I swam watched me from their holes as though I were a sea monster on the prowl. And I really felt rather like one as I swam along, filled with the lust of the chase, looking for new adventures, with my harpoon ready. I stopped beneath a high, jagged cliff. From this vantage ground I had a clear view of the corals to right and left and of the abyss. I could not foresee at the time that this rock was destined to come within an ace of representing my tombstone.

At the rear of the cavity, which formed a kind of recess, I saw a fine golden perch, lying motionless and calmly looking at me. As it couldn't get away, I could have easily harpooned it. But I didn't in the least want to do so. I was only interested in those silly "boobyfish" which had been so impudently wheeling round and round the harpoon.

I didn't have to wait long for a chance at them. Here, too, I had already been spotted by one of their shoals and it came dancing right up to me. I aimed at the fattest and harpooned it. As before, the fish dashed frantically off, but this time the wire and line held, and I myself was straddling the corals in such a way that the creature could tug and wriggle as much as it liked but couldn't get free. It drifted in space like a flag, at the end of the taut line.

A torrent of fish poured over us while I was doing my best to haul in the catch and get hold of it. At last I had the creature by the tail and finished it off with my knife. A cloud of blood spread out above us. Then a black shadow came gliding diagonally down, from one side.

I was so busily engaged in working the point loose, as it had gotten stuck in the fish, that I didn't see the shadow until it was within a couple of yards of me. When I looked up, I saw a phalanx of threatening pairs of eyes directed upon me. No less than forty barracudas, each five feet long, were coming straight at me in a silent wedge.

I had met these dreaded killers of the seas before, in the West Indies. We had come across even bigger specimens there, but always solitary rovers, which had not attacked us. I had never seen such a shoal as this before; perhaps Bill, Mahmud, and all the rest of them had not been so mistaken, after all, to warn me as seriously against barracudas as against sharks.

It is true that barracudas do not, like sharks, bite off whole limbs at once; nevertheless, their habit is to rush upon their victim from all directions and tear his flesh from his bones into strips, the taste of blood exciting them to a state of utter frenzy. A lady I knew was only about thirty feet away from a man when the latter was attacked, at Bali in water only up to his hips, by barracudas. Though several persons at once rushed to his assistance, and got him ashore, he was so badly wounded that a leg had to be amputated and in the end he succumbed.

The innumerable teeth in the jaws of a barracuda resemble little daggers. I regarded the creatures with a certain uneasiness as they, with their staring, expressionless eyes, made steadily toward me.

I got a firm hold on the shaft of my harpoon — the point was still stuck in the "boobyfish," which lay on the corals at my feet — and backed away into the recess. I was at bay now, like a rat in its hole.

The barracudas patrolled the entrance tirelessly, back and forth, coming a little nearer to me each time they turned. It was a regular siege. But they had not yet made up their minds to give the signal for the assault. Just as when I had been surrounded by the shoal in the harbor, I now, too, had the feeling that I was not confronted by individual creatures but by a sort of superego, with a steadily mounting common will. I could see no escape and began to lose my composure. I started jabbing viciously, in all directions, at one fish after another, with the blunt end of the iron shaft.

I damaged a few of them, but the reaction to this move was to increase the weird horror of the scene. The fish described a circle at lightning speed and were back again in their original order the next moment, just as though they were all enclosing an electrical field, each member keeping relentlessly to its appointed position.

In this situation an unexpected ally came to my rescue. I saw a great gray shape come gliding through the circle of barracudas, followed closely by a second. Sharks! They were about eight feet long, well proportioned, and had white tips to their back and tail fins. The sight of them caused the barracudas to cower like dwarfs. For a moment I plucked up courage; I dashed suddenly in among the barracudas, simultaneously making as much noise as I could by puffing against the water. The shoal scattered in all directions, and my repeated antics prevented it from reassembling. The common will that so mysteriously and invisibly dominated them went to pieces.

Sharks! There they were at last! A third was just approaching from the left, zooming up, like an aircraft, between two towers of coral. He glided nearer, across a ravine of coral, and swam past me, a bare six feet above my head. Then he turned, so as to focus me with his laterally placed eyes. It was the first time I had seen a shark vertically, from below: his belly, with the pectoral fins standing out from it like pointed wings, was snow-white; at its forward end, behind the tapering snout, showed a clear, semilunar outline — the jaws.

I felt marvelously self-confident again. No, these sharks, I perceived immediately, were no different from those I already knew. They were, so to speak, old friends, whose actions and behavior I could rely on without question. At last the suspense under which I had so long labored was at an end — the fabulous bogies, capable of every atrocity, had turned into ordinary creatures of flesh and blood with which I was perfectly familiar from hundreds of previous encounters. For the first time I no longer felt myself to be a surreptitious invader of these reefs, but their ruler. Like a protective, invulnerable coat of mail, a feeling of power and security enveloped me.

The first three sharks had now disappeared and a smaller one, darkly colored, had risen from the abyss. I swam toward him and he turned sluggishly away. The battle was over! The barracudas hung in a motionless cloud a hundred feet away. Perhaps that malign instrument was again playing upon a uniform will, that common electrical vibration directed to the annihilation of a new victim. I swam to the edge of the abyss and looked down into the black, unknown depths, where I could see the shapes of more sharks. Then the risen tide of my confidence ebbed again, and I decided to call it a day. I went back to the rock under which the golden perch was still hovering and fetched my dead "boobyfish," which probably weighed a good fifteen or twenty pounds. Then I glided up the coral precipice, with considerable relief.

LAURENCE LIEBERMAN

From *The Unblinding,* 1968

TARPON

Five shadows in heavy motion, lumbering half-seen,
    pass me on either side, shark
panic slowly leaving my fluttered breath pumping as I make

    out the tarpons' armored plate scales,
diamonded in silvery weave, the undershot bulldog
    jaw, his thick cylindrical body,

a wingless fuselage, famed for muscling twelve foot
    leaps in the air on his tail's pole
vault — when hooked, and broadjumping thirty feet at a bolt,

    many times, in Kodak-flash succession.
Now some thirty tarpon pass, in clusters of three to six.
    Still mindful of shark fins, I half-spin

radially, peering from side to side, with metronomic
    evenness of rhythm, kicking to and fro
to sustain a stable axis of pivot, the only way to keep

from drifting blindly out of shore's safe
keeping, my attention fastened undivertedly to the man-sized
   passersby. I scrutinize the larger specimens,

ruling out the offchance of a lone predator, prowling.
   I take heart finally, as the school thins
out, a few last (three foot!) small fry trailing behind,

   solitarily, one pausing just under my legs,
looking after the others, and up at me disconcertedly,
   finally edging up to my spear for a closer

view... a being more innocent, quiet, curious – more frail
   than myself. My hand, before my very eyes,
puts down claws: all the violence I so dreaded to find,

   moments before, in a fancied pursuer, now
surging in my arm, up my back and neck, and finally,
   shaking my eyes in my skull like false

teeth in a cup. I hang back. The loaded speargun,
   its three rubbers taut for release,
jiggles between us, seemingly playful, fish-chumming

   away the tarpon's caution, a kinship
springing up between us; my hand still shaking its fury,
   becomes a strange brute thing, self-motivated,

disengaged, yet clinging still to my wrist, tugging
   at my joints as a mad dog on a leash,
yearning for a sickening engagement: *my eyes fix*

   on a point above his head, drilling in.
A brain shot would yank him up, so much limp flesh
   hung on a spit; a tail shot implode

all fierceness inside him, our two nerve cords thrown
    into a queer freedom of naked contact,
as though our bodies had fallen away, and the nerves

    danced and leapt and wound about each
other like quivering vines... I have been here before.
    I have dreamed the death of friends, died

in a friend's dream, and come back. For love, I could
    kill, or be killed. I'll always return,
as a fish perhaps, as myself turned fish. Fish-friend,

    I drop my spear. All terror, love, thee
I spare, who can tow a twenty-foot sailing smack
    for hours, or twist and snap a heavy

duty wrought-iron spear like a pretzel, or tug
    an ill-fated spearfisherman to breath-
less lung-forfeiting depths... In seconds flat.

Bucky McMahon

From *Outside* magazine, October 1996

THE MOLE TRIBE

It's a horror hole, just a depression full of springwater with a scum of hydrilla coating its surface and muddy banks that have been stomped by wild hogs. The small, oval mouth of the spring, some twenty feet down, is spitting out gravel, and a large fallen cypress tree, its tangled gray roots clawing at the air, slants deep into the pool. For anyone with the arcane propensity to give a damn, a good guess would be that under the tannin-dark water, at the bottom of the hole, there is forest debris and possibly unseen horror things: a medusa's head of cottonmouths, perhaps, or a hog-fed gator.

And maybe there's a cave.

On this cool fall evening, with a full moon launched high in the red sky, the Moles stand around the rim of the beckoning pool, wondering whether it "goes" — that is, connects to a larger cave system.

"This is a pretty one," says Wes Skiles, who at thirty-eight is probably the most experienced cave diver in this tribe of elite aquanauts. Hooded in expedition fleece and chomping on a Honduran cigar, he looks something like Anthony Quinn in *Lawrence of Arabia*. Skiles studies the surface of the pool, running his hand over it like a book of Braille. After more than twenty-two years and three thousand cave dives, Skiles has an intimate feel for the invisible world beneath the Florida limestone: how much water is down there, how it behaves, where it's going. "There's gotta be big water moving down there," he says in his thick, swamp-country drawl. "We'll find it."

The Moles, as they call themselves, are among the best cave divers in the world, a loose fraternity of middle-aged men who've devoted a good portion of their lives to mapping the aqueous labyrinth that braids through the porous crust of north central Florida. This intricate waterscape was formed by the Floridan Aquifer, the largest underground river system in the United States. Patiently following its leads tunnel by tunnel, sump by sump, the Moles have been responsible for piecing together many of the aquifer's bigger riddles. But there are still question marks, still a few speleological mysteries to be solved. And so for the past week this group of half a dozen friends — Lamar Hires, Woody Jasper, Mark Long, Tom Morris, Ron Simmons, and Skiles — has been poking around the back-woods of Suwannee County, about an hour's drive northwest of Gainesville, searching for the holy grail of cave diving: a virgin passage, some hereto-fore untouched connection to the remarkable honeycombs of karst that lie beneath the fruit stands and bayous, the used car dealerships and putt putt courses, of Florida civilization.

Here at this pulsing hole, hidden on a patch of private property along the bluffs of the Suwannee River, Skiles thinks they may have stumbled on the portal to their next big find.

The problem, as always, will be getting in. The passageways in these spring caves seldom dead-end. Instead, they plunge into depths beyond the reach of today's technology. Or, more intriguingly, they keep narrowing into tighter and tighter cavities that for the diver can induce horrendous psychological stress. "The small stuff," the Moles call these claustrophobic cellars.

Should they succeed in slipping through the initial opening, they'll probably have to unclip their scuba tanks and push them out ahead, butt-first, like battering rams. The water will be a confusing swirl of leaves, wood bits, and silt. As they move on in total blackness, unseen obstacles will snag at their hoses, press on their chests and shoulders. They'll be engulfed in bubbles as they drop down into mud and water and stone. And then, if they're lucky, they'll wriggle through the last of the restrictions and break into the robin's-egg blue of the Floridan Aquifer, briskly flowing water fit for designer bottling.

Since this particular site is well marked with No Trespassing signs, the Moles decide to christen it Posted Spring. Skiles nominates Long — a soft-spoken lighting fixtures salesman from Leesburg, Florida — to take the first plunge. Long is a classic Florida backwoodsman who has logged some fifteen hundred hours of cave diving and has lately been making quite a reputation for himself with his solo rampages through the remotest nooks of the aquifer.

"I'll do it," Long says gamely as he pulls on a hooded wetsuit, a crash helmet with a headlamp, and a steel tank clipped to a side-mount harness. He pays out some line from his exploration reel and ties the end to a tree root. All at once, he jackknifes forward into the water and kicks for the bottom. We see his fin-tips churning the surface. Then he's down. Then his feet are back out. Then down again. Everyone is silent as the bubbles rise to the surface, roiling the weeds.

"Give him a minute," Skiles whispers. "He'll get in there."

In the murk below we can see Long's dark legs scissoring. A panicked turtle breaks for cover, leaving a puff of brown silt. Soon Long's bubbles cease percolating to the surface of the pool, which means he's made it through the first major restriction and is now on the move somewhere beneath us.

Skiles peers into the water and takes another puff on his stogie. "If the virgin system is down there," he says, "it'll be one hell of a rib-cracking squeeze."

With a high domed forehead and barrel chest, Skiles doesn't look like the sort of guy who could squirm through geological keyholes. And yet he's squashed that physique into places scarcely imaginable, places with names like the Basketball Restriction and Russell's Rub, places not much larger than a mailbox.

Today Skiles is hunkered over a table in the map room at Karst Environmental Services, his place of business, which is housed in a modest red-brick building on a quiet stretch of blacktop outside High Springs, Florida. He has plucked several cardboard tubes from a rack of blueprints and unfurled the survey charts of different caves throughout the Floridan Aquifer — charts that are the painstaking work of Skiles and a few of his Mole brethren. He's fitting the pieces together, part of the process he calls "doing the water budget." On one of the maps, he points out a stretch of land along the west bank of the Suwannee River, where, suspiciously, no caves have yet been discovered. This tantalizing territory is where he feels certain the next virgin cave is going to he bagged. "The missing link," he calls it.

"The first generation of explorers, people like (the late Florida explorer) Sheck Exley, hit all the big, obvious caves," Skiles says. "They thought the rest were scraps. But the scraps really told the true story of the Floridan Aquifer — karst plane by karst plane."

Fanning across the northern third of the state, from Wakulla Springs in the Panhandle all the way south to Orlando, the Floridan Aquifer holds ninety percent of the state's drinking water. Like water everywhere, it likes to make space for itself, chewing away at the rock, creeks becoming streams, streams becoming rivers. Wherever it finds cracks and the water pressure is sufficient, it surges to the surface as a spring. Or else it nibbles away capriciously at the surface soil until the roof comes crashing down as a sinkhole. In 1981 near Orlando, one such sinkhole swallowed a swimming pool, several houses, and a Porsche dealership.

Listening to his animated talk about the nuances of the aquifer, one quickly realizes that Wes Skiles is one of those rare, fortunate souls who's managed to carve out a living doing precisely what he loves most, deftly blurring the distinction between office and playground. Karst Environmental Services, which he owns and operates, is a sort of cave exploratory firm. Over the years, various government agencies and conservation groups have contracted Skiles's outfit to map and study spring caves in order to learn what's going on with the water supply. As part of his service, Skiles and some of his fellow Moles go down into caves and perform dye traces, measure volume and flow, take water samples, make detailed maps, and study the complex dynamics and hydrogeology at play. It's the kind of meticulous but also adventurous work that seems perfectly suited to Skiles, whose odd personality type might best be described as Fastidious Redneck. "Yep," he drawls as he pores over one of his blueprints. "I'm definitely the anal one of the bunch."

Skiles also runs a photography and filmmaking company, Karst Productions, that's in demand at underwater venues from Puerto Rico to southern Mexico to Australia. Whether as a photographer or explorer, Skiles has participated in some of the most ambitious cave-diving expeditions on the planet, including Bill Stone's 1994 push into Mexico's Huautla cave system.

Skiles made his first cave dive as a fifteen-year-old in 1973, right about the time that the Great Florida Cave Rush, as he calls it, was just heating up. Back then a frontier atmosphere of balls before brains prevailed. Equipment was primitive and fatalities were frequent, reaching a state-wide high of twenty-six for the year 1974. By the late seventies, Skiles had emerged as an expert in cave-diving safety, his knowledge growing from his own close calls and from the onerous duty of recovering more than thirty bodies from flooded caves all across the Southeast and the Caribbean. In 1980, he became one of the designers of the National Speleological Society's cave-diving certification program, which has done much to halt the waste of life.

It was also during the early eighties that Skiles began to meet other cave divers of like-minded intensity — people such as Morris and Jasper — and the exploits of the Moles began in earnest.

Tom Morris started cave diving when he was thirteen, easing into the darkness with a flashlight in a plastic bag. Now forty-nine, he serves as Skiles's key grip and business partner and is a freelance biologist with an encyclopedic knowledge of subterranean flora and fauna. He's a bearish man with curly gray hair and the perpetually cheerful outlook of the country boy who loved chasing animals and is still chasing them.

Woody Jasper, also forty-nine, got into cave diving after a series of motocross mishaps wrecked his knees and forced him to use a wheelchair and crutches for the better part of a year. An industrial engineer who designs water purification systems, he's always been a tinkerer — "your basic junkyard engineer," Skiles calls him — with a talent for improvising that often comes in handy during the Moles' hastily arranged nocturnal expeditions.

Later, Skiles hooked up with Ron Simmons, a technical wizard who now is a state-of-the-art machinist at the University of Virginia, and Lamar Hires, a dive instructor who worked for a spell at the chemical company that makes the little dots of "Retsyn" that go into Certs. Today, Hires is a vice-president of a diving equipment company called Dive-Rite.

As the Moles started diving together, they quickly found they shared the same curious amalgam of personalities — part techie, part explorer, part contortionist. But above all, they were romantics, for whom virgin sites meant everything. And they were more than willing to construct their entire lives around their sport. Most of the Moles' wives and girl-friends became certified cave divers, if not full-fledged explorers, a shrewd accommodation to their mates' passion. "Dive with us," as Skiles puts it, "or don't see us."

Since he founded his business in 1983, Skiles and his buddies have managed to acquire the political know-how and connections needed to gain access to caves long sequestered on private land, and their explorations have gradually shaded from sport to science. They've sometimes played the role of biologists, documenting the odd species that swim in the stygian gloom of the aquifer. "There are some seriously strange creatures living in our drinking water," Morris says, such as the blind, white isopods and amphipods that feed off the natural chemicals in sunless water. *Procambarus morrisi* is the name the Smithsonian Institution gave a new species of crayfish that Morris discovered in Florida's Devil's Sink. In other caves, there is a delicate, spidery creature, known as *Troglocambarus maclani,* that is held together by water pressure and disintegrates when you try to bring it to the surface.

Karst Environmental has provided the Moles with some interesting work and has even paid a few bills, but in the end what has fueled their nearly lifelong obsession with Florida's spring caves is the simple thrill of figuring out where the great maze leads, discerning its master design. "The Floridian Aquifer is like a giant mega-3-D puzzle in the earth," Skiles says, as he scrolls up the last of the maps and stashes them in the archives. "It's the most dynamic of all the underground river systems in the world. We're not into breaking records here. We're just a bunch of old friends trying to follow down this outrageous maze."

It's easy to underestimate the dangers of venturing into a water-filled cavity of the earth. A single misplaced fin-kick can stir up a cloud of silt that almost immediately reduces visibility to nil. A couple of detours down tempting tunnels, and the whole physical world has a way of rotating, like a trick bookcase in a haunted house, so you'd swear that in is out. And always the clock is ticking, the gauges running down. In 1976, a veteran Florida cave diver named Bill Hurst, realizing he'd made a fatal wrong turn that consumed the air he needed for his exit swim, took out his slate and used his last minutes to compose a farewell letter to his family.

Thirty-five minutes have now elapsed at Posted Spring, and Mark Long is still down there. The Moles know he's tapped into something significant by now. Either that or he's trapped and dying and drafting his own sayonara on a slate.

But just when the Moles are starting to get a little antsy, a pallid light winks at the murky bottom and a form comes hissing up from the depths like some mutant submarine.

It's Long, whipping off his mask, spitting, gasping. "Phawh! Graagh!" He looks up at his fellow Moles and beams. "Wow — that's a kick-ass flow! Forty feet straight down to a sand restriction, and flowing like a son-of-a-gun!"

"Any line in there?" Skiles asks, meaning, was the cave virgin after all?

"There is *now*," Long laughs.

That's enough of a briefing to set the rest of the Moles in motion. Soon Skiles and Jasper have strapped on their multicolored dry-suits and lamps and side-mount tanks, looking as if they're heading out for some formal function in the fifth dimension. Before long, they're dropping down into the hole, one after the other, softly lighting up the black water like a candlelight procession.

A half-hour or so later they reemerge, hot-wired with adrenaline, gesturing wildly. "We ran out of line, big-time," Skiles says, showing his empty reel. "I was pushing through this gnarly passage, all branches and leaves, when I saw what I thought was somebody swimming down toward me — no light, no tank, just this black wet-suit. *Bam!* It smacks into my lamp. Then I realize, it's not a human, it's a six-foot gator! I think he was as scared as I was."

Everybody is raving about *the flow, the flow!* "I was brought to a standstill," Morris says after returning from his dive. "I was pulling for all I was worth and wasn't moving. I figured I had something snagged."

"That's about as pretty a virgin cave as you'll ever see," Skiles says.

"Just think," Jasper muses. "It was right under our noses all these years!"

The Moles have seen enough for tonight, so they hop into their boats and head back to camp, not far away on the bluff of the Suwannee River by a well-known spot called Sandbag Spring. It's a perfect bivouac site, the spring radiating a tender grandeur as it burbles out of the earth between two enormous tan boulders. Above us, a century-old live oak, its elephantine roots clutching limestone, holds out its hoary, moss-draped arms in benediction.

Fifty yards from our tents, a group of locals is holding a heavy-metal hoedown around a crackling bonfire, strains of Bon Jovi and Metallica invading the dark woods. "We'll drown 'em out," Skiles vows, and even before they light the campfire, the Moles stake their claim with the classic licks of the Allman Brothers. First things first.

Skiles has brought along a big Ziploc bag of gourmet barbecue, and there's a bottomless cooler of Coronas. It's been a few months since the Moles have had an outing together, and they have a lot of catching up to do.

A week ago, Morris and Skiles were in the Yucatan, laying line in Nohoch Nah Chich, the world's largest underwater cave. Hires has just returned from a cave-diving trip in Japan, while Jasper and Long have been pushing leads in their own secret caves closer to home, somewhere in the Floridan Aquifer. They really don't want to say too much about it — not even among the tribe.

Living as they do over the world's premier cave-diving pits, the Moles are constantly hosting out-of-town explorers, and expedition meetings tend to turn into parties where the talk always winds back to the old Suwannee County days and twice-told tales, like the one about the Telford Ghost.

"There were two old friends," Skiles begins, "who became lost while diving in a place not far from here called Telford Sink. They got separated in the cave and one of them found the exit and called for help."

The sheriff's department organized a search, which went on for days. As one of the principal explorers of the Telford cave system, Skiles was the best hope for recovering the drowned friend.

"He must've made a hell of a swim in the wrong direction, because we never found a trace of him," Skiles says. "Meanwhile, the police discovered that the drowned diver had been on probation, and they started to suspect that the two friends had planned the whole thing, and that maybe the missing guy was on his way to Canada.

"Four years later, I'm sitting in a local restaurant eating breakfast, and Roger Warner, an old cave-diving buddy of mine, burst in: 'Wes, Wes, I found him!' And I'm going, 'Who, Roger? Who did you find?' 'The guy in Telford!' 'What guy in Telford?' It turns out, Roger was way back in some little side tunnel laying exploration line, and looked up and saw this skeletonized hand reaching down toward him."

Skiles makes an Edvard Munch face and imitates a gargled underwater scream.

"With Roger's next breath, the exhaust bubbles broke up the skeleton, and the bones came pouring out of the wetsuit, pelting down on him. A few days later, a couple of divers went back there and removed the guy's body. They kept his tank and tried everything to get the stench out. In the end, they just had to throw it away."

The woods are eerily silent now. The Moles have partied down the metalheads. "Sounds like they've run out of steam over there," Hires says, with evident pride.

We stare for a long while into the glowing embers of the fire and start to feel spooked. Twenty years ago, the Moles recall, there was a beautiful colonial-style mansion overlooking the Suwannee River here at Sandbag Spring. It fell into disrepair, then ruin. Local legend tells that a man was electrocuted as he tried to pirate the copper wire in the house. For as long as the mansion stood derelict, cave divers kept spotting the man's ghost — the Sandbag Ghost, as he came to be known.

But over the years, campers cannibalized the house for firewood. Overzealous party animals finally burned the hulk to its foundations, and now not a trace remains, an illustration of the river's essential lesson: Erosion never rests.

The landowner is not pleased. Her arms are sternly folded across the ample bosom of her floral-printed dress, and she's staring down at several of the Moles, who're in full wetsuits and preparing to plunge into a certain sinkhole, not far from Posted Spring, that's squarely on her property: Caught in the act.

Skiles sheepishly approaches the woman and brandishes an official-looking waiver, presigned by the Moles.

"I know you won't sue me," counters the landowner, whose name, we learn, is Mrs. Clara L. "You'll be dead. But what about that wife of yours?"

It doesn't take long for the Moles to "Yes, Ma'am" and "No, Ma'am" her into butter-soft compliance.

"Oh, all right, I suppose," Mrs. L says. "Only don't stay down there more than an hour, hear?"

Now the Moles are free to follow the Posted Spring clues wherever they may lead. Over the past two days, the Moles have succeeded in extending the cave in all directions, laying several thousand feet of line. The Moles shake Mrs. L's hand, and then turn their attention back to the sinkhole, a little foxhole of green slime that the Moles feel certain will connect with Posted Spring.

This time, I'm going in too.

I follow Skiles as he kicks for the bottom, unreeling line as he goes. Swimming behind him and holding on to the line as it descends into the spring, I remember the childhood hand-game that involves dropping a marble into an opaque maze, listening as it rolls and natters down through invisible gaps into the many mysterious levels of the contraption.

Once inside the cave, the visibility opens up, and Skiles gestures graciously for me to precede him. I find myself winding down a beautiful chimney of ancient stone. The ceiling is dark, with pendulous knobs that look like coffee stained dentures. The passage dips down to fifty feet, where we come to the first serious restriction. The space is only about foot and a half high, but Skiles has taught me how to stretch out and assume the Mole posture.

Still, for a few long moments it feels like I'm wedged in. I look behind me — a big mistake, much like looking down when you're climbing a sheer cliff. All I can see is the dim glow of my own light. I've stirred up a thick cloud of sediment. I feel like a bug crushed between two colossal slabs of peanut brittle, and I want out.

So this is "the small stuff," I think, trying not to panic. I can hear my own galloping heartbeat and the constant cascade of bubbles. I remember a story that Woody Jasper once told me about being trapped deep in a cave much like this one. For inspiration, he recalled the words of Harry Houdini: "There's always slack somewhere." I'm wallowing in slack and just don't know it.

Sure enough, after the silt settles, I do find the slack and somehow shimmy through. Now Skiles and I cruise over steep ski slopes of sand, through galleries of clear blue water and gleaming limestone. We shine our lights into enticing side tunnels and fractures in the roof. Not only does this cave connect up to Posted Spring; it goes on and on and on. The Moles don't know how far yet, but it's getting more spacious as it drops ever deeper, tapping into the full flood of the Floridan Aquifer.

It's everything Skiles had been hoping for, the Missing Link he was dreaming about back in his map room.

When we sail out of the exurgence and pop out into daylight with Mrs. L peering down at us, arms akimbo, I feel the momentary euphoria one feels after narrowly avoiding a lethal car crash.

"How'd you like that?" Skiles asks.

I liked it, I say, meaning it.

"Yeah," Skiles says, with a laugh. "Restrictions are a hell of a lot of fun."

It's cold on the boat ride back to Branford. The Suwannee River is the hard navy blue of Catholic school uniform sweaters. Before the sun goes down, Wes Skiles wants to show me one more cave which the Moles walled-out some years ago. He cuts the engine and we sink into a deep, gliding turn, coasting into the still waters of Rock Bluff's spring run. We take up oars and pole upstream in the shallows lined on both sides by a collonade of heavy-hipped cypresses.

"You see that tree there?" Tom Morris drawls rhetorically. Of course we see it: it's a tremendously tall old-growth cypress snag that rockets up from the first stone tier of the natural amphitheater that is the Rock Bluff Spring basin. Generations of boys have made a Moby Dick of this tree, grappling the great gray beast with rope swings and bolted come-along cables and hammered-in two-by-four steps, most of which are rotted now down to barnacle-like clusters of rusted nails.

Chance has almost aligned the huge tree with a deep, water-filled fracture, like the Washington Monument and its reflecting pool, but it's still a tricky angle shot for daredevils — out and over a ways. The oval spring pool itself is very shallow, no more than three feet deep. Death or the wheelchair is the price of a missed landing from halfway up the tree or higher, where the wooden steps peter out.

"Gosh, it must be nearly thirty years ago now," Morris resumes. "I remember it was a Saturday, the summer before my junior year at the University of Florida. I don't think I even had any scuba gear with me. I was just diving off that tree."

The land is posted now, but back then the spring would've brought plenty of cars and trucks rumbling up from the dusty dirt roads of rural Suwannee County. Wild-haired hippie wizards and semi-naked nymphs from the university town of Gainesville would've mixed with rustic swains and country belles in modest bikinis. Dope smoke and beer fumes and orange Frisbees pursued by bandana-collared dogs would've ridden the same hot puffs of feeble breeze. Splashes and screams and country music from a radio on somebody's towel would've steadily diminished as college boy Tom Morris, not much changed from how he looks now at forty-nine, scales the great tree, which appears as a dark spire against bright cumulus castles piled up high in the blue heat of a north Florida summer sky.

"I do a couple of medium-height dives, and then this guy comes striding out of the crowd across the grass. You can tell by how he walks he's an alpha male. He's wearing blue jean cutoffs and a kind of aluminum chain-mail vest he made for himself out of beer can pull-tabs."

Morris laughs, still surprised by the memory of that backwoods armor.

"Well, he isn't about to let anybody dive off his tree without him doing one a little higher. So I do a dive, and he beats it by a little bit, and then I do one higher than his, and he does one a little higher than that. And then I climb up to the top, to that crook up there..."

The spindly, attenuated crotch must be sixty, seventy feet above the pool, the water-filled crack — a knight's move out and over — no more than four or five feet wide. I look skeptically at Wes Skiles, who, of all the Moles, has probably known Morris best these by-gone three decades.

"Tom was a gymnast in college," Skiles explains. "He's one of those guys who're big but still super-coordinated."

"...and I stick a one and a half in that crack," Morris says. "He knew he couldn't do that. He just had to walk away. Afterwards, these little kids come up to me, and one of them says, 'Man, I'm glad you did that. Ain't nobody round here ever showed up Bobby Joe before.'"

The Moles, who've heard the story before, smile indulgently and turn their attention back to the fracture in the stone, and the small cave entrance twenty-five feet below the surface, an oval like a catfish's mouth, spitting bits of gravel in the considerable flow. It's a cave you wouldn't even get into with the old back-mount technology — strictly side-mount, on your belly, scratching at the grit with an Army-surplus trenching tool. A very interesting dive.

But I'm mesmerized by Morris's story, that soaring, phallic tree, the placid, limpid pool, the scene laid out as if in a Medieval allegory. I see in my mind's eye the strutting spring champion in pop-top chain-mail, and Tom Morris blowing him out of the water with the clean clearance of that splendid dive. It stands in my mind as an outward sign of inner grace, for all the unseen risks the Moles have taken, for the astringent relish of the tight squeeze conquered. Never mind who saw it. It must've been a wonderful dive.

DAVID POYER

From *Down To A Sunless Sea,*
a novel, 1996

ORANGE GROVE SINK

It was an hour-and-a-half ride to Peacock Springs through largely rural countryside. Scovill drove. Galloway rode shotgun, while July Toll and the student divers curled up with the gear in back.

There were six students, four men and two women. The van was noisy and packed full and there wasn't much talking. Everyone seemed preoccupied. One dark-haired, knife-faced girl couldn't stop moving. Every time he looked back, she was jiggling a skinny leg or playing with her hair.

The roads were long, level, straight, and empty except for the occasional pickup or slowly trundling tractor. He stared out for a while at passing fields dotted with ant mounds, abandoned motels, horse farms, little backcountry churches. Then fished around in the glove compartment and came up with a cave-diving map.

Starting near Orlando, the springs stretched northwest in a broad band up into the Panhandle. There were divable ones pimpled across the northwest, but the biggest cluster was where they were headed, between Gainesville and the Gulf. There weren't any cities there, just towns he'd never heard of: Luraville, Branford, High Springs, Williston. He found

Peacock, where they were going. The map said it was a state park on the Suwannee River, with a dozen sinks and springs.

He looked out again, to see Mayo going by, awninged brick storefronts along a main street, sidewalks empty in the glare of noon. A heavy man stared unwelcomingly at them through the front window of an antique store. Scovill paused at a crossing, then turned left.

Past a weathered SITE OF THE FUTURE MAYO BAPTIST CHURCH sign, a modern blue steel suspension bridge x'd the sky. It looked out of place among the hammocks and pine woods. The Suwannee River. One of the students whistled a few bars of Stephen Foster. The dark-haired girl laughed, sandal flapping on her jiggling foot. Water the color of iced coffee swirled between vines, ferns, and wild orchids that grew right down to the banks. Past that, they made a right turn opposite the Luraville Country Store. They passed burned-over fields, acres of still-smoking char, as if a volcano had just erupted.

"We're here," July announced. "Cough it up. Park fee, dive fee, hand it up."

The students sat up, blank, inward-turned looks hardening. A round-faced guy chewed on a sandy mustache; sweat glistened on his forehead. They passed cash up front. Scovill folded it into an envelope and dropped it into an unattended box.

The Peacock Springs State Recreation Area was a sandy washboard road through deep piney woods. Scovill turned off at a wooden sign that read TO ORANGE GROVE SINK. A quarter of a mile on, he braked at a widening in the sand.

The doors slid open, the sound echoing from the trees, and they emerged into a dense, still, enervating heat. He was sweating, too, now. The forest was silent except for the distant shriek of a scrub jay.

"Here we are," said Scovill jovially. He slapped the back of the guy with the blond mustache. "How you feeling, Orr?"

"Fantastic." The man's adam's apple bobbed as he swallowed.

They pulled on wet suits and set up gear in front of another sign. This one informed them forty-five divers had died in these springs. Tiller handed out the students' equipment till the van was empty, then set up his own — tanks, regulator, BC, gauges. He swung it onto his back and humped it after the others past a rail fence and down a little root-choked path.

Past a tilted picnic bench, cypresses stood with outstretched arms. Palmetto fronds clicked in the faintest breath of wind. A bird called far off, harsh and startlingly loud. He rounded a clump of brush and there it was.

The spring pool was surprisingly small, a rough oval beneath a gnarled limestone cliff. He could have chucked a softball across underhanded. Fluorescent green slime lay bright and still under pin oaks and cypresses dripping long beards of Spanish moss. The slime covered every inch of the surface, save for a small patch of slowly stirring dead black fluid.

"Yuk," a voice murmured beside him. Not the nervous girl, the other one — a stocky blonde with a broad face. Gloria, he remembered. Some kind of therapist, from Gainesville. "They want us to dive in that?" Another student, a thin fellow with a brown-and-gray ponytail, sat and began kicking his fins, driving the duckweed back. Slowly, the green curtain parted. Tiller squatted to peer through the surface.

Both the opacity and the darkness were illusions. Beneath the glare of sun, the water was clear and deep and green as old glass. Tiny black fish darted restlessly above a bottom of tumbled pale rock. He tested it with his hand. Cold compared to the summer heat, but not bitterly so. Near seventy, at a guess. He was wearing Farmer John bottoms and a long-sleeved jacket top. The thick black neoprene was already heating up even in the shade.

He swung his gear down on a patch of bare rock and went off to water the palmettos. When he got back, the divers were seated in a circle. As he came up, Scovill was saying, "Remember to illuminate the hand that's giving the signal. Down there, no one's going to see what you're saying otherwise. Basic hand-signal review: *Attention. Emergency. Okay. Look at that.*" He demonstrated each. "The other signals you need to know: *Turn around. Hold it. Slow down. Surface.*"

Galloway found a seat on a limestone outcrop. Scovill glanced at him and went on to review light signals. A circle meant *okay;* vertical movements, *attention;* rapid horizontal strokes, *emergency.* "Then, if you've got something more complex to communicate, you've got your slate. Everybody hold up his slate. Good."

They listened in silence as July outlined the emergency procedures: what to do in case they lost the line, had difficulties with their air supply, got stuck in a restriction, experienced silting, or lost their lights. She sounded distant, almost preoccupied. Or maybe he was reading something else into her dispassionate matter-of-factness.

"Any questions? Okay, the dive plan. Orange Grove Sink, which runs back under this cliff, goes back about a thousand feet to Challenge Sink. It interconnects there with the rest of the Peacock system. There are twenty-eight thousand feet of underwater passages. We will not take the complete tour today."

Toll waited out uneasy snickers, then went on. "Remember our two-thirds rule. We breathe our air supply down to two-thirds starting pressure, then turn the dive and head back. That not only gives you a safety margin in case there's a problem on the way out; it lets you take a buddy with you if he experiences a gear failure."

Scovill said, "Now, there's no reason to be nervous or not enjoy this. This isn't a test of either your *cojones* or your ability. Since this is y'all's first time in a close, real live overhead environment, we're going to take it nice and slow and not go in all that far. You read the cave description in your manuals, so you know what it's gonna be like."

"I didn't," said Tiller.

Scovill's mouth turned down. "Okay, quick review. The cave opening, and then the big room. Up near the ceiling of the big room, about seventy feet by your depth gauge, there's a corridor leads off in a northeasterly direction. We'll follow it to what we call the Throne Room. That'll put us about two hundred feet back, and that'll be our turnaround point. We should all still have plenty of air then, so if everybody's copacetic, we'll do some shared-air drills. Any questions?"

Gloria: "What if we need more weight, when we're on the bottom?"

July said, "You probably won't. Those steel tanks are a lot heavier than the aluminum ones you're used to. That's why we don't carry weight belts like you did in open-water work."

The third man, a freckle-faced redhead who hadn't said a word the whole trip up to now, grunted, "How are we organized?"

"You got your buddy, right, Kevin? Orr, you're his buddy? And Jack and

Scott, so everybody's got a partner. Gloria and Kay are the lead team. Gloria's lead reel. I'll be 'up.' Mr. Galloway —" Their eyes turned to him.

"Tiller."

"July, how about we let Tiller take over the assistant instructor's position, let him follow the last team in. You can be our safety this first dive."

She hesitated, then nodded with the faintly sad expression he'd noted she often had. Scovill went over a couple more things, then said that was about it; they'd check their buoyancy and gear on the bottom before cave entry. The divers began buckling on their last items of gear.

Tiller zipped his suit and bent for the rest of his equipment.

Scovill had told him to take the display set he'd looked at that morning at the store. Twin tanks, dual manifold, dual regulators. He'd left the oxygen and the stage tanks in Tallahassee, since this wouldn't be a deep-penetration dive. For the same reason, he hadn't bothered with a computer. He hoisted it to his shoulder and finished the rigging, making sure everything was tucked back and clipped off, nothing dangled, and that he knew where every thing was. A separate pouch held dive tables, a folding knife, two spare handheld dive lights, and a few plastic line markers.

He picked up his fins, then checked on how the students were doing. Kevin and Gloria were already in the water. His eye stopped on Kay. The dark-haired girl was jerking on her crotch strap and muttering to herself. Scovill frowned at him. Help her out, he mouthed.

He went over, told her to stand, made sure the straps were tight on her backpack, then bent to fix the crotch strap. She had heavy tanks, the same size as his, although she wasn't but half his size and he could see her knees quivering. "You sure you're ready for this?" he asked her in a low voice.

"I'm all right."

"Better get in, then. Cool off, and let the water help you carry that."

She nodded quickly, managing a smile. As he watched her waddle away, he thought, Keep an eye on that one.

Back to his own gear, sweat running down into his eyes. The suit felt as if it were shrinking in the sun, shrink-wrapping him like a supermarket eggplant. He gathered up fins, mask, and line reel, then picked his way down the worn limestone shelf that led into the pool.

The others floated here and there in the water. The abrupt hisses as they tested their regulators echoed beneath the cypresses like the threats of dinosaurs. Steel clanged on steel as Jack backed into Orr.

"See you on the bottom," Scovill yelled. Tiller noticed he wore a yellow wet suit, unlike the others, which were black with colored accents. The instructor thrust his regulator into his mouth and sank from sight. Hardly a ripple marked where he'd floated. The duckweed stirred uneasily, closing in again. Then a gush of rising bubbles pushed it back again in a slowly widening circle.

Galloway stepped carefully down from rock to slick rock into the water and bent to slip his fins on. They felt tight over the booties and socks, but they'd loosen as he swam. He was checking his gauges when July surfaced. "Buddy check on the bottom," she said, and vanished again.

Suddenly alone, he rinsed out his mask and fitted it to his face. He looked around once more at the woods, the slowly stirring weed, the burning sun directly above. A crow cawed. Cicadas buzzed. He heard a distant crunching roar as a truck went by far off.

He tucked his regulator into his mouth, sucked a quick breath of dry air, and slid down into the blue.

Breathing slowly, he sank through a warm layer at the surface into a crystalline light that reached out in all directions. The water felt cold at first, iciclemelt filtering between his skin and the suit, the gloves, the booties. Then it warmed, held by the close-fitting rubber. He swallowed and worked his jaw, and his ears cleared with a fizzing snap.

Around him, moss that looked soft enough to pet waved slowly from tumbled white rock. The spring bowl sloped down into indigo depths where huge limbs and tree trunks lay woven into a crisscrossed jumble. He was astonished at the visibility. He could see every rock on the bottom, could see bubbles drifting up on the far side of the spring with perfect clarity.

Still sinking, clearing his ears again, he looked up to a wavering mirror. Sunfish and chub drifted in mobile clouds against the silvery green surface, the needle-nosed silhouette of a gar cruising slowly among them like some new high-tech weapon.

When he looked down again, the others were scattered across the bottom, hovering a few feet above head-sized rocks and white sand and fallen trees. Mercury jellyfish rocked upward from their bent heads, their exhaled breath racing to rejoin the outer air. They were checking one another's gear. Scovill swam among them, tapping a strap here, yanking on a fin. His faceplate flashed as he glanced up toward Tiller.

Galloway was looking past them, at the cave.

At sixty feet, its entrance was a malignant gape, an evil black grin. A waterlogged palm trunk was wedged across it, barring it like a last warning. It was just wide enough to drive a full-sized car in with enough room on either side to be comfortable. He looked back toward the surface, then toward the cave again. For the first time, uneasiness wormed down his spine. Past the mouth was nothing but black, rimmed by palely glowing rock and writhing weed. A fluttering curtain of fish glittered like rain in sunlight as they moved restlessly in the deepening blue.

He flicked his main light on, and the spot of hot light reassured him. He checked his pressure gauge next: 3,100 psi. Shit, he thought. Long as we've got light and air, what can go wrong?

Scovill, grabbing his arm, pointed toward the students. He nodded, getting the message. He pumped a little more air into his buoyancy compensator — no, the cavers called them "wings" — and swam toward them.

One diver rose, shrouded momentarily in the mingled plume of rising bubbles from the others, then fell again. It was Kay. She was floating upward, venting too much air, then dropping like a stone. Up and down, on the elevator. She stabbed clumsily at the dump valve, shaking her head. He waved, but she didn't seem to see him. He swam around in front of her and pushed his hand down, indicating, Slow down; take it easy. Dark eyes stared past him through her mask. Then they focused. He gave her the okay sign, and after a moment, she returned it.

Scovill pointed toward the entrance, beckoned, held up one finger. Hesitantly, the number-one team moved toward him: Gloria and Kay. Gloria had the line, a caged arrangement like an oversized fishing reel. She sank toward the fallen palm trunk, then fumbled there for what seemed like minutes while her fins kicked up a white hurricane of sand.

When she rose again, the guideline was tied off, and a pale spider thread spun out. He wondered why Scovill let the girls lead. Then he thought, Shit, why not. It didn't strike him as that tough. What was so frigging dramatic about it?

The first team's lights probed the entrance, then darted inside. Finning slowly, reeling out the line, they went in. He saw their lights moving around, outlining weird knobs and hollows of rock with flickering shadow.

Jack and Scott went in next, with Scovill trailing a couple of feet above them. Then the last team, number three, Kevin and Orr.

His turn. He flicked his light back on, geared his breathing back to slow, and kicked slowly toward the entrance. Bubbles roared in his ears. The black mouth grew, yawning until it surrounded him, slowly drawing a cold barrier of shadowy rock between him and the last silver shimmer of the liquid sky.

His eyes searched the dark, chasing the spot of his light. He glided ahead slowly, following the flame flicker of fins ahead, craning around as his sight adapted to the grayish gloom.

He floated above an enormous room, falling away below him into a lightless depth. It looked big as the whole outer basin, though distances were deceptive in water this clear. The crystalline lens magnified each rock and outcropping as it thrust out toward him. But Billy Graham could have held a revival in this arched cavern, floored with canted flat boulders and the occasional waterlogged limb. The spring outflow was a steady wind in his face. He wondered, Did the current ever reverse? Maybe when the rains were heavy?

He peered at his depth gauge in the gloomy gray-blue light that still washed in from behind him. Eighty feet. He realized he was lagging, and followed his light downward.

The others were at the far end of the cavern already. Their lights moved slowly across tortured craggy walls of black-stained rock. He swam a little faster. As it grew darker, the water seemed to chill, as if a darker fluid were gradually replacing the liquid light that had first filled his suit. Craning his head upward, he saw air pooled in the irregular roof. It shimmered in the rays of his light, tiny silver replicas of the great bubble that was the world outside.

The manual he'd glanced through back at the shop called caves an "overhead environment." That was the overhead, right up there, and it was the reason so many people died in caves. In open water, you could bail out when things went to shit. You didn't even have to know which way was up. Just dump your weight belt, pop your buoyancy, and sail back up to the surface.

If things went sour down here, there was no quick way out.

He looked back, to see July silhouetted against the irregular crack of blue-silver light. The rays streamed in around her, outlining her body and gear like a painting of a descending angel. It was so achingly beautiful, he had to exert a conscious effort to turn back to the darkness.

Finning downward again, he checked his depth. The green needle nudged ninety, and still dropping. The room was deeper than he'd thought. The divers at the far end had to be a hundred feet down. And all around them, blackness, growing more impenetrable as each cycle of his fins drove him onward, as the walls and floor sucked in the last particles of light.

His light spot caught a white thread, followed its taut zigzag from rock to rock. Then he slowed, sinking as he reached the trailing team. A flash of yellow showed him Scovill. The instructor was pointing upward, making rapid hand motions.

Intent on him, Tiller flinched as his fin tip brushed the floor. He stifled his first impulse to kick himself upward and instead hit the inflator for a quick shot of air. He rose slowly, corrected, and came to a balanced halt four feet off the silty bottom. A flick of his light showed a rolling cloud of darkness where his fin had touched.

The two women, indistinguishable in suits and gear from the men except by their smaller size relative to their tanks, rose slowly along the face of the far wall. Their lights roved about, probed into recesses, then focused together on a saffron-colored guideline, already set, leading into an oval five-by-eight-foot blackness.

He finned slowly upward, eyeing the tunnel opening, suddenly conscious again of being a hundred feet back under the rock. If the air hissing through his regulator stopped, he'd either have to get help or make it back that hundred feet and up another sixty without another breath. His fingers searched his chest for the spare regulator, the "octopus." If he lost a first stage, he'd have to close the manifold valve fast or all his air would dump. What if he tore his wings on one of these rocks? He'd have to drop his weights.... No, no weights. He'd have to crab-crawl back along the bottom. He loosened the grip his teeth were indenting into the mouthpiece and forced himself on, following the student divers as one by one they filed into the tunnel.

Now the last remnant of light disappeared, and the only illumination was what they carried.

The passage was so narrow, he could touch both sides at once. It wound along, narrowing and opening, the ceiling dropping and rising. Bubbles skittered along it like live things trying to escape. He couldn't see the divers ahead, just the flicker of their lights and occasionally a writhe of fin.

He imagined the eight of them strung out along the length of the tunnel and was suddenly glad he wasn't in the middle, closed in above and below and to both sides by rock, and ahead and behind by other divers. Surrounded and walled in, and each individual isolated, separate, dependent on the steady flow of compressed air through valves and hoses and diaphragms for life itself. Shit, it was getting to him. His bubbles were roaring out too fast. He forced his breathing back to a slow, steady rhythm, put his light on his gauges, ran through the checklist in his head. Eighty plus feet deep, two hundred feet in, the guideline leading ahead into the darkness.

He was wondering how much farther it was to this Throne Room when the fins of the diver ahead suddenly flailed around his head, knocking his mask askew. He grabbed an outthrust of rock, clutching at his mask as he drifted toward the ceiling. When he had it adjusted and cleared, he pointed his light down.

Not the diver in front of him, but the one before *him,* Kevin, the big freckled guy. He was shaking his head, hand on his regulator, as if he wasn't getting air. Then he pulled it out of his mouth. It tumbled free, gushing bubbles for a moment before it cut off.

Then he saw the yellow circle of the backup regulator, and he relaxed as Kevin tucked it under his mask. His buddy, Orr, eased up on him, feeling for his own octopus. A plume of bubbles mushroomed against the ceiling as Kevin purged the backup regulator.

Then the redheaded diver was shaking his head again, craning it back, sinking toward the floor of the tunnel.

Orr didn't move to help. Maybe he didn't see. So Tiller swam forward, past and over him, jerking his own octopus free from the rubber keeper loop. He held it out as Kevin's mask came around. Bubbles roared up from his regulator, but Kevin was shaking his head again. As his widened eyes caught Galloway's he made the slit-throat gesture: out of air.

Orr chose that moment to lunge in, and his head hit Galloway's left hand. It knocked the light head out of his grasp. It fell away, bounced off a rock, flared once, and went out.

Crap, he thought. But meanwhile, Kevin had reached out for his proffered regulator.

Now they were linked. He had to stay with the man he was sharing air with.

But to his astonishment, the big man shook his head again. In the flickering shadow, his eyes were white-rimmed. Great bursts of bubbles stormed upward, straight into Tiller's mask, making it impossible to see even if he'd had light.

He was marveling how rapidly things could turn to crap when Kevin lunged up and wrenched the primary from between Tiller's teeth.

He was on an out breath when it was jerked out, and his throat closed instantly against the flood of cold water. Galloway swallowed rapidly, floating upward as bursts of bubbles beat softly at his chest. Strange flickers lit the rock walls. The big redhead was yanking on Tiller's primary hose, pulling so hard that he had to roll with it, afraid the son of a bitch was going to pull it right out of the housing. Now everything was dark. He was losing his updown orientation. He caught a flicker of the guideline, but that wasn't what he was worried about. He had to get some air in his empty lungs.

Kevin yanked on Galloway's hose again. Tiller reached back to his manifold, found where the whip came off the first stage, and ran his hand rapidly down it. His fist slammed into the other man's face. Then a hand gripped his, forcing it back. They rolled locked together, crashing into the rock.

Tiller broke free at last, but he still didn't have any air. He swallowed.

That usually helped, but it didn't seem to now. He couldn't find his octopus, though it had to be out there somewhere. He jackknifed suddenly and shoved himself into where he figured Kevin was again. His outstretched hand brushed a regulator, drifting there in midtunnel.

He was groping frantically for it when he crashed into another soft body, and lost it. It was roaring bubbles — he could hear it venting — but his splayed fingers scraped rock instead. Fire flickered around the edge of his vision. The dark contracted like a squeezing fist.

He hit another diver and grabbed, got what felt like a shoulder. Something smashed him in the face, almost cracking his mask. Something else closed around his shoulders and grew tight as he struggled. The black fist crimped down on his sight. He struggled weakly, staring into the dark.

Light burst around them, brilliant and white, flooding the tunnel and showing him Kevin, Galloway's orange octopus in his mouth, his back against the ceiling of tormented rock. His light dangled free, illuminating a roiling brown cone of silt. Before Galloway could lunge, a yellow arm reached between him and the other diver. It carried a regulator, and it was only after Galloway had jammed it into his mouth and purged it that he recognized it as his own primary.

Scovill grabbed Kevin by the manifold and spun him around. He tore Galloway's octopus out of the student's mouth and jammed his own in. The redhead struggled, but Scovill just tightened the hammerlock. The instructor tapped his purge valve, giving him bursts of air. Then, as the student's struggling lessened, Scoville slid around to face him. He stared into Kevin's mask, both hands on the other man's shoulders. He was holding eye contact. Without breaking it, he pointed quickly to Tiller, then pointed ahead along the tunnel and held up a clenched fist, indicating, hold them up. Then he pointed to himself and Kevin and jerked a thumb upward. We're surfacing.

Tiller nodded, sucking air with hungry rapidity. He tucked the broken light head under his harness and pulled out his spare. He swam rapidly down the line, till the tunnel opened again, widened, and the ceiling lifted.

The first two teams were hovering in the center of a large room, above a smooth dark floor littered with more fallen rock. Four faceplates swung toward him as he finned in, still sucking air so hard, his regulator squeaked and thudded. His heart was hammering so loudly that the walls of the cave seemed to vibrate. That had been close.... He gave them a quick thumbs-up, the signal to end the dive. They glanced at one another, then fell dutifully into line. He waved them on, checking each as he or she passed.

Gloria was the last to exit. She held the reel out, but he waved her on impatiently. She offered it again, then shrugged and moved off into the dark, the gears going *ratchety ratchety* as she cranked in the line. He glanced around one last time — the Throne Room, hell, he didn't see the attraction — and turned to follow her out.

His beam reached out two feet, then ended in a black wall of silt.

Oh shit, he thought. He lunged quickly toward the ratcheting sound and collided with her fins. The water was lightless, murky, making the lights useless.

He suddenly realized there were seven people between him and the surface now, in that pipe straw of a tube. And he was sucking gas like there was no tomorrow. He throttled back again, forced his frenzied consumption into a smooth in, out, in, out.

He followed her fins with one arm outstretched, back along the tunnel. When they exited into the main room, the silt cleared as if by magic. His beam leapt across it, picking out the silhouettes of the others making for the jagged crack of blue far above, outlined against the light as if they were ascending into a heaven gained despite their sins.

As he broke the surface, he squinted at his pressure gauge. He had four hundred pounds of air left.

When he pulled his mask off, treading water, Scovill and Kevin were sitting at the edge of the pool. The redhead looked shaken. Scovill was saying, "Yeah, but if you got a problem, you got to solve it right there, where you are. This isn't like an open-water dive."

"I done lots of wreck diving. Never had any trouble —"

"Well, this isn't a wreck. You feel better now?"

"I don't know."

Tiller got to the brink and pulled his fins off and threw them up onto the shore. He got his feet set and grabbed a rock and pulled himself out, then walked heavily, bent over, up to where he could unbuckle his harness and swung his tanks down to the ground. He still felt shaky.

Scovill came over and squatted down beside him. "Thanks, Colten," Tiller said, hating it, but knowing it was better this way, say it flat out. "Guess I dicked up."

"A guy starts to freak, hit him from behind. Give him air, but don't let him start grabbing on you."

"Okay."

"Or use a backup. I always carry one." Scovill swung his tank set down and pointed to a little separate bottle-and-regulator setup just the size, Tiller thought, of a fifth. "Hand 'em the Spare Air and back off. It won't last forever, but it gives them time to calm down. It's saved my butt once or twice.... But you kept your cool; you did okay for your first time in a cave." He unzipped his jacket and stood, raising his voice to the others. "Glory, you did real good up front. Kay, Jack, Scott — good dive; y'all looked fine down there. Orr, Kevin, let's go back to the van. I need to talk to you guys for a second."

They had to stay out for a while before the second dive, a surface interval till they dropped to a lower decompression group. Meanwhile, they had lunch. Tiller hadn't brought anything, but Gloria shared fried chicken and biscuits. "Take it. I need to lose a little," she told him. With the top of her wet suit off, he had a good view as she leaned forward, carefully dividing everything down the middle with a gleaming little dive knife. He kept looking toward the parking lot. He was curious to see how Scovill had handled Kevin. But when they came back, there was nothing to see, no fireworks. The redhead slogged along behind Orr and Scovill, not speaking any more than he had on the ride down.

When their surface interval was up, they went in again, this time checking out a side passage and practicing emergency drills. July moved up as Orr's buddy. Kevin didn't go in with them on the second dive. He sat holding his knees by the pool. Tiller saw his head bent thoughtfully at the edge of the circle of light as they sank away, deeper and deeper, into the all-encompassing dark.

DIANE ACKERMAN

From *Lady Faustus,* 1983

CAVE DIVING IN THE TROPICS

A mile's drive from the ocean
through hip-high snarls
of liana, frangipani,
dark, thorny creepers,
and poison ivy keen with hell-sap,
the earth yawns
into a towering deep grotto
canted below ground,
with its own small sea
and boulder-strewn beach
where once, long ago,
Arawak Indians sheltered
under the vaulted ceiling
and bat-crusted walls,
knowing nothing perhaps
of what lay beneath
the water we ski into now
with masks and scuba-gear,
finding:

limestone spires of gothic beauty,
high mesas, and mud-dark plummets
where blind fish grope,
their eye frames blank
from long disuse,
tunnels twirling fine as bird bone
through rock, trenches
of chinchilla-soft mud,
ceilings ripped like English muffins
alcoves atwitch with gargoyles,
batheads, fangs of limestone,
spiderweb rock,
stalactites and stalagmites
reeling at one another
as if the walls were jousting,
the halocline: a blurry film
where warm salt, and fresh cold, waters
meet like dowagers,
flirt and cloy, but refuse to mate,

and, above all, as you sink
down the gourd-neck entrance
deep into the cave's swollen belly,
rolling on your back,
you see shimmering overhead,
clearer than any sweet dreams of reason,
a fluke in the sunlight:
a blue cathedral
through whose stained glass window
sun gushes wide corridors of light,
each searching the abyss,
construing the gloom, while skindivers
rise and fall among them
like mute choirs of the heavenbound.

A scant moment, I hang
in the twilight,
watching the Creation scene
overhead: a vision
that could blister doubt:
and want to rise through the blue
on glittery sun drapes.

Beside me, a guide floats
hatchet-faced in the murk,
his gear an Arawak in profile.
The yellow stripe rimming his mask
sheds light:
a thin, hand-daubed glow,
and his cheeks look strong as plinths.
Will you come now,
he motions, *deeper into the cave,*
or will you stay here
with the uprushing foils of gold light?

Air bubbles pour above us
for long, dark seconds,
then flood the shallows
where light lies, and drift away
bright as doubloons.
What mattered to the Arawaks
was food, raincover, sun,
fresh water: their mysticisms
worked the oracle of Earth.
And mine? I wonder,
as, plunging away from the vision,
I fin down the cave
into the cold argument
of fresh and salt waters,
through firmaments
chillier than steel on ice.

Touch pioneers,
as we probe the cluttered avenues,
rainbows of rock, carp,
time-tortured pillars,
and plush wallows of womb-soft mud.

Too soon, round a bend
where stalagmites tower
rigid as bamboo,
we slip over a ledge
and find ourselves again
below the main hall's chandelier sun
that molds high darkness
into the cathedral
and, at our depth, pales water
from mink-brown to grey.
Through a silty blur
the guide motions
Up now, long enough.
He points to three divers
lilting toward the surface
on crystal beacons,
their angel-wings folded
tight as aqualungs.

Surface, the guide motions,
but I am already far away
where light breeds light,
spring herbs hearten my tongue,
and, out of the tropic vetch
I can hear, clear as a bell
over water, like an old spiritual,
life's green anthem.

ANDREW TODHUNTER

From *The Atlantic Monthly*, January 1994

BENEATH THE ICE

It takes a saw with an eighteen-inch bar to get through the ice in the middle of the lake. When the chain reaches the water, it throws back a clear, arcing fount as thick as my thumb.

I cut a triangle six feet on each side. When I'm finished, I press down on a corner with my boot: nothing. I sink the saw back into the notch and take another inch, rocking the bar. Another shove with the heel. Now the slab rocks, water pushing up through the cracks and pooling along the perimeter. Two of us sink the floe with our weight and slip it to one side beneath the ice. On the black surface of the water, drops of oil twist into paisleys of electric green and plum. Beside them, upside down, float the reflected summits of the High Sierra.

Over the expedition-weight Capilene underwear, a rag sweater, two pairs of wool socks, and a pile-jumpsuit known as a woolybear comes the dry suit. Of coated nylon, airtight, it seals with rubber gaskets at the neck and wrists. Then comes the brass-tinged body harness, followed by the weight belt: some twenty-five pounds of lead shot. Over this is an inflatable vest, called a buoyancy compensator, and then the tank, the regulator, neoprene mittens and hood, the fins, and the mask.

We clip lines to the rings on our harnesses. Flashlights, secured by lanyards, are tucked into pockets in our vests. Inflator hoses are coupled with valves on the vest and the dry suit, and the air is turned on. We look at our gauges: 2,250 pounds of air; depth, 0; dive time, 0; residual nitrogen, 0. The compass swivels freely in its chamber of oil.

We are about to go ice-diving, which as a recreational sport is relatively new but is beginning to develop a following. Ice-diving is done professionally by ice salvage divers, who make a fair sum winching trucks and snowmobiles out of lakes. Search-and-rescue divers with the same skills save several lives nationwide every year. To their ranks one can now add hundreds of Americans who go diving under the ice not because they have to but because they want to. Two of the nation's largest diving organizations, the Professional Association of Diving Instructors and the National Association of Underwater Instructors, now offer instruction and certification in ice-diving, the prerequisites for which generally include certifications in open-water and advanced open-water diving.

Ice-diving as a recreational sport is practiced wherever conditions allow, from frozen lakes and quarries in divers' home states to the serpentine ice caverns that can be found beneath the polar ice caps.

But whether done at the North Pole or beneath the surface of a more accessible location, ice-diving offers displays and physical sensations that one can experience in no other way.

There are two of us who will make this dive, and a support team of four. Bobbing in the water, we go over the signals with our line-tenders. The slow bleed of adrenaline has sharpened the landscape. Low clouds tear their bellies on the peaks. We turn to the sun, gathering heat. Then we let the air out of our dry suits and descend.

In the first seconds the unprotected skin around the face protests and then goes numb. We sink, watching for the bottom. At fifty feet the mud plain looms out of the darkness. We pump a blast of air into the dry suits and arrest our descent, hovering with our fin tips five feet from the bottom. Had we landed in the silt, or even brushed it with our fins, we would have sent a cloud of decaying organic matter in all directions. As it is, the pulses of current from our fin blades strike the membranous surface of the silt. It quivers without tearing, like the coating on milk that has been boiled in a pan.

Far above, the triangle is aglow in the dimly translucent field of ice. Our lines stretch upward, vanishing. I give a firm tug: "Okay." A tug comes back from my tender: "Acknowledged." The trail of air bubbles works its way to the surface without hurry, rumbling faintly. I take a deep breath and expel it with one quick contraction of my diaphragm. The bolus of air breaks into three spheres that flatten into mushrooms the diameter of dinner plates, expanding as they climb.

We send two tugs up the lines: "Going out, give us slack." Keeping our distance from the silt, we move across the bottom. We follow a bearing due north. If we are separated from our lines, a 180-degree turn should bring us within sight of the hole.

A school of fingerling trout hangs motionless above a meadow of fresh-water grass. We could pick them like apples if we cared to, collect them in a bag. They're sleeping out the winter, drunk with cold. I touch one with a mitten tip. A tremor in the gills, the tail flickers once, then nothing.

Farther on is a dinghy, perfectly intact. Right side up, it sits becalmed on the surface of the silt. As if abandoned on a winter beach, gathering snow, the benches and deck are blanketed with pale sediment. We sweep our lights beneath the benches, looking for a tackle box, an unopened bottle of beer. This wreck surrenders nothing — a sign of other divers here before us, or else a thorough abandonment of ship.

When we have used a third of our air, we ascend to the ice, still five hundred lateral feet from the hole. We come up gradually, hands raised to cushion the landing. Our breaths lie pinned against the ice in shimmering pools. Expanding as we add to them with each exhalation, they elongate, break apart. Following ravines and valleys too subtle for the eye, they seek the highest place.

The ice seems to glow from its core. Palpable as mist, it is a pale light in which no shadows fall. The ice is smoked through with minute bubbles. Cracks lost deep within glitter like bayonets.

I inflate the dry suit until I am buoyant enough to "fall" upward and lie flat on my stomach against the ice. I crawl a few feet upside down on my hands and knees. With the heels of my fists I pound the ice. *Whump.*

Whump. When struck, the ponds of air leap and scatter into quicksilver, spiraling in the current of the blow.

Pushing off the ice, I stand upside down and join my partner. Our exhalations tumble along our chests and break down our fins. There is a moment of vertigo before the inner ear accommodates the artificial gravity of this inverted world. Then we accept the illusion that we're standing upright on the ice.

The atmosphere above our heads — the deepening lake — is green darkening to black. The luminescent plain at our feet is as perfect and featureless as a glacier in the half light of a gathering storm. The horizon is uniform, impenetrable. My hands are getting colder.

We check our air. It's time to head back to the hole. Turning south, we take the lines in hand and send a fast series of tugs. We brace, leaning back.

On the other side of the ice our tenders set off like sled dogs at a run. The lines go taut and we begin to move, gaining speed. Howling through our regulators, we ski upside down across the ice.

The wedge of blue sky suddenly appears, hurtling toward us. As I dive head first through the triangle, I'm blinded. I look straight down into the sun.

JACK DRISCOLL

From *Language of Bone,* 1979

DIVING UNDER THE ICE

When you first enter through the dark hole
pretend you are looking for home. If the rope
around your waist should ever break
or tear loose, do not come up
clawing the roots of ice. You must sit there

in darkness, listening to the cold wind
in the clearing of your ear. There are shanties
spread out across the lake
and sometimes you can hear the slap of an axe
in the ice. Underwater

some men break out in a sweat
and kick frantically, following sounds
carried miles inside the current. They are found
in Spring, their eyes still open
behind their masks, air lodged deep
in their throats. But

if you simply drift
across the quiet bottom
you might see lights floating from a house
built close to the lake. Crawl up shallow.
A dog, hearing your bubbles rise,
will circle and bark. And soon
some old mother stooping with a flashlight
will find you, naked in your black wetsuit,
staring back through the clear ice.

SUSAN FAWCETT

From *Abandoned House*, 1988

THE DIVER

After the drowning of his firstborn son
my father learned to dive —
deep, in a thick black rubber suit
with tanks to breathe for him in the dark
quarries of Ohio.

He'd flipper and fin, ogling fish,
the rusting hulks of cars
lying precariously on their sides
in green prismatic swaying
tons of water, truly aquamarine —
like the stone I wear upon my throat,
this tiny block of stopped sea water,
my charm against the drowned.

Was my father learning
not to loathe his own competence or blame
his son for dying — bumbler,
violator of natural laws,
who dared to swim in ice cold springs,
bobbed, predictably, three times,
went down?

After the comedy of salvation,
after strangers pulled my brother from the weeds
and laid him face up on the bank, the water
pooling in his throat,
after they botched the resurrection —
resuscitator ill-assembled, never used —
my father disappeared
into his grief. He went down

hand over hand on the small ladder, down
zone by zone of cold,
searching the bottom, examining
the fish who hung there, cold-blooded, stupid,
graceful as angels drifting to his mask, torn
as he was, between curiosity and fear.

He never spoke about these journeys,
how he disappeared into the water and came back, but over
and over he came back, permitting me
to fill his arms.

NEAL BOWERS

From *The Golf Ball Diver*, 1983

THE GOLF BALL DIVER

When the golf ball diver comes to town
with his wet suit draped across the back seat
like a spare life, the boys at the Skelly station
spread the word and half the population
shows up at the country club just in time
to see him slip into the water hazard,
the way something once stepped into a thicket
at the side of the road beyond the headlights
of the sheriff's car and a dog in a nearby yard
set up a howl so mournful and so long
the neighbors spent most of the night searching,
cursing sawbriars and mosquitoes.

What they found was how darkness curved back on itself,
kept them walking in circles, each man pacing
the inside circumference of his own black bin.
In the morning they laughed to see
how the trampled weeds lay like fairy rings,
but they brought nothing with them out of that field,
just a few chiggers and beggar lice
and a dew heavy in their clothes.

Now they wait with others on the fairway above
the pond strewn with algae and frog spawn,
watching the diver's bubbles, conjuring
things lost years ago — a hat left on the hook
in a Kansas cafe, remembered in Iowa, too late
to turn around; a ring missed at Kentucky Lake;
three forks gone without a clue from the silverware tray;
keys dropped through a corner grate; a letter,
used to mark the page, left in a library book —
so many regrets, so many unsolved mysteries.

For thirty cents a ball, the diver will grope
all afternoon amid beer cans and bottles,
golf gloves waving like tentacles
in the thin light on the bottom,
and each time he surfaces the gallery
will whistle and applaud, happy
to have even this much returned.

JOHN BARR

From *The Hundred Fathom Curve*, 1997

DIVING THE EAST RIVER

NYPD divers, who like their work,
can't like diving the murk of what New York
has urinated, belched, expressed.
I think of them, rather, as men who lower
to the actual to see how it compares.

Chalk to *mouse* to *charcoal* they see
feelingly the dropped this, thrown that.
Ooze rich in shopping carts, cash registers,
cars — "quite a few occupied" —
always they find that what they can imagine
falls short of what drops off Manhattan's table.

Crime is the excuse for these descents
which we lack license to attempt,
but where else can the living
walk the bottoms of their dreams?

At earth's edge, where streets cease,
the river that is East plows south,
under the urge to be Atlantic
carries the question to the sea.

BUCKY McMAHON

From *Esquire*, July 2000

EVEREST AT THE BOTTOM OF THE SEA

You toss in your seaman's bunk and dream the oldest, oddest beachcomber's dream: Something has siphoned away all the waters of the seas, and you're taking a cold, damp hike down into the world's empty pool. Beer cans, busted pipes, concrete blocks, grocery carts, a Cadillac on its back, all four tires missing — every object casts a long, stark shadow on the puddled sand. With the Manhattan skyline and the Statue of Liberty behind you, you trek due east into the sunrise, following the toxic trough of the Hudson River's outflow — known to divers in these parts as the Mudhole — until you arrive, some miles out, at Wreck Valley.

You see whole fishing fleets asleep on their sides and about a million lobsters crawling around like giant cockroaches, waving confounded antennae in the thin air. Yeah, what a dump of history you see, a real Coney Island of catastrophes. The greatest human migration in the history of the world passed through here, first in a trickle of dauntless hard-asses, and then in that famous flood of huddled masses, Western man's main manifest destiny arcing across the northern ocean. The whole story is written in the ruins: in worm-ridden middens, mere stinking piles of mud; in tall ships chewed to fish-bone skeletons; five-hundred-foot steel-plated cruisers plunked down onto their guns; the battered cigar tubes of German U-boats; and sleek yachts scuttled alongside sunken tubs as humble as old boots.

You can't stop to poke around or fill your pockets with souvenirs. You're on a journey to the continent's edge, where perhaps the missing water still pours into the Atlantic abyss with the tremendous roar of a thousand Niagaras. Something waits there that might explain, and that must justify, your presence in this absence, this scooped-out plain where no living soul belongs. And you know, with a sudden chill, that only your belief in the dream, the focus of your mind and your will on the possibility of the impossible, holds back the annihilating weight of the water.

You wake up in the dark and for a moment don't know where you are, until you hear the thrum of the diesel and feel the beam roll. Then you realize that what awakened you was the abrupt decrease of noise, the engine throttling down, and the boat and the bunk you lie in subsiding into the swell, and you remember that you are on the open sea, drawing near to the wreck of the *Andrea Doria*. You feel the boat lean into a turn, cruise a little ways, and then turn again, and you surmise that up in the pilothouse, Captain Dan Crowell has begun to "mow the lawn," steering the sixty-foot exploration vessel the *Seeker* back and forth, taking her through a series of slow passes, sniffing for the *Doria*.

Crowell, whom you met last night when you hauled your gear aboard, is a big, rugged-looking guy, about six feet two inches in boat shoes, with sandy brown hair and a brush mustache. Only his large, slightly hooded eyes put a different spin on his otherwise gruff appearance; when he blinks into the green light of the sonar screen, he resembles a thoughtful sentinel owl. Another light glows in the wheelhouse: a personal computer, integral to the kind of technical diving Crowell loves.

The *Seeker*'s crew of five divvies up hour-and-a-half watches for the ten-hour trip from Montauk, Long Island, but Crowell will have been up all night in a state of tense vigilance. A veteran of fifty *Doria* trips, Crowell considers the hundred-mile cruise — both coming and going — to be the most dangerous part of the charter, beset by imminent peril of fog and storm and heavy shipping traffic. It's not for nothing that mariners call this patch of ocean where the *Andrea Doria* collided with another ocean liner the "Times Square of the Atlantic."

You feel the *Seeker's* engine back down with a growl and can guess what Crowell is seeing now on the forward-looking sonar screen: a spattering of pixels, like the magnetic shavings on one of those draw-the-beard slates, coalescing into partial snapshots of the seven-hundred-foot liner. What the sonar renders is but a pallid gray portrait of the outsized hulk, which, if it stood up on its stern on the bottom, 250 feet below, would tower nearly fifty stories above the *Seeker*, dripping and roaring like Godzilla. Most likely you're directly above her now, a proximity you feel in the pit of your stomach. As much as the physical wreck itself, it's the *Doria* legend you feel leaking upward through the *Seeker's* hull like some kind of radiation.

"The Mount Everest of scuba diving," people call the wreck, in another useful catchphrase. Its badass rep is unique in the sport. Tell a fellow diver you've done the Great Barrier Reef or the Red Sea, they think you've got money. Tell 'em you've done the *Doria*, they know you've got balls. Remote enough to expose you to maritime horrors — the *Seeker* took a twenty-five-foot wave over its bow on a return trip last summer — the *Doria's* proximity to the New York and New Jersey coasts has been a constant provocation for two generations. The epitome, in its day, of transatlantic style and a luxurious symbol of Italy's post-World War II recovery, the *Andrea Doria* has remained mostly intact and is still full of treasure: jewelry, art, an experimental automobile, bottles of wine — plus mementos of a bygone age, like brass shuffleboard numbers and silver and china place settings, not so much priceless in themselves but much coveted for the challenge of retrieving them.

But tempting as it is to the average wreck diver, nobody approaches the *Doria* casually. The minimum depth of a *Doria* dive is 180 feet, to the port-side hull, well below the 130-foot limit of recreational diving. Several years of dedicated deep diving is considered a sane apprenticeship for those who make the attempt — that, plus a single-minded focus that subsumes social lives and drains bank accounts. Ten thousand dollars is about the minimum ante for the gear and the training and the dives you need to get under your belt. And that just gets you to the hull and hopefully back. For those who wish to penetrate the crumbling, mazelike interior, the most important quality is confidence bordering on hubris: trust in a lucid assessment of your own limitations and belief in your decision-making abilities, despite the knowledge that divers of equal if not superior skill have possessed those same beliefs and still perished.

Propped up on your elbows, you look out the salon windows and see the running lights of another boat maneuvering above the *Doria*. It's the *Wahoo*, owned by Steve Bielenda and a legend in its own right for its 1992 salvage of the seven-hundred-pound ceramic Gambone Panels, one of the *Doria*'s lost art masterpieces. Between Bielenda, a sixty-four-year-old native of Brooklyn, and Crowell, a transplanted southern Californian who's twenty years younger and has gradually assumed the lion's share of the *Doria* charter business, you have the old King of the Deep and the heir apparent. And there's no love lost between the generations.

"If these guys spent as much time getting proficient as they do avoiding things, they'd actually be pretty good" is Crowell's backhanded compliment to the whole "Yo, Vinny!" attitude of the New York-New Jersey old school of gorilla divers. Bielenda, for his part, has been more pointed in his comments on the tragedies of the 1998 and 1999 summer charter seasons, in which five divers died on the *Doria*, all from aboard the *Seeker*. "If it takes five deaths to make you the number-one *Doria* boat," Bielenda says, "then I'm happy being number two." He also takes exception to the *Seeker*'s volume of business — ten charters in one eight-week season. "There aren't enough truly qualified divers in the world to fill that many trips," Bielenda says.

To which Crowell's best response might be his piratical growl, "Arrgh!" which sums up his exasperation with the fractious politics of diving in the Northeast. He says he's rejected divers who've turned right around and booked a charter on the *Wahoo*. But, hell, that's none of his business. His business is making the *Seeker*'s criteria for screening divers the most coherent in the business, which Crowell believes he has. Everyone diving the *Doria* from the *Seeker* has to be Tri-mix certified, a kind of doctoral degree of dive training that implies you know a good deal about physiology, decompression, and the effects of helium and oxygen and nitrogen on those first two. That, or be enrolled in a Tri-mix course and be accompanied by an instructor, since, logically, where else are you gonna learn to dive a deep wreck except on a deep wreck?

As for the fatalities of the last two summer seasons — "five deaths in thirteen months" is the phrase that has been hammered into his mind — Crowell has been forthcoming with reporters looking for a smoking gun onboard the *Seeker* and with fellow divers concerned about mistakes they might avoid. "If you look at the fatalities individually, you'll see that they were coincidental more than anything else," Crowell has concluded. In a good season, during the fair-weather months from June to late August, the *Seeker* will put about two hundred divers on the *Doria*.

Nobody is more familiar with the cruel Darwinian exercise of hauling a body home from the *Doria* than Crowell himself, who has wept and cursed and finally moved on to the kind of gallows humor you need to cope. He'll tell you about his dismay at finding himself on a first-name basis with the paramedics that met the *Seeker* in Montauk after each of the five fatalities — how they tried to heft one body still in full gear, until Crowell reached down and unhooked the chest harness, lightening the load by a couple hundred pounds. Another they tried to fit into a body bag with the fins still on his feet.

But beyond their sobering effect on those who've made the awful ten-hour trip home with the dead, the accidents have not been spectacularly instructive. Christopher Murley, forty-four, from Cincinnati, had an outright medical accident, a heart attack on the surface. Vince Napoliello, a thirty-one-year-old bond salesman from Baltimore and a friend of Crowell's, "just a good, solid diver," was a physiological tragedy waiting to happen; his autopsy revealed a 90 percent obstructed coronary artery. Charlie McGurr? Another heart attack. And Richard Roost? A mature, skilled diver plain shit-out-of-luck, whose only mistake seems to have been a failure to remain conscious at depth, which is never guaranteed. Only the death of Craig Sicola, a New Jersey house builder, might fit the criticism leveled at the *Seeker* in Internet chat rooms and God knows where else — that a supercompetitive atmosphere, and a sort of taunting elitism projected by the *Seeker*'s captain and his regular crew, fueled the fatalities of the last two seasons.

Did Sicola, soloing on his second trip, overreach his abilities? Maybe so, but exploring the wreck, and yourself in the process, is the point of the trip.

"You might be paying your money and buying your ticket just like at Disney World, but everybody also knows this is a real expedition," says Crowell. "You've got roaring currents, low visibility, often horrible weather, and you're ten hours from help. We're pushing the limits out here."

All this you know because, like most of the guys on the charter, you're sort of a *Doria* buff... Well, maybe a bit of a nut. You wouldn't be out here if you weren't. A lot of the back story you know by heart. How on the night of July 25, 1956, the *Andrea Doria* (after the sixteenth-century Genoese admiral), 29,083 tons of *la dolce vita*, festively inbound for New York Harbor, steamed out of an opaque fogbank at a near top speed of twenty-three knots and beheld the smaller, outbound Swedish liner *Stockholm* making straight for her. The ships had tracked each other on radar but lined up head-on at the last minute. The *Stockholm's* bow, reinforced for ice-breaking in the North Sea, plunged thirty feet into the *Doria's* starboard side, ripping open a six-story gash. One *Doria* passenger, Linda Morgan, who became known as the miracle girl, flew from her bed in her nightgown and landed on the forward deck of the *Stockholm*, where she survived. Her sister, asleep in the bunk below, was crushed instantly. In all, fifty-one people died.

Eleven hours after the collision, the *Andrea Doria* went down under a froth of debris, settling onto the bottom on her wounded starboard side in 250 feet of cold, absinthegreen seawater. The very next day, Peter Gimbel, the department-store heir (he hated like hell to be called that) and underwater filmmaker, and his partner, Joseph Fox, made the first scuba dive to the wreck, using primitive double-hosed regulators. The wreck they visited was then considerably shallower (the boat has since collapsed somewhat internally and hunkered down into the pit the current is gouging) and uncannily pristine; curtains billowed through portholes, packed suitcases knocked around in tipped-over staterooms, and shoes floated in ether. That haunted-house view obsessed Gimbel, who returned, most famously, for a monthlong siege in 1981. Employing a diving bell and saturation-diving techniques, Gimbel and crew blowtorched through the first-class loading-area doors, creating "Gimbel's Hole," a garage-door-sized aperture amidships, still the preferred entry into the wreck, and eventually raised the Bank of Rome safe. When Gimbel finished editing his film, *The Mystery of the Andrea Doria*, in an event worthy of Geraldo, the safe was opened on live TV. Stacks of waterlogged cash were revealed, though much less than the hoped-for millions.

In retrospect, the "mystery" and the safe seem to have been invented after the fact to justify the diving. Gimbel was seeking something else. He had lost his twin brother to illness some years before, an experience that completely changed his life and made of him an explorer. He got lost in jungles, filmed great white sharks from the water. And it was while tethered by an umbilicus to a decosphere the divers called Mother, hacking through shattered walls and hauling out slimed stanchions in wretchedly constrained space and inches of visibility, always cold, that Gimbel believed he encountered and narrowly escaped a "malevolent spirit," a spirit he came to believe inhabited the *Doria*.

But while Gimbel sought absolute mysteries in a strongbox, salvagers picked up other prizes — the *Andrea Doria*'s complement of fine art, such as the Renaissance-style life-sized bronze statue of Admiral Doria, which divers hacksawed off at the ankles. The wreckage of the first-class gift shop has yielded trinkets of a craftsmanship that no longer exists today — like Steve Bielenda's favorite *Doria* artifact, a silver tea fob in the form of a locomotive with its leather thong still intact. A handful of Northeastern deep divers who knew one another on a first-name basis (when they were on speaking terms, that is) spread the word that it was actually fun to go down in the dark. And by degrees, diving the *Doria* and its two-hundred-foot-plus interior depths segued from a business risk to a risky adventure sport. In the late eighties and early nineties, there was a technical-diving boom, marked by a proliferation of training agencies and a steady refinement of gear. Tanks got bigger, and mixed gases replaced regular compressed air as a "safer" means of diving at extreme depths.

Every winter, the North Atlantic storms give the wreck a rough shake, and new prizes tumble out, just waiting for the summer charters. The *Seeker* has been booked for up to three years in advance, its popularity founded on its reputation for bringing back artifacts. The most sought-after treasure is the seemingly inexhaustible china from the elaborate table settings for 1,706 passengers and crew. First-class china, with its distinctive maroon-and-gold bands, has the most juju, in the thoroughly codified scheme of things. It's a strange fetish, certainly, for guys who wouldn't ordinarily give a shit about the quality of a teacup and saucer. Bielenda and Crowell and their cronies have so much of the stuff that their homes look as if they were decorated by maiden aunts.

Yet you wouldn't mind a plate of your own and all that it would stand for. You can see it in your mind's eye — your plate and the getting of it — just as you saw it last night on the cruise out, when someone popped one of Crowell's underwater videos into the VCR. The thirty-minute film, professionally done from opening theme to credits, ended beautifully with the *Seeker*'s divers fresh from their triumphs, still blushing in their dry suits like lobsters parboiled in adrenaline, holding up *Doria* china while Vivaldi plays. A vicarious victory whose emotions were overshadowed, you're sorry to say, by the scenes inside the *Doria*, and specifically by the shots of *Doria* china, gleaming bone-white in the black mud on the bottom of some busted metal closet who knew how far in or down how many blind passageways. Crowell had tracked it down with his camera and put a beam on it: fine Genoa china, stamped ITALIA, with a little blue crown. The merit badge of big-boy diving, the artifact that says it best: I fuckin' did it — I dove da *Doria!* Your hand reaches out ...

The cabin door opens and someone comes into the salon, just in time to cool your china fever. It's Crowell's partner Jenn Samulski, who keeps the divers' records and cooks three squares a day. Samulski, an attractive blond from Staten Island who has been down to the *Doria* herself, starts the coffee brewing, and eyes pop open, legs swing out over the sides of the bunks, and the boat wakes up to sunrise on the open sea, light glinting off the steely surface and the metal rows of about sixty scuba tanks weighing down the stern.

On a twelve-diver charter, personalities range from obnoxiously extroverted to fanatically secretive — every type of type A, each man a monster of his own methodology. But talk is easy when you have something humongous in common, and stories are the coin of the lifestyle. You know so-and-so? someone says around a mouthful of muffin. Wasn't he on that dive back in '95? And at once, you're swept away by a narrative, this one taking you to the wreck of the *Lusitania*, where an American, or a Brit maybe — somebody's acquaintance, somebody's friend — is diving with an Irish team. He gets entangled, this diver does, in his own exploration line, on the hull down at 280 feet. His line is just pooling all around him and he's thrashing, panicking, thinking — as everybody always does in a panic — that he has to get to the surface, like *right now*. So he inflates his buoyancy compensator to the max, and now he's like a balloon tied to all that tangled line, which the lift of the b.c. is pulling taut. He's got his knife out, and he's hacking away at the line. One of the Irish divers sees what's happening and swims over and grabs the guy around the legs just as the last line is cut. They both go rocketing for the surface, this diver and his pumped-up b.c. and the Irishman holding on to him by the knees. At 160 feet, the Irishman figures, Sorry, mate, I ain't dying with you, and has to let him go. So the diver flies up to the top and bursts internally from the violent change of depth and the pressurized gas, which makes a ruin of him.

Yeah, he should never have been diving with a line, someone points out, and a Florida cave diver and a guy from Jersey rehash the old debate — using a line for exploration, the cave diver's practice, versus progressive penetration, visual memorization of the wreck and the ways out.

Meanwhile, a couple of the *Seeker*'s crew members have already been down to the wreck to set the hook. The rubber chase boat goes over the bow, emergency oxygen hoses are lowered off the port-side rail, and Crowell tosses out a leftover pancake to check the current. It slaps the dead-calm surface, spreading ripples, portals widening as it drifts aft. Because the *Doria* lies close to the downfall zone, where dense cold water pours over the continental shelf and down into the Atlantic Trench, the tidal currents can be horrendously strong. Sometimes a boat anchored to the *Doria* will carve a wake as if it were underway, making five knots and getting nowhere. An Olympic swimmer in a Speedo couldn't keep up with that treadmill, much less a diver in heavy gear. And sometimes the current is so strong, it'll snap a three-quarter-inch anchor line like rotten twine. But on this sunny July morning, already bright and heating up fast, Crowell blinks beneath the bill of his cap at the bobbing pancake and calculates the current at just a couple of knots — not too bad at all, if you're ready for it.

Crowell grins at the divers now crowded around him at the stern. "Pool's open," he says.

You can never get used to the weight. When you wrestle your arms into the harness of a set of doubles, two 120-cubic-foot-capacity steel tanks yoked together on metal plates, you feel like an ant, one of those leaf-cutter types compelled to heft a preposterous load. What you've put on is essentially a wearable submarine with its crushed neoprene dry-suit shell and its steel external lungs and glass-enclosed command center. Including a pony-sized emergency bottle bungee-strapped between the steel doubles and two decompression tanks clipped to your waist, you carry five tanks of gas and five regulators. You can barely touch your mittened hands together in front of you around all the survival gear, the lift bags, lights, reels, hoses, and instrument consoles. And yet, for all its awkwardness on deck, a deep-diving rig is an amazing piece of technology, and if you don't love it at least a little you had better never put it on. It's one thing you suppose you all have in common on this charter — stockbrokers, construction workers, high school teachers, cops — you're all Buck Rogers flying a personal ship through inner space.

The immediate downside is that you're slightly nauseated from reading your gauges in a four-foot swell, and inside your dry suit, in expedition-weight socks and polypropylene long johns, you're sweating bullets. The way the mind works, you're thinking, To hell with this bobbing world of sunshine and gravity — you can't wait to get wet and weightless. You strain up from the gearing platform hefting nearly two hundred pounds and duckwalk a couple of steps to the rail, your fins smacking the deck and treading on the fins of your buddies who are still gearing up.

Some of the experienced *Doria* divers from Crowell's crew grasp sawed-off garden rakes with duct-taped handles, tools they'll use to reach through rubble and haul in china from a known cache. Crowell gestures among them, offering directions through the *Doria*'s interior maze. Your goal is just to touch the hull, peer into Gimbel's Hole. An orientation dive. You balance on the rail like old Humpty-Dumpty and crane your neck to see if all's clear on the indigo surface. Scuba lesson number one: Most accidents occur on the surface. There was a diver last summer, a seasoned tech diver, painstaking by reputation, on his way to a wreck off the North Carolina coast. Checked out his gear en route — gas on, take a breath, good, gas off — strapped it on at the site, went over the side, and sank like a dirt dart. His buddies spent all morning looking for him everywhere except right under their boat, where he lay, drowned. He had never turned back on his breathing gas.

And there was a diver on the *Seeker* who went over the side and then lay sprawled on his back in the water, screaming, "Help! Help!" The fuck was the matter with the guy? Turns out he'd never been in a dry suit before and couldn't turn himself over. Crowell wheeled on the guy's instructor. "You brought him out here to make his first dry-suit dive on the *Doria?* Are ya *crazy?*" Then the instructor took an underwater scooter down with him, and he had to be rescued with the chase boat. *Arrgh!* Crowell laments that there are divers going from Open Water, the basic scuba course, to Tri-mix in just fifty dives; they're book-smart and experience-starved. And there are bad instructors and mad instructors, egomaniacal, gurulike instructors.

"You will dive only with me," Crowell says, parodying the Svengalis. "Or else it's a thousand bucks for the cape with the clouds and the stars on it. Five hundred more and I'll throw in the wand."

"Just because you're certified don't make you qualified" is Steve Bielenda's motto, and it's the one thing the two captains can agree on.

You take a couple of breaths from each of your regs. Click your lights on and off. You press the inflator button and puff a little more gas into your buoyancy compensator, the flotation wings that surround your double 120's, and experience a tightening and a swelling up such as the Incredible Hulk must feel just before his buttons burst. Ready as you'll ever be, you plug your primary reg into your mouth and tip the world over ... and hit the water with a concussive smack. At once, as you pop back up to the surface, before the bubbles cease seething between you and the image of the *Seeker*'s white wooden hull, rocking half in and half out of the water, you're in conflict with the current. You grab the floating granny line and it goes taut and the current dumps buckets of water between your arms and starts to rooster-tail around your tanks. This is two knots? You're breathing hard by the time you haul yourself hand over hand to the anchor line, and that's not good. Breath control is as important to deep divers as it is to yogis. At two hundred feet, just getting really excited could knock you out like a blow from a ball-peen hammer. As in kill you dead. So you float a moment at the surface, sighting down the parabola of the anchor line to the point where it vanishes into a brownish-blue gloom. Then you reach up to your inflator hose and press the other button, the one that splutters out gas from the b.c., and feel the big steel 120's reassert their mass, and calmly, feetfirst, letting the anchor line slide through your mitts, you start to sink.

For the thin air of Everest, which causes exhaustion universally and pulmonary and cerebral events (mountain sickness) seemingly randomly, consider the "thick" air you must breathe at 180 feet, the minimum depth of a dive to the *Doria*. Since water weighs sixty-four pounds per cubic foot (and is eight hundred times as dense as air), every foot of depth adds significantly to the weight of the water column above you. You feel this weight as pressure in your ears and sinuses almost as soon as you submerge. Water pressure doesn't affect the gas locked in your noncompressible tanks, of course, until you breathe it. Then, breath by breath, thanks to the genius of the scuba regulator — Jacques Cousteau's great invention — the gas becomes ambient to the weight of the water pressing on your lungs. That's why breathing out of steel 120's pumped to a pressure of seven thousand p.s.i. isn't like drinking out of a fire hose, and also why you can kick around a shallow reef at twenty feet for an hour and a half, while at a hundred feet you'd suck the same tank dry in twenty minutes; you're inhaling many times more molecules per breath.

Unfortunately, it's not all the same to your body how many molecules of this gas or the other you suck into it. On the summit of Everest, too few molecules of oxygen makes you light-headed, stupid, and eventually dead. On the decks of the *Doria*, too many molecules of oxygen can cause a kind of electrical fire in your central nervous system. You lose consciousness, thrash about galvanically, and inevitably spit out your regulator and drown. A depth of 216 feet is generally accepted as the point at which the oxygen in compressed air (which is 21 percent oxygen, 79 percent nitrogen) becomes toxic and will sooner or later (according to factors as infinitely variable as individual bodies) kill you. As for nitrogen, it has two dirty tricks it can play at high doses. It gets you high — just like the nitrous oxide that idiot adolescents huff and the dentist dispenses to distract you from a root canal — starting at about 130 feet for most people. "I am personally quite receptive to nitrogen rapture," Cousteau writes in *The Silent World*. "I like it and fear it like doom."

The fearsome thing is that, like any drunk, you're subject to mood swings, from happy to sad to hysterical and panicky when you confront the dumb thing you've just done, like getting lost inside a sunken ocean liner. The other bad thing nitrogen does is deny you permission to return immediately to the surface, every panicking person's solution to the trouble he's in. It's the excess molecules of nitrogen lurking in your body in the form of tiny bubbles that force you to creep back up to the surface at precise intervals determined by time and depth. On a typical *Doria* dive, you'll spend twenty-five minutes at around two hundred feet and decompress for sixty-five minutes at several stopping points, beginning at 110 feet. While you are hanging on to the anchor line, you're off-gassing nitrogen at a rate the body can tolerate. Violate deco and you are subject to symptoms ranging from a slight rash to severe pain to quadriplegia and death. The body copes poorly with big bubbles of nitrogen trying to fizz out through your capillaries and bulling through your spinal column, traumatizing nerves.

Enter Tri-mix, which simply replaces some of the oxygen and nitrogen in the air with helium, giving you a life-sustaining gas with fewer molecules of those troublesome components of air. With Tri-mix, you can go deeper and stay longer and feel less narced. Still, even breathing Tri-mix at depth can be a high-wire act, owing to a third and final bad agent: carbon dioxide. The natural by-product of respiration also triggers the body's automatic desire to replenish oxygen. When you hyperventilate — take rapid, shallow breaths – you deprive yourself of CO_2 and fool the body into believing it doesn't need new oxygen. Breath-hold divers will hyperventilate before going down as a way to gain an extra minute or two of painless O_2 deprivation. But at depth (for reasons poorly understood), hypercapnia, the retention of CO_2 molecules, has the same "fool the brain" effect. It's a tasteless, odorless, warningless fast track to unconsciousness. One moment you are huffing and puffing against the current, and the next you are swimming in the stream of eternity.

Richard Roost, a forty-six-year-old scuba instructor from Ann Arbor, Michigan, one of the five *Doria* fatalities of the last two seasons, was highly skilled and physically fit. His body was recovered from the *Doria's* first-class lounge, a large room full of shattered furniture deep in the wreck. It's a scary place, by all accounts, but Roost seemed to be floating in a state of perfect repose. Though he had sucked all the gas from his tanks, there was no sign that he had panicked. Crowell suspects that he simply "took a nap," a likely victim of hypercapnia.

So it is that you strive to sink with utter calm, dumping a bit of gas into your dry suit as you feel it begin to vacuum-seal itself to you, bumping a little gas into the b.c. to slow your rate of descent, seeking neutrality, not just in buoyancy but in spirit as well. Soon you've sunk to that zone where you can see neither surface nor bottom. It's an entrancing, mystical place — pure inner space. Things appear out of nowhere — huge, quick things that aren't there, blocks of blankness, hallucinations of blindness. Drifting, drifting ... reminds you of something Steve Bielenda told you: "The hard part is making your brain believe this is happening. But, hey, you know what? It really is happening!" You focus on the current-borne minutiae — sea snow, whale food, egg-drop soup — which whizzes by outside the glass of your mask like a sepia-colored silent movie of some poor sod sinking through a blizzard.

Your depth gauge reads 160 feet, and you hit the thermocline, the ocean's deep icebox layer. The water temp plunges to 45 degrees and immediately numbs your cheeks and lips. Your dry suit is compressed paper-thin; you don't know how long you can take the cold, and then something makes you forget about it completely: the *Doria*, the great dome of her hull falling away into obscurity, and the desolate rails vanishing in both directions, and a lifeboat davit waving a shred of trawler net like a hankie, and the toppled towers of her superstructure. And it's all true what they've said: You feel humbled and awed. You feel how thin your own audacity is before the gargantuan works of man. You land fins-first onto the steel plates, kicking up two little clouds of silt. Man on the moon.

You've studied the deck plans of the Grande Dame of the Sea — her intricacy and complexity and order rendered in fine architectural lines. But the *Doria* looks nothing like that now. Her great smokestack has tumbled down into the dark debris field on the seafloor. Her raked-back aluminum forecastle decks have melted like a Dalí clock in the corrosive seawater. Her steel hull has begun to buckle under its own weight and the immense weight of water, pinching in and splintering the teak decking of the promenade, where you kick along, weaving in and out of shattered windows. Everything is moving: bands of water, now cloudy, now clear, through which a blue shark twists in and out of view; sea bass darting out to snatch at globs of matter stirred up by your fins. They swallow and spit and glower. Everywhere you shine your light inside, you see black dead ends and washed-out walls and waving white anemones like giant dandelions bowing in a breeze.

You rise up a few feet to take stock of your location and see that on her outer edges she is Queen of Snags, a harlot tarted up with torn nets, bristling with fishermen's monofilament and the anchor lines of dive boats that have had to cut and run from sudden storms. She's been grappled more times than Moby Dick, two generations of obsessed Ahabs finding in her sheer outrageous bulk the sinews of an inscrutable malice, a dragon to tilt against. In your solitude you sense the bleak bitch of something unspeakably larger still, something that shrinks the *Doria* down to the size of Steve Bielenda's toy-train tea fob: a hurricane of time blowing through the universe, devouring all things whole.

On the aft deck of the *Wahoo*, Steve Bielenda, a fireplug of a man, still sinewy in his early sixties, is kicked back in his metal folding-chair throne. He wears his white hair in a mullet cut and sports a gold earring. He was wild as a kid, by his own account, a wiseguy, wouldn't listen to nobody. The product of vocational schools, he learned auto mechanics and made a success of his own repair shop before he caught the scuba bug. Then he would go out with fishermen for a chance to dive — there weren't any dive boats then — and offered his services as a salvage diver, no job too small or too big. When he sold his shop and bought the *Wahoo*, it was the best and the biggest boat in the business. Now, as the morning heats up, he's watching the bubbles rise and growling out *Doria* stories in his Brooklyn accent.

"When you say Mount Everest to somebody," he says, "you're sayin' something. Same with da *Doria*. It was the pinnacle wreck. It was something just to go there."

And go there he did — more than a hundred times. The first time in
'81, with a serious *Doria* fanatic, Bill Campbell, who had commissioned a
bronze plaque to commemorate the twenty-fifth anniversary of the sinking;
and often with maritime scholar and salvager John Moyer, who won salvage rights to the *Doria* in federal court and hired the *Wahoo* in '92 to put
a "tag" on the wreck — a tube of PVC pipe, sealed watertight, holding the
legal papers. Tanks were much smaller then, dinky steel 72's and aluminum
80's, compared with the now-state-of-the-art 120-cubic-foot-capacity tanks.
"You got air, you got time," is how Bielenda puts it. And time was what
they didn't have down at 180 feet on the hull. It was loot and scoot. Guys
were just guessing at their decompression times, since the U.S. Navy Dive
Tables expected that nobody would be stupid or desperate enough to
make repetitive dives below 190 feet with scuba gear. "Extrapolating the
tables" was what they called it; it was more like pick a lucky number and
hope for the best. But Bielenda's quick to point out that in the first twenty-
five years of diving the *Doria*, nobody died. Back then the players were all
local amphibians, born and bred to cold-water diving and watermen to
the *n*th degree. Swimming, water polo, skin diving, then scuba, then deep
scuba — you learned to crawl before you walked in those days.

A thousand things you had to learn first. "You drive through a toll-
booth at five miles an hour — no problem, right? Try it at fifty miles an
hour. That hole gets real small! That's divin' da *Doria*. To dive da *Doria* it's
gotta be like writin' a song," the captain says, and he hops up from his
chair and breaks into an odd little dance, shimmying his 212 pounds in a
surprisingly nimble groove, tapping himself here, here, here — places a
diver in trouble might find succor in his gear.

"And you oughta wear yer mask strap under yer hood," he tells a
diver who's gearing up. "There was this gal one time ..." and Bielenda
launches into the story about how he saved Sally Wahrmann's life with that
lesson.

She was down in Gimbel's Hole, just inside it and heading for the gift
shop, when this great big guy — John Ornsby was his name, one of the
early *Doria* fatalities — comes flying down into the hole after her and just
clobbers her. "He rips her mask off and goes roaring away in a panic,"
Bielenda says. "But see, she has her mask under her hood like I taught

her, so she doesn't lose it. It's still right there around her neck."

The blow knocked Wahrmann nearly to the bottom of the wreck, where an obstruction finally stopped her fall seven sideways stories down. But she never panicked, and with her mask back on and cleared, she could find her way out toward the tiny speck of green light that was Gimbel's Hole, the way back to the world. "She climbs up onto the boat and gives me a big kiss. 'Steve,' she says, 'you just saved my life.'"

As for Ornsby, a Florida breath-hold diver of some renown, his banzai descent into Gimbel's Hole was never explained, but he was found dead not far from the entrance, all tangled up in cables as if a giant spider had been at him. It took four divers with cable cutters two dives each to cut the body free. Bielenda has been lost inside of wrecks and has found his way out by a hairbreadth. He and the *Wahoo* have been chased by hurricanes. One time he had divers down on the *Doria* when a blow came up. He was letting out anchor line as fast as he could, and the divers, who were into decompression, they were scrambling up the line hand over hand to hold their depth. The swells rose up to fifteen feet, and Bielenda could see the divers in the swells hanging on to the anchor line, ten feet underwater but looking down into the *Wahoo!* A *Doria* sleigh ride — that's the kind of memories the *Doria*'s given him. Strange sights indeed. He knows he's getting too old for the rigors of depth, but he's not ready to let go of the *Doria* yet, not while they still have their hooks in each other.

Up in the pilothouse of the *Seeker*, Dan Crowell is fitting his video camera into its watertight case, getting ready to go down and shoot some footage inside the wreck. He tries to make at least one dive every charter trip, and he never dives without his camera anymore if he can help it.

The more you learn about Crowell, the more impressed you are. He's a voracious autodidact who sucks up expertise like a sponge. He has worked as a commercial artist, a professional builder, a commercial diver, and a technical scuba instructor, as well as a charter captain. His passion now is shooting underwater video, making images of shipwrecks at extreme depths. His footage of the *Britannic* was shot at a whopping depth of four hundred feet. When Crowell made his first *Doria* dive in 1990, a depth of two hundred feet was still Mach I, a real psychological and physical barrier. He remembers kneeling in the silt inside Gimbel's Hole at 210 feet and scooping up china plates while he hummed the theme from *Indiana Jones,* "and time was that great big boulder coming at you."

In '91, Crowell didn't even own a computer, but that all changed with the advent of affordable software that allowed divers to enter any combination of gases and get back a theoretically safe deco schedule for any depth. "In a matter of months, we went from rubbing sticks together to flicking a Bic," Crowell says. It was the aggressive use of computers — and the willingness to push the limits — that separated the *Seeker* from the competition. When Bill Nagle, the boat's previous captain, died of his excesses in '93, Crowell came up with the cash to buy the *Seeker.* He'd made the money in the harsh world of hard-hat diving.

Picture Crowell in his impermeable commercial diver's suit, with its hose-fed air supply and screw-down lid, slowly submerging in black, freezing water at some hellish industrial waterfront wasteland. The metaphorical ball cock is stuck and somebody's gotta go down and unstick it. Hacksaw it, blast it, use a lift bag and chains — the fuck cares how he does it? Imagine him slogging through thigh-deep toxic sludge hefting a wrench the size of a dinosaur bone. His eyes are closed — can't see a damned thing down there anyway — and he's humming a tune to himself, working purely by touch, in three-fingered neoprene mitts. Think of him blind as a mole and you'll see why he loves the camera's eye so much, and you'll believe him when he says he's never been scared on the *Andrea Doria.*

"Well, maybe once," Crowell admits. "I was diving on air and I was pretty narced, and I knew it. I started looking around and realized I had no idea where I was." He was deep inside the blacked-out maze of the wreck's interior, where every breath dislodges blinding swirls of glittering rust and silt. "But it just lasted a few seconds. When you're in those places, you're seeing things in postage-stamp-sized pieces. You need to pull back and look at the bigger picture — which is about eight and a half by eleven inches." Crowell found his way out, reconstructing his dive, as it were, page by page.

You've always thought that the way water blurs vision is an apt symbol of a greater blurring, that of the mind in the world. Being matter, we are buried in matter — we are buried alive. This is an idea you first encountered intuitively in the stories of Edgar Allan Poe. Madman! Don't you see?

cries Usher, before his eponymous house crashes down on top of him. And the nameless penitent in "The Pit and the Pendulum" first creeps blindly around the abyss, and then confronts the razor's edge of time. He might well be looking into Gimbel's Hole and at the digital readout on his console; he is literature's first extreme deep diver, immersed in existential fear of the impossible present moment. But the diver's mask is also a miraculous extra inch of perspective; it puts you at a certain remove from reality, even as you strike a Mephistophelian bargain with physics and the physical world.

You're twelve minutes into your planned twenty-five-minute bottom time when the current suddenly kicks up. It's as if God has thrown the switch — *ka-chung!* — on a conveyor belt miles wide and fathoms thick. You see loose sheets of metal on the hull sucking in and blowing out, just fluttering, as if the whole wreck were breathing. If you let go, you would be whisked away into open sea, a mote in a maelstrom. The current carries with it a brown band of bad visibility, extra cold, direly menacing. Something has begun to clang against the hull, tolling like a bell. Perhaps, topside, it has begun to blow. Keep your shit together. Control your breath. Don't fuck up. And don't dream that things might be otherwise, or it'll be the last dream you know. Otherwise? Shit ... this is it. Do something. Act. Now! You're going to have to fight your way back to the anchor line, fight to hold on for the whole sixty-five minutes of your deco. And then fight to get back into the boat, with the steel ladder rising and plunging like a cudgel. What was moments ago a piece of cake has changed in a heartbeat to a life-or-death situation.

Then you see Dan Crowell, arrowing down into Gimbel's Hole with his video camera glued to his eyes. You watch the camera light dwindle down to two hundred feet, 210, then he turns right and disappears inside the wreck. Do you follow him, knowing that it is precisely that — foolish emulation — that kills divers here? Consider the case of Craig Sicola, a talented, aggressive diver. On his charter in the summer of '98, he saw the crew of the *Seeker* bring up china, lots of it. He wanted china himself, and if he'd waited, he would've gotten it the easy way. Crowell offered to run a line to a known cache — no problem, china for everybody. But it wouldn't have been the same. Maybe what he wanted had less to do with plates than with status, status within an elite. He must've felt he'd worked his way up to the top of his sport only to see the pinnacle recede again. So he studied the *Doria* plans posted in the *Seeker*'s cabin and deduced where china ought to be — his china — and jumped in alone to get it. He came so close to pulling it off, too.

Dropping down into Gimbel's Hole, he found himself in the first-class foyer, where well-dressed passengers once made small talk and smoked as they waited to be called to dinner. He finessed the narrow passageway that led to the first-class dining room, a huge, curving space that spans the width of the *Doria*. He kicked his way across that room, playing his light off lumber piles of shattered tables. Down another corridor leading farther back toward the stern, he encountered a jumble of busted walls, which may have been a kitchen — and he found his china. He loaded up his goody bag, stirring up storms of silt as the plates came loose from the muck. He checked his time and gas supply — hurry now, hurry — and began his journey back. Only he must have missed the passage as he recrossed the dining room. Easy to do: Gain or lose a few feet in depth and you hit blank wall. He would've sucked in a great gulp of gas then — you do that when you're lost; your heart goes wild. Maybe the exit is inches away at the edge of vision, or maybe you've got yourself all turned around and have killed yourself, with ten minutes to think about it.

Sicola managed to find his way out, but by then he must've been running late on his deco schedule. With no time to return to the anchor line, he unclipped his emergency ascent reel and tied a line off to the wreck. Which was when he made mistake number two. He either became entangled in the line, still too deep to stop, and had to cut himself free, or else the line broke as he ascended. Either way, he rocketed to the surface too fast and died of an embolism. Mercifully, though, right up to the last second, Sicola must have believed he was taking correct and decisive action to save himself. Which, in fact, is exactly what he was doing.

But with a margin of error so slender, you have to wonder: Where the hell does someone like Crowell get the sack to make fifty turns inside that maze? How can he swim through curtains of dangling cables, twisting through blown-out walls, choosing stairways that are now passages, and taking passages that are now like elevator shafts, one after another, as relentlessly as one of the blue sharks that school about the wreck? By progressive penetration, he has gone only as far at a time as his memory has permitted. Only now he holds in his mind a model of the ship — and he can rotate that model in his mind and orient himself toward up, down, out. He's been all the way through the *Doria* and out the other side, through the gash that sank her, and brought back the images. This is what it looks like; this is what you see.

But how does it feel? What's it like to know you are in a story that you will either retell a hundred times or never tell? You decide to drop down into the black hole. No, you don't decide; you just do it. Why? You just do. A little ways, to explore the wreck and your courage, what you came down here to do. What is it like? Nothing under your fins now for eighty feet but the mass and complexity of the machine on all sides — what was once luminous and magical changed to dreary chaos. Drifting down past the cables that killed John Ornsby, rusty steel lianas where a wall has collapsed. Dropping too fast now, you pump air into your b.c., kick up and bash your tanks into a pipe, swing one arm and hit a cable, rust particles raining down. You've never felt your attention so assaulted: It is everything at once, from all directions, and from inside, too. You grab the cable and hang, catching your breath — bubble and hiss, bubble and hiss. Your light, a beam of dancing motes, plays down a battered passageway, where metal steps on the left-hand wall lead to a vertical landing, then disappear behind a low, sponge-encrusted wall that was once a ceiling. That's the way inside the *Doria*.

There is something familiar about that tunnel, something the body knows. All your travels, your daily commutes, the Brownian motion of your comings and goings in the world, straining after desires, reaching for your beloved — they've all just been an approach to this one hard turn. You can feel it, the spine arching to make the corner, a bow that shoots the arrow of time. In the final terror, with your gauges ticking and your gas running low, as dead end leads to dead end and the last corridor stretches out beyond time, does the mind impose its own order, seizing the confusion of busted pipes and jagged edges and forcing them into a logical grid, which you can then follow down to the bottom of the wreck and out — in a gust of light and love — through the wound in her side? Where you find yourself standing up to your waist in water, in the pit the current has gouged to be the grave of the *Andrea Doria*. Seagulls screech in the air as you take off your gear piece by piece and, much lightened, begin to walk back to New York across the sandy plane. And it comes as no surprise at all to look up and behold the *Seeker* flying above you, sailing on clouds. On the stern deck, the divers are celebrating, like rubber-suited angels, breaking out beers and cigars, and holding up plates to be redeemed by the sun.

ADRIENNE RICH

From *Diving Into The Wreck*, 1973

DIVING INTO THE WRECK

First having read the book of myths,
and loaded the camera,
and checked the edge of the knife-blade,
I put on
the body-armor of black rubber
the absurd flippers
the grave and awkward mask.
I am having to do this
not like Cousteau with his
assiduous team
aboard the sun-flooded schooner
but here alone.

There is a ladder.
The ladder is always there
hanging innocently
close to the side of the schooner.
We know what it is for,
we who have used it.
Otherwise
it's a piece of maritime floss
some sundry equipment.

I go down.
Rung after rung and still
the oxygen immerses me
the blue light
the clear atoms
of our human air.
I go down.
My flippers cripple me,
I crawl like an insect down the ladder
and there is no one
to tell me when the ocean
will begin.

First the air is blue and then
it is bluer and then green and then
black I am blacking out and yet
my mask is powerful
it pumps my blood with power
the sea is another story
the sea is not a question of power
I have to learn alone
to turn my body without force
in the deep element.

And now: it is easy to forget
what I came for
among so many who have always
lived here
swaying their crenellated fans
between the reefs
and besides
you breathe differently down here.

I came to explore the wreck.
The words are purposes.
The words are maps.
I came to see the damage that was done
and the treasures that prevail.
I stroke the beam of my lamp
slowly along the flank
of something more permanent
than fish or weed

the thing I came for:
the wreck and not the story of the wreck
the thing itself and not the myth
the drowned face always staring
toward the sun
the evidence of damage
worn by salt and sway into this threadbare beauty
the ribs of the disaster
curving their assertion
among the tentative haunters.

banyans. Hot knots of waiting petitioners discover each other and put their cases over and over again, ever more articulate, ever more impassioned, scattering in the sunlight gems of rhetoric whose brilliance goes unrecorded. Squeezing through the press of people the tea boys come and go with battered tin trays and dirty glasses with half an inch of undissolved sugar in them. Wholly unconcerned with legal wranglings, they form a noisy subcommunity of their own, their cries and whistles joining the birds'. Everywhere is a prodigality of speech and gesture and smell, and from it all a distillation leaks out in a steady trickle of files containing depositions typed shakily on yellowed paper.

An old man wearing spectacles mended with fuse wire gathers them up every so often and takes them inside the great building, through a back entrance and gloomy passageways, climbing flights of worn steps until, having knocked on a door, he enters a remarkable room. It is not particularly big, but the open windows are spacious and it is the light coming through them which gives the room its quality. This must be the back of the building, facing away from the hubbub downstairs which had seemed to besiege it on all sides. The air is quiet. The windows open into a cage of leaves, as if the room were built in the heart of a tree. Through them filters a serene undersea glow pricked with spicules of dazzling sunlight, one stray beam laying the spectrum in a bar of colors across the windowsill. At a bare table before the window sits a scholarly man — a judge, possibly — staring out into the greenery and watching the hop and flitter of small birds among the branches. The old messenger lays the files in silence on the judge's desk and in silence withdraws, closing the door gently behind him. Maybe something of the din below is audible after all, for there is a faint but constant background noise, a soft roaring like a distant sea. The judge sighs, opens the top file and begins to read. It is hard to connect the orderly, formulaic sentences with the whizzing and tumultuous lives which, in some garbled form, they partly express.

One needs to drift in the green undersea light day after day, month after month, maybe for years, until almost bored. Or maybe not bored but blocked. Looking and listening, the conviction grows that something is missing, some dark matter hidden but deduced. It is an absence which to an animal privileging the visual leads to the idea that it must be *located* if only it could be found. Somewhere behind the next outcrop (vaguely right-angled, like the wing of a somber old palace) must be a forgotten courtyard containing a great assemblage, a tumult, the core and center of this submarine complex. Until it is found one will go on missing the point, ears stuffed with water and eyes straining behind glass, too immured in a scholarly attention to detail and too intent on deciphering easily apprehended messages which purport to tell the whole story. What is needed is a sideways shift, a skidding off into a different position entirely.

Some black art may be needed for dealing with reefs, one I have never discovered. All my experiments with them, while having suggested themselves as serious, ended up as parodic or whimsical. When diving off coral reefs it would be useful to learn how to judge the direction and speed of a nearby boat rather than run the risk of surfacing for air directly in its path. Even after so many years I still cannot do this reliably. Sound underwater becomes omnidirectional, reflected off rocks, off the shelving sea floor, even back down from the surface. Depth, too, makes a difference. The more distant a boat is, the farther down one has to go to hear it. Sometimes a fishing boat will pass directly above. The silveredged lozenge scoots overhead — black, very sharp and swift — and the whirring disc of its propeller mutes itself for an instant, like an electric fan which is quieter heard edgeways on than from in front or behind. What, then, would be the effect of hearing a sound from a source vertically below instead of overhead?

Having borrowed a cassette player with a loudspeaker, I swathed it in many plastic bags and walked into the sea, its owner watching and torn between consternation and ridicule. I swam down about twenty feet and set the machine on a ledge among corals. The pressure flattened the layers of polyethylene in a secondary diaphragm across the speaker grille and it was possible to believe equally that this might conduct the sound better or else muffle it. I wanted to see what effect music had on fish and other reef creatures, but also how well it would sound underwater. It turned out to be disappointing, ethereal only in so far as it was inherently weird to hang in water twenty feet down and hear Mozart's G-Minor Quintet coming from behind an outcrop of *Acropora*. It was not so much attenuated as muted, the higher frequencies suffering most. With the cassette player on its back the sound, as heard from the surface directly above, was definitely feebler than at the same distance away horizontally. This was probably due to the focusing effects of rocks and the sea floor. As for the creatures, they paid the music no obvious heed, with the exception of a damselfish which braved the ecstatically depressed sounds to dart at the polyethylene. They are highly territorial, and the player was probably in its backyard. Since fish have excellent hearing, it is likely that this dim source of noise was at all the wrong frequencies to be interesting. It certainly was muffled. This maybe had something to do with water pressure deadening the air column inside the speaker and even slightly inhibiting the vibrations of the paper cone itself. Altogether, it was a pathetic substitute for a GLORIA transponder.

On other days I experimented with making high-frequency noises by partially inflating condoms and trying to make them squeak underwater. It was necessary to wash off the silicone lubricant, otherwise my fingers would skid greasily without making a sound. I finally coated my hands with a resin used locally as the basis of incense and tried inflating the bladders to different dimensions to obtain different frequencies. This, too, was a failure. At best I achieved a brief grunting sound, though it was uncertain whether this was generated manually. Anyone who has ever tried swimming underwater holding an inflated condom will appreciate the difficulties involved.

There are fish which are blind and others which have no olfactory organs, but they all have some variety of acoustico-lateralis system. That is, they have "ears" or sound receptors as well as lateral line organs. A fish's lateral line runs from its head along both sides, its course often marked with a pigmented stripe. It is made up of tiny hairlike sensors which respond to changes in the water caused by local movement and currents. In addition to having "ears" some species of fish have the capacity to make sounds, generally in one of two ways. They either drum on the wall of their swim bladder or, like a cricket, stridulate two bony surfaces together. It is presumed that such abilities are used for courting and mating rituals. Species which have some sort of connection between their swim bladder and their inner ear must have exceptionally acute hearing since the air sac would act like a diaphragm and efficiently collect sound. As for the noises made by marine creatures, some are very loud indeed. Apart from the celebrated carrying qualities of cetacean sound, the sharp snapping of a pistol shrimp is enough to make a swimmer jump, while the grunts of toadfish have been known to set off acoustic mines.

Such things are the background to another experiment, one performed so often as to become a habit. This is to swim out to the edge of the reef on a moonless night, head down into the depths and, holding on to a rock near the bottom, simply concentrate on all that can be heard and seen until the air in the lungs runs out. This is the best way I have yet discovered of apprehending a reef and it has become the central ritual of my explorations. To save blundering painfully into corals, stinging hydroids and sea urchins, one needs to take a sealed flashlight, but it must be used sparingly, otherwise the light destroys the eyes' rhodopsin and leaves one blinder and — strangely — deafer as well. Obviously it is better to choose a reef whose layout and fauna are familiar. Knowing what to expect, it is less of a shock when a stingray explodes off the bottom in a cloud of silt, pelting wings flashing quick beats of white underside as it vanishes into the blackness. It is *necessary* to be alone and it is necessary to be apprehensive. When the night is overcast and the wide drench of tropical starlight falls uselessly into an upper bed of soft cloud and nothing below it can be seen, not even the shore: then is the time to take a deep breath and swim down, grains of luminescence streaming back from fingertips, down and down.

It was whale song which mariners heard filtering through their vessels' resonant wooden hulls and which they took for the Sirens' voices, beckoning them to disaster. To have lain in one's bunk at night and heard on the other side of a few inches of oak and copper sheathing those directionless, distanceless cries must have been to feel the chill of utter melancholy and dissolution. Also, to have felt one's nakedness. This is the effect of listening to reef sounds at night, too. It is more than just the nakedness of wearing next to nothing, and it is more than vulnerability. It is the sensation of animal messages passing *through* one as if, being seven-tenths water, one's body were transparent.

At first it is too unnerving to permit concentration. After a time, when nothing life-threatening has happened, the rhythm of swimming down, waiting, and coming back up for air becomes soothing. The sea is warm. With the clamp of water over one's ears and the blackness pressing up against one's mask, conditions approximate very slightly to those of controlled sensory deprivation, a disorienting and eventually unhinging technique fashionable in torture and interrogation circles some years ago. But there is no real comparison. There is too much sensation, too much physical effort in holding the breath, in staying down rather than floating up, in seeing and hearing. It is never more than mildly hypnotic for a few minutes (but with a vanishing of time which makes those moments impossible to calculate). Steady in the background is the loud white noise of uncounted crustaceans stridulating with pincers, horny plates, mandibles, who knows what. Very occasionally it stops dead, and in the ensuing silence a chill passes over the body because a million crabs and prawns have all heard something attention-grabbing which one has missed completely. What is it out there? Out here? The frogs in the paddies do it, too. Nightly they crank up their ranarian machine until it is turning over at a constant speed. It goes for an hour, then abruptly stops. A beat or two, then a few brave ones try to turn it over, are joined by others until it catches and settles back into its rackety tick-over. Crickets will do the same.

Out here we are on the edge of something: of drowning, fear, understanding. The huge unseen city itself seems always on the cusp of vanishing, it is so delicate and its true nature so elusive. It is a place whose strangeness is far greater than we can know even as we painstakingly try to identify each snapping shrimp, each grunting fish, the soft concussion — like a cloth being flapped — of a sizable fish taking evasive action somewhere nearby. *Whup*. But then we, too, are stranger than we imagine. We hang here in the depths with granules of cold fire prickling around us as creatures and currents stir dinoflagellates into luminescence. We hang here, inquisitive carbon-based life-forms, knowing that every atom of carbon now in our bodies was once in the interior of a star. For an instant we dissolve, are without form, become nothing but the point at which the three axes plotting this three-dimensional borderland intersect. The three dimensions of a fringing coral reef are as follows. *Horizontally*, it marks a border between sea and land. The flats at low tide baking for hours in sunlight support a variety of marine animals which can survive out of water and resist a wide temperature range. *Vertically*, the seaward cliff of a reef face reaches to within inches of the surface and may plunge 3,000 feet in a precipitous slope, its initial descent marked by a steady change in colors and life-forms. *Obliquely*, a reef exists at other wavelengths than those we can perceive. The hidden courtyard with its tumult, the babble and rhetoric, the colors and unimagined smells, all are tucked away in great bright pockets of the electromagnetic spectrum which are closed off to us, in sounds we cannot hear, in pheromones our nostrils cannot detect. This knowledge makes us ache, sea creatures that we once were, as for a country we have lost on the far side of a frontier we can barely even discern. We are left with our narrow, thickened senses. We are also left resorting to fossil gestures. I find myself opening my mouth underwater, the better to hear. It works on land, but not noticeably beneath the sea, where a proportion of sound reaches one via direct conduction through the bones of the skull. It is the gesture of a creature with a phylogenetic memory, as if some ancestor with a different otopharyngeal arrangement had opened its mouth to let messages in and out, grinding chattily away with a set of bones at the back of its throat. I also track down a dimly surviving fragment of my lost lateral line, maybe. In daylight one day I notice tiny plumes of silt pulsing from a hole at the foot of a coral outcrop about thirty feet down. I do not know what particular worm or shrimp is busily excavating inside but have the sudden urge to feel this minute puffing as well as to watch it. I put my fingertips half an inch away but can detect nothing. Without thinking I maneuver awkwardly so that my head is close to the hole. The puffing stops for a few seconds but then starts again. Gently I move so that I am almost kissing the hole and can just feel the tiny waves of energy from the unseen creature's fins or pedipalps break against my upper lip. It is the underwater version of that uncon-scious gesture which makes people press their laundry beneath their noses to feel how dry it is: ex-weanlings whose haptic sense for moisture and movement was designed for the breast.

The reef's vertical axis is most vividly revealed in terms of light, ranging from the brilliance of sunlight to the inkiest depths. The sea is both lit and heated by the sun's energy, which is absorbed and scattered from the moment it penetrates the surface. The uppermost meter of the sea effectively absorbs all ultraviolet and infrared, respectively those wavelengths shorter and longer than the visible. Thereafter seawater absorbs the longer wavelengths first and at about thirty feet down most of the surviving energy is in the blue-green part of the spectrum. From here downward, increasing numbers of reef creatures are colored in various shades of red. With almost no visible red light remaining they look dark or black and in still dimmer waters farther down become almost invisible. In these top ten meters the simplest experiments show how much light the water absorbs. Slightly dull objects take on fabulous colors as one swims toward the surface with them. Likewise, a bloodcolored anemone becomes pale and anemic as one swims away from it.

At a depth of fifty meters only five percent of the sun's energy still penetrates. If the water is exceedingly clear, there is enough light for photosynthesis in plants and algae down to 150 meters. Below that, ordinary plant life cannot exist, which is why there are no great prairies of seaweed covering the deep ocean beds.[1] Generally speaking, the hundred-meter mark defines the bottom of the euphotic ("well lit") zone, the most productive part of the sea. Coincidentally, it also marks the theoretical limit to unaided diving by creatures of the upper air. Certain free divers have exceeded this by a few meters but it is at around this point that pressure collapses the lungs. Well before that, the strain of keeping them inflated will have begun to rupture small blood vessels. In splendid violation of a supposed boundary auks (razorbills and guillemots) have sometimes been seen from submersibles at one hundred meters, while the bird diving record is easily held by the emperor penguin with a recorded eighteen-minute dive to 265 meters, or 870 feet. In any case this hundred-meter zone effectively denotes the end of the reef as an ecosystem. Below this its dead corals become a habitat for scattered sponges and, of course, the sundry twilight animal species.

---

[1] This statement wants qualifying. Plant-like structures may occur in the deep and highly specialized ecosystems of vent communities. These grow up around "black smokers" at volcanic sites and are not based on photosynthesis. The bacteria of vent communities, on which populations of tube worms, huge crabs and oysters, and other creatures depend, have metabolisms which use sulphur in place of oxygen. Hence these strange pockets of life have nothing to do with the upper world and its biochemistry. Meanwhile, the greatest depth at which conventional plant life has been found is 269 meters, a clump of maroon algae in exceptionally transparent water off the Bahamas.

Underwater photography naturally has to take into account this absorption of light energy by water. Even if there is enough ambient light for filming, color values will be increasingly affected by the progressive filtering out of the warm and comforting wavelengths: first red, then orange, then yellow. "Correct" color values can be restored by carefully calculated artificial lighting. Any approach to the question of human vision underwater leads back to the fact that the narrow waveband in which our eyes operate corresponds very markedly with how sunlight is transmitted in seawater. Quentin Huggett at IOS has wondered whether this setting of our visual "window" reflects our aquatic origin. In air the bandspread is much wider. Several species of insect see at ultraviolet wavelengths, while the pit viper uses infrared sensing to detect warm prey in the dark. Had *Homo* developed differently he might have "seen" a different world.

It is sad that we cannot smell things underwater, though now and then something lodges in a taste bud or receptor to produce the simulacrum of a smell, a pungent impression located somewhere in the muzzle part of the face, neither precisely smell nor taste. Sad, too, that our hearing is not very acute, and with a limited range from about sixteen cycles per second up to twenty thousand cps. A mere cat has three times this range, a bat six. The pitch at which human ears are at their most sensitive is that of "a child's or woman's cry," according to Yi-fu Tuan, who thinks this suggests that our ear is adapted to favor our species's survival rather than hunting.[2] This is most aggravating to those reef haunters who have no wish to listen to children and women crying, either above or below water, nor any interest in the survival of their own species, but who would dearly like to eavesdrop among the courthouses, malls, temples, palaces, and suburbs of their passion.

My lame experiments sound foolish. *Are* foolish to scientists like those aboard *Farnella*, who could suggest any amount of gear for increasing my sensing ability. Yet in the early days of submarine warfare the help of people with musical knowledge and perfect pitch was sought in order to classify the sounds made by submerged craft. In World War I the composer and conductor Sir Hamilton Harry was called in by the British Admiralty's

[2] Yi-fu Tuan, *Topophilia* (1974).

Board for Invention and Research to identify the most likely frequency bands of hull and propeller noises, "anticipating by a whole war a similar attempt in America, where the conductor Andre Kostelanetz was approached for much the same purpose..."[3] Ernest Rutherford also took a colleague with perfect pitch out in a small boat as part of the war effort. At a prearranged spot one of the great names in atomic physics took a firm grip of his companion's ankles while this man stuck his head into the Firth of Forth and listened to the engine note of a British submarine. Hauled back into the dinghy and toweling his head he announced it was a submersible in A-flat and he would recognize it anywhere.[4]

Today with an ultrasound detector I could wiretap the citizens of this submarine city, but it would not be the same. As with medical diagnostic equipment such apparatus can also blunt other responses. Ironically, part of the problem of the tropical reef is its very visibility. It famously stands as the icon of marine exoticism: brilliant colors, profusion of species, intricacy of shape and design. To make all this more easily seen by means of scuba gear, or more easily heard with ingenious electronics, is somehow too facile to be serious, except for detailed scientific work. Scuba equipment is, of course, indispensable for any work below forty or fifty feet and down to two hundred feet. It is a marvelous invention.[5] However, it has certain disadvantages which are not compatible with traveling alone in remote parts of the world, since it is heavy to lug around, expensive to replace when stolen, and limited by the local availability of a reliable compressor, to say nothing of the obligatory diving companion. Apart from wishing to be quite alone in the sea, I dislike scuba gear for two

---

[3] R.V. Jones, *Reflections on Intelligence* (1989).

[4] See *New Scientist* 1768, p. 80.

[5] Scuba gear is a vast improvement on all its predecesssors, although the tonic effects of oxygen seem not to be as pronounced nowadays as they used to be. In a report in the New York *Daily Times* (24 August 1854) the writer considers the newly developed diving suits of the day, which were made of leather and rubber and entailed the divers carrying "a box of condensed air." "The condensed air they are forced to breathe furnishes them a greater quantity of oxygen in a given time, and increases their strength very much for the time being. A diver, at a depth of ninety feet under water, at Portsmouth, England, was known to bend nearly double an iron crowbar in his work, which resisted the strength of four men at the surface." Presumably the proposition here is that if oxygen gives life, a lot of oxygen will give a lot of life.

additional reasons. It is awkward to wear, all the time making me conscious of itself, of bits of metal and tube, of tanks as bulky as a growth, of
belts and dials and rubber straps and harness. But even more important, I
cannot hear with it. Breaths and bubbles rattle and roar in the ears, the
very heart drums in the air hose. It all gets in the way as much as it
facilitates, and on most occasions it is preferable to sacrifice depth for the
immediacy and greater effort of free diving. The immediacy is whatever
transcends discomfort and inconvenience, leaving one uncluttered on
borrowed time. By making certain things too easy, scuba equipment gives
rise to that curious paradox: The more accessible a thing becomes, the
harder it can be to see.[6]

Besides, we are not trying to push outward the frontiers of science, but
our own. We are content to have identified the calm room with the big
windows letting in the blue-green undersea light and to know that whatever we learn is only a part of what goes on in its corridors and undercrofts
and courtyards. It is a consoling pleasure to have hung about this cityscape
at night and watched the lights winking to codes unguessed at, to the roar
of conversation in a universe off at an angle. It is enough to have clung to
the roots of a reef at sunrise and watched the dark gradually bleach from
the water. The night shift changes, silence falls. Then the creatures of day
emerge and all around the dawn chorus starts, as if invisible behind still-
misty water a great banyan were spreading its branches.

---

[6] C.F. Wallace Stevens's poem "The Creations of Sound," in which he chides an imaginary
writer whose poems "do not make the visible a little hard/To see..."

ROBERT STONE

From *A Flag for Sunrise*, a novel, 1981

IT'S OUT THERE

With the air tank tucked into the gunwales under the bench on which he sat, Holliwell smoked and watched the green coastline — palm groves, banana plants strayed from the plantations, beach heliotrope of outsized luxuriance. Sandy, the dive master, ran his thirty-six-footer at full throttle, slapping the hull over the placid water; the bow took spray over the windward side that soaked the STP jacket Holliwell had worn against the sun.

Sandy was a long, spare man with a freckled English country man's face darkened by the suns of Tecan and West Africa. He lounged in the stern, one loose hand over the stick, one elbow on the rail, leaning out to see the water ahead. His long black hair was bleached at the crown, parted at the middle of his skull like a nineteenth century Russian peasant's, and this with his sharp black eyes deep-set under thick low brows brought a kind of dervish flair, a Rasputin intensity, to his appearance.

In the boat with Holliwell was a family of five Cuban-Americans from Miami. The father was stocky and muscular, his hair worn in a brush cut, his jaw jowled and pitted from relentless shaving. His wife was buxom and fleshy-faced yet with a long-legged trim frame, a Floridian body honed by dieting and Gloria Stevens. There were three boys between twelve and seventeen — the oldest vulpine with a nearly complete mustache and muscular like his father, the two younger quite like their mother; over the waist of each of their bathing suits sagged a tube of buttery fat. The parents spoke to each other in Spanish, the boys in American Adolescent. All of them ignored Holliwell.

"Could be seein' turtle over this reef," Sandy told the boys. "Good place to see dem."

"Aw-*right*," said the middle boy with enthusiasm.

"Would they bite you?" asked the smallest boy.

Sandy laughed. "Turtle bite you? Turtle don't bite you. Maybe take you for a ride."

"Hey," the seventeen-year-old said, "I could go for that."

When the children's parents spoke to Sandy it was in a formal and imperious way, as though they were used to service. Sandy answered them with deference.

Three hundred yards offshore, Sandy killed his engine and hopped forward to put the anchor line down. Everyone looked over the side. The sky's light sparkled back at them, reflected and refracted from the reef tops below — a long line of peaks curving out toward open ocean.

Sandy gave them the dive plan. The current was southerly. They would dive straight out from the stern, up-current. Then they could follow a semi-circle of reef tops, cross a sandy bottom and follow the edge of a drop back to the boat with the current behind them. There was black coral there, Sandy told them. The site was called Twixt by the people of the coast.

Holliwell stared down at the liquid light of the white reefs. They were, after all, what he had come to see. He took a deep breath and put on his buoyancy compensator, his backpack tank, and bent to wrestle on his weight belt. Sandy put his own tank on with the ease of a man donning a sweater. The Cuban-American bustled about, trying stays and buckles — the head of the house overseeing procedure. The woman and the youngest boy were not going down. While Holliwell put his boots and fins on, Sandy checked out the gear of the younger of the two boys who were diving.

"Ever see any sharks around here?" the younger boy asked, as casually as he could. Holliwell admired his sangfroid. Testing his own regulator, he turned to watch Sandy answer.

"No sharks here," Sandy said simply.

It turned out that the younger boy was diving with Sandy, the oldest with his father. It had been so ordered.

"Want to come with us?" the dive master asked Holliwell.

"I'll just follow along," Holliwell said. "I'll be all right." He was not in fact a very experienced diver but the dive seemed easy enough.

Holliwell went over last, carrying two five-pound weights, wearing trunks and a tee shirt to ease the shoulder straps on his sunburned back. On the jump-off, his mask filled almost to eye level; he let the water rise in it, pinching his nostrils to equalize pressure. When he saw the reef tips rising around him, he cleared his mask and checked the depth gauge on his wrist. He was forty-five feet below the surface. He settled over a punch-bowl depression on the bottom; his fin tips stirred the milk-white sand there. The visibility at this depth was marvelous — over a hundred feet, perhaps two hundred. Black and golden angelfish swarmed around him as though they expected to be fed. There were parrot fish and convict tangs in uncountable numbers. The reef descended in terraces from its highest peaks, from each terrace elkhorn coral stretched in tortured fantastical shapes between the domes of brain coral. Below him wrasse and groupers glided by, a boxfish watched him shyly from behind two prongs of elkhorn. When he paddled out from the plateau on which he had rested, two trumpet fish came along with him like scouts. He swam clear of the next terrace and let the weights take him deeper; on the edge of vision he saw a barracuda — fairly small, certainly under three feet — prowling the edge of the swarm to pick off stragglers. When he leveled off, he was at sixty feet and the ocean floor still sloped downward under his fins. Far off and about forty feet above him he saw Sandy and the Cuban boy outlined against the shimmering curtain of the surface, swimming away from him.

On the next terrace he saw the black coral. There seemed to be acres of it, dappled with encrusting yellow infant sponges, and circling down he felt as though he were flying over a lava field grown with daisies. When he was closer, he could see the coral's root and branch patterns. It was sublime, he thought. He could feel his heart beating faster; his blood coursed through him like a drug. The icy, fragile beauty was beyond the competency of any man's hand, even beyond man's imagining. Yet it seemed to him its perfection provoked a recognition. The recognition of what? he wondered. A thing lost or forgotten. He followed the slope of the coral field. Down.

It had been years since he had taken so much pleasure in the living world.

At about ninety feet, he confronted the drop. The last coral terrace fell away and beyond it there was nothing, an immensity of shadowy blue, an abyss. He was losing color now. The coral on the canyon wall read blue-gray as he descended; the wrasse, the butterflies, the parrot fish looked as dun as mackerel. A gray lobster scurried along the cliff. Enormous gray groupers approached to have a look at him. In a coral crevice, a spotted moray drew back at his approach, then put its head out to watch his bubble trail with flat venomous eyes. The surface became a mirage, a distant notion.

He was at 110 and his pressure gauge, which had pointed twenty-five hundred p.s.i. at the jump-off, now read slightly under eight hundred. It was all right, he thought, the tank had no reserve and no J valve; he would have enough to climb back as the pressure evened out. At 120, his exhilaration was still with him and he was unable to suppress the impulse to turn a somersault. He was at the borders of narcosis. It was time to start up.

As soon as he began to climb, he saw shimmers of reflected light flashing below his feet. In a moment, the flashes were everywhere — above and below. Blue glitters, lightning quick. The bodies of fish in flight. He began pumping a bit, climbing faster, but by the book, not outstripping his own bubble trail.

Some fifty feet away, he caught clear sight of a school of bonito racing toward the shallows over the reef. Wherever he looked, he saw what appeared to be a shower of blue-gray arrows. And then it was as if the ocean itself had begun to tremble. The angels and wrasse, the parrots and tangs which had been passing lazily around him suddenly hung in place, without forward motion, quivering like mobile sculpture. Turning full circle, he saw the same shudder pass over all the living things around him — a terror had struck the sea, an invisible shadow, a silence within a silence. On the edge of vision, he saw a school of redfish whirl left, then right, sound, then reverse, a red and white catherine wheel against the deep blue. It was a sight as mesmerizing as the wheeling of starlings over a spring pasture. Around him the fish held their places, fluttering, coiled for flight.

Then Holliwell thought: It's out there. Fear overcame him; a chemical taste, a cold stone on the heart.

He started up too fast, struggling to check his own panic. Follow the bubbles. Follow the bouncing ball.

As he pedaled up the wall, he was acutely aware of being the only creature on the reef that moved with purpose. The thing out there must be feeling him, he thought, sensing the lateral vibrations of his climb, its dim primal brain registering disorder in his motion and making the calculation. Fear. Prey.

He was running out of air — overbreathing and overtaxing the expanding contents of his tank. The sound of his own desperate respirations furthered panic.

When he had worked out a breathing pattern and reached the first terrace, he found that he had enough to curve his ascent with the slope of the coral. At forty feet, he saw a sandy punch bowl like the one in which he had stopped but the forests of elkhom were everywhere the same and the anchor line was nowhere in sight. Looking up, he saw Sandy outlined against the surface, coming down at him.

Sandy grabbed Holliwell's pressure gauge, read it and shook his head in reproach. He pointed to the right and upward along the slope. Holliwell followed the coral ridges as long as he could. The fish in the shallows swam placidly, unperturbed. When he found himself sucking hard on the regulator mouthpiece, he eased up the next thirty feet taking three breaths on the way. And there, in another dimension altogether, the boat rocked gently, the youngest of the Cuban boys leaned over the side to watch the shifting surface, lost in reverie; his mother thumbed through *Cosmopolitan.* The shoreline glowed green beyond the hot blur of the beach, the line of banana jungle broken only by a white wooden building on a solitary hill, surmounted with a cross. Holliwell turned over on his back and swam to the boat's ladder.

The boy and his mother watched as he took off his gear. Before disconnecting the regulator from the tank he checked the gauge once more; it read just a hair over empty at sea level.

"That's as empty as it gets," he told the people in the boat. The charge of primary process he had experienced at 110 feet put him in danger of becoming garrulous.

The boy looked at the gauge. "None left at all?"

"Empty," Holliwell said. "Just like it says." He was ill at ease with the boy and he sensed a certain artificiality in his own manner. His own children had not been this age for five years or more; he had forgotten what it was like. Out of touch again, he thought.

"How come is that?" the woman asked.

"Just ran it out," Holliwell told her cheerfully.

"What did you see?" the boy asked him.

"Lots of great fish," he said. "And beautiful black coral."

"And we can't take any," the woman said. "Such a shame because it's so beautiful."

"I'm sure it looks prettier where it is," Holliwell heard himself say pompously.

The woman inflated her cheeks and shrugged. She was not a bad sort, Holliwell decided. They chatted for a few minutes. The family's name was Paz; they lived in Miami, had lived there since 1961. All of their sons were born there. The man was a dentist, she herself was in real estate. They were visiting her brother, who had five hardware stores in Tecan. Holliwell told her that he was a professor; she had lived in the States long enough to remain unimpressed.

Sandy and the middle son were next up; the boy climbed aboard and fixed a smirk on Holliwell. The dive master got out of harness in a single easy motion.

"Now what you want down theah, mistuh?" he asked Holliwell. He was smiling. "I nevah tol' you go down theah."

"Just wanted a look, I guess."

"Sandy made him get out of the water," the middle son announced. Señora Paz and the youngest boy gave Holliwell dutifully accusatory looks. Then Señora Paz asked sharply after her husband and eldest son. They were under the boat, Sandy assured her, playing among the elkhorn coral.

After a few minutes, the dentist surfaced and climbed aboard. He was elated after his dive and his amiability extended even to Holliwell.

"Where the hell were you?" Dr. Paz asked Holliwell. "I never even saw you." His English was almost completely unaccented.

"Sandy made him get out of the water," the middle son said.

"Just down too deep," Sandy said soothingly. "A bit too deep and de air run out faster."

"What's the attraction down there?" the dentist asked.

"Just the drop," Holliwell said.

"How far you think she drop off dere!" Sandy asked him, laughing.

"A long way," Holliwell said.

"Nine hundred meters," Sandy said.

"Is that possible?" Holliwell said.

Sandy let his smile fade. His nod was solemn, his eyes humorous with certainty.

"I'm tellin' you, mon. Nine hundred meters."

When the youngest boy wanted to know how far that was in feet, Sandy was uncertain.

"It's about two thirds of a mile," the dentist said. "I thought they taught you that in school."

"Yeah, dummy," the middle son said to his brother.

"How about that," Holliwell said.

Then the oldest boy surfaced with an empty tank.

"Orca, orca," the two younger boys shouted. "Orca surfaces at last."

The youth's eyes were shining as he climbed up the ladder. It was hard to dislike anyone, Holliwell thought, when you watched them come up from a dive.

"Gosh," the boy said to Holliwell, "we didn't see you anywhere."

"Sandy made him get..."

Señora Paz hushed her middle son with a frown and a raising of her chin.

They motored back to the hotel dock making small talk. At the dive shack, Sandy, who knew a big tipper when he saw one, helped the Pazes wash and stow their gear and was jolly with the boys. Holliwell put his own gear away and sat down on the dock. After a while Sandy wandered down and joined him.

"How long you been divin'?" Sandy asked him.

"I've been certified for two years. I don't do it much anymore."

Sandy looked out to sea. "Lost a mon on dat drop other year. I follow him dom near two hundred meters but when I turn off de mon still goin' down."

"Suicide," Holliwell said.

"Das right. Mon take de sleepin' pills and go down."

"It must have happened more than once."

Sandy nodded. "I don' lose nobody," he said. "Got to be dere own chosen will."

Holliwell felt himself shudder. "Did you think that's what I was doing?"

"Oh, no," the dive master said quickly. He touched Holliwell on the shoulder in the Caribbean way but avoided his eye.

"I won't make the dive this afternoon," Holliwell told him. "Maybe you could leave me off around French Harbor. I'd like to snorkel down there."

Sandy guessed that it would be all right. French Harbor was on the way. He told Holliwell that if he requested it, the Paradise kitchen might pack a lunch for him. They walked together toward the hotel buildings.

"There was something down that drop this morning," Holliwell said. "A big shark, maybe."

Sandy stopped walking and looked at Holliwell, holding his hand on his brow to shield his eyes from the sun.

"You see any shark?"

"No."

"Then don' be sayin' shark if you don' see one."

"Something was happening down there."

"I tell you don' go down that far, Mistuh Holliwell. I give you de dive plan. When you down so far, das not a good place."

"Why's that?"

Sandy walked on; Holliwell followed him.

"Dat drop, people see things, den dey don' know what dey seen. Dey be frightened after."

"Was it always like that?"

"Jus' dangerous divin', das all. Surface current and de drop is cunnin'. You get deeper den you know."

"So pretty, though."

"Jus' as pretty on de top," Sandy said. "Always prettier in de light."

"Yes," Holliwell said. "Yes, of course."

SUSAN FAWCETT

From *Poetry,* 1992

BLACK WATER DIVING

I am the woman in black rubber
frog-kicking
through the cold weight of the water,
tranced with apprehension.

A mask clears the world before me
as I listen to my crashing breath
and tug the lead, two longs — I'm here,
I'm fine — kicking deeper.

My strobe funnels through the haze,
illumines drifting particulates,
a grouper of no color
whose meditative mouth and gills pump

silently as my tanks hiss.
I could be one of Klee's clumsy angels,
pallid, unlucky, ogling
predictable wonders:

blue octopus, sand shark,
seven refrigerators without doors
aglitter with coral, silt, small fish.
Would it begin with itching,

scales breaking out like cellophane chips
or gelatinous flowers,
the transformation: woman into fish?
I try a forceful sacral thrust,

legs together like a tail —
no flailing human arms and legs,
no head battered by thoughts.
Then simply sway, inert,

as in a smooth last box.
Cutting the strobe,
I let the black embrace me.
All the apparatus — mask, hoses, clamps —

seem my body now.
Phosphorescent glimmerings spill
like diamond chips from black silk,
and one faint vessel, pinkish

blue as a Deco vase, glows in the pitch.
My mind pauses like a fish,
knowing it holds a blackness
inside blackness.

Ascending, I am nearly happy
though embolism threatens like a bomb,
though bearing a dark star inside me,
random as grief, compact as a wish.

I rise toward the line coming down to me,
toward the hull of a boat,
a ceiling of light
heaving like molten glass.

MICHAEL CRICHTON

From *Travels*, 1988

BONAIRE

The setting sun glowed red off the ocean as we waded clumsily out from the beach with our scuba tanks and lights. We paused, waist-deep in water, to put on our face masks and adjust the straps. Behind us, at the Hotel Bonaire, people were heading for the dining room to eat.

I said to my sister, "Hungry?"

She shook her head. My sister had never been night-diving before, and she was a little apprehensive about it.

We had come to Bonaire for a two-week diving holiday in the summer of 1974. Kim had just finished her second year of law school, and I had completed a draft of my next novel; we both looked forward to a good rest and a lot of superb diving.

Bonaire is a Dutch island fifty miles off the coast of Venezuela. The island is actually a sunken mountain peak with sheer sides; twenty yards from the sandy beach, the crystal-clear water was a hundred feet deep.

This made night-diving easy: just walk out from the hotel beach at sunset, and drop on down to a hundred feet. You could make your night dive for an hour and be back at the hotel dining room in time for dinner.

This was our plan.

My sister put her mouthpiece between her teeth, and I heard the hiss as she sucked air. She clutched her shoulders and pantomimed that she was cold; she wanted to get started. I bit my mouthpiece.

We sank beneath the surface.

The landscape is deep blue, small fish flicking like shadows over the sand and heads of coral. I hear the burble of my air bubbles sliding past my cheek. I look over at Kim to see how she is doing; she is fine, her body relaxed. Kim is an accomplished diver, and I have been diving for more than ten years.

We go deeper, down the slope into blackness.

We turn on the lights, and immediately see a world of riotous, outrageous color. The corals and sponges are all vivid greens, yellows, reds.

We move deeper, through black water, seeing only what is illuminated in the glowing cone of light from the flashlights. We find large fish sleeping beneath overhanging shelves of coral. We can touch them, something you can never do during the day. The night animals are active; a black-and-white-spotted moray eel comes out of its hole to flex its powerful jaws and peer at us with beady black eyes. An octopus scurries through my beam, and turns bright red in irritation. In a niche of coral we find a tiny red-striped crab no larger than my little finger.

On this dive I plan to take photographs, and so I have my camera around my neck. I take a few shots, and then my sister taps me on the shoulder and gestures she wants the camera. I take the strap from around my neck and hold it out to her. I'm moving slowly; with a flashlight dangling from my wrist, things seem awkward. Kim pulls the camera away.

Suddenly I feel a sharp yank at my jaw, and my mouthpiece is torn from my lips. My air is gone.

I know at once what has happened. The camera strap has caught on the air hose. My sister, in pulling the camera away, has also pulled out my mouthpiece.

I have no air. I am hanging in ink-black water at night and I have no air.

I remain calm.

Whenever you lose your mouthpiece, it invariably drops down the right side of your body. It can always be found hanging in the water alongside your right hipbone. I reach down for it.

The mouthpiece isn't there.

I remain calm.

I keep feeling for it. I know it is down there somewhere near my hip. It has to be. I feel my tank. I feel my weight belt. I feel my backpack. My fingers run over the contours of my equipment moving faster and faster. The mouthpiece isn't there. I am sure now: it isn't there. The mouthpiece piece isn't there.

I remain calm.

I know the mouthpiece hasn't been ripped from the air hose, because if it had I would be hearing a great blast of air. Instead, I am in eerie black silence. So the mouthpiece is around me, somewhere. If it hasn't fallen to my right side, it must be behind my neck, near the top of the air tank. This is a little more awkward to reach for, but I put my hand behind my neck and feel around for the air hose. I can feel the top of the tank, the vertical metal valve. I feel a number of hoses. I can't tell which is my air hose. I feel some more.

I can't find it.

I remain calm.

How deep am I? I check my gauges. I am in sixty feet of water now. That's okay. If I can blow out my air in a slow, steady stream and make it to the surface. I am sure I can. At least, I am pretty sure I can.

But it would be better to find the mouthpiece now. Down here.

My sister is hanging in the water five feet above me, her fins kicking gently near my face. I move up alongside her, and she looks at me. I point to my mouth. Look: something's missing. No mouthpiece, Kim.

She waves at me, and gives me the high sign that everything is all right with her. She busies herself with putting the camera around her neck. I realize that in the darkness she probably can't see me very well.

I grab her arm. I point to my mouth. No mouthpiece! *No air!*

She shakes her head, shrugs. She doesn't get it. What is my problem? What am I trying to tell her?

My lungs are starting to burn now. I blow a few air bubbles at her, and point again to my mouth. Look: no mouthpiece. For God's sake!

Kim nods, slowly. I can't see her eyes, because light reflects off her glass face mask. But she understands. At least, I think she understands.

My lungs are burning badly now. Soon I am going to have to bolt for the surface.

I am no longer calm.

In the darkness, she swings slowly behind me. Her light is behind my head, casting my shadow on the coral below. She is picking around my air hoses, near my neck. Sorting things out. Now she is over on my left side. Not my left side, Kim! It's got to be somewhere on the right! She moves slowly. She is so deliberate.

My lungs are burning.

I know I am going to have to bolt for the surface. I am telling myself, over and over: remember to breathe out, remember to breathe out. If I forget to exhale on the way up I will burst my lungs. I can't afford to panic.

Kim takes my hand. She gives me something in her slow, deliberate way. This is not the time to be giving me something! My fingers close on rubber: she has put the mouthpiece into my hand! I jam it between my teeth and blow out.

Water gurgles, then I suck cold air. Kim looks at me tentatively. I suck air, and cough a couple of times. Hanging in the water beside me, she watches me. Am I all right?

I suck air. My heart is pounding. I feel dizzy. Now that everything is okay, I feel all the panic I have suppressed. My God, I almost died! Kim is looking at me. Am I all right now?

I give her the high sign. Yes, I am all right. We finish the dive, though I have trouble concentrating. I am glad when it is over. When we get to the beach, I collapse. My whole body is shaking.

"That was weird," she says. She tells me that somehow the air hose has gotten twisted around, so that it was hanging down behind my left shoulder. "I didn't know that could happen," she says. "It took a while to find it. Are you all right'"

"I think so," I say.

"You're shivering."

"I think I'm just cold."

I take a hot shower. Alone in my room, I have a terrible urge for sex, a compulsive desire. I think, This is a cliché — escape death and seek procreation. But it's true. I am feeling it. And here I am with my sister, for Pete's sake.

By the end of dinner, I have calmed down. The next couple of days are more ordinary. We make another night dive. Nothing bad happens. I settle into the novels I have brought. I work on my suntan. For the next week, we have a good time. And we do all of the standard dive spots that every diver does in Bonaire.

But I want to do more.

"I won't tell you where it is," the divemaster said, when I asked about the wreck. I had read there was an interesting wreck somewhere on the north shore of the island.

"Why not?"

"You'll die if you go there," the divemaster said.

"Have you been there?" I asked.

"Sure."

"You didn't die."

"I knew what I was doing. The wreck's deep, the shallowest part is 140 feet. At that depth, no-decompression limits are four minutes."

"Is it really a paddle-wheeler?"

"Yes. Iron-hull. Nobody knows when it was wrecked, maybe around the turn of the century."

I tried to get him talking about it, hoping that he would drop enough clues so I could find my way.

"The ship rolled down the incline?" I had read that, too. Bonaire is surrounded on all sides by a steep drop-off, an incline that goes from the shore almost straight down two thousand feet in some places.

"Yeah. Apparently the ship originally crashed on the shore — at least there're some fragments from it near shore, in about thirty feet of water — and then sank. When the ship sank, it rolled down the incline. Now it's on its side, 140 feet down."

"Must be something to see."

"Oh yeah. It is. Hell of a big wreck."

"So there're fragments in thirty feet of water, near the shore?"

"Yeah."

"What kind of fragments?"

"Forget it," he said.

Finally I said, "Look, I know what I'm doing; I've been diving with you guys for over a week, so you know I'm okay. You don't have to sanction what I'm doing, but it's unfair of you not to tell me where this famous dive is."

"Yeah?" he said. "You think you're up to this dive?" He got truculent. "Okay, here's how you do it. Drive east five miles until you find a little dock. Then load up, jump in with all your gear on, and swim north from the dock about a hundred yards, until you pass a green house on the shore. When the house gets to be about two o'clock to you, start looking down in the water. You'll see a spar and cables in thirty feet of water, right below you. Swim down to the spar, and then go right over the edge and straight down the incline as fast as you can go. When you get to ninety feet, leave the incline and swim straight out into the open ocean. You think you're swimming straight, but actually you'll be dropping, and you'll hit the wreck about 140 feet down. It's huge. You can't miss it. Okay! Still want to go?"

The directions sounded difficult, but not impossible. "Yes," I said. "Sure."

"Okay. Just remember, if anything happens to you, I'll deny I told you where it is."

"Fine."

"And remember, at that depth you'll be narked, so you have to pay attention to your time; remember, your no-decompression limits only give you four minutes down there. The wreck is so huge there's no way you can see it in four minutes — don't even try. Make sure you observe all the stops on the way up. There isn't a decompression chamber within eight hours' air time of Bonaire, so you don't want to screw up. If you get the bends, there's a good chance you'll die. Got it?"

"Got it," I said.

"Another thing — if you do decide to go, remember to leave your camera. Your Nikonos is only certified to 160 feet, you'll warp the case."

"Okay," I said. "Thanks for your help."

"Take my advice," he said. "Don't go there."

I asked my sister what she thought about it.

"Why not?" she said. "Sounds interesting."

The next day we drove up to have a look at the site.

There was a sort of industrial pier that went a few yards out into the water. It looked broken-down, disused. There were several ratty houses along the shore, none green. Still farther north, there was some sort of refinery or industrial complex, with big ships tied up. The water by the dock was murky and unappealing.

I was all for giving it up. I asked my sister what she thought. She shrugged. "We're here."

"Okay," I said. "At least we can look for the mast."

We put on our gear, inflated our vests, and floated north. It was a fairly strenuous swim; I kept watching the houses on the shore. I had about decided that the divemaster had given us bad instructions when I suddenly saw, at two o'clock as I looked back, a green door. It was not visible from the dock.

I looked down in the water. Directly below us was a heavy mast and spar, some metal cables draped over the coral. It looked almost new.

"Think that's it?" I asked my sister.

She shrugged. "Looks like what he described."

I asked her what she thought we should do.

"We've come this far," she said.

"Okay, let's go," I said. We put in our mouthpieces, deflated our vests, and went down to the spar.

Up close, the spar was big — forty feet long, a foot in diameter. It had very little marine growth on it. We swam along its length, moving out from the shore. Then we ducked over the edge, and plunged down the incline.

That's always an exciting moment, to drop over an undersea ledge, but my heart was pounding now. The landscape was ugly, with heavy pollution from the nearby industrial site. The water was cloudy and visibility was poor; we were swimming in crud. There wasn't a lot of light, and it got quickly darker the farther down we went. And we had to go fast, because we had to conserve our air.

At ninety feet, I looked out at the open ocean and decided the instructions were wrong. Anyway, it was difficult to leave the scummy incline and head straight out into the cloudy murk. I decided to go deeper before heading out. At 120 feet, I headed outward. I couldn't see more than a few feet ahead of me, but once I had left the incline behind, it was difficult to know where to focus my eyes. There was nothing to look at except the milky strands of crud suspended in the ocean.

I was chiefly concerned that we would miss the wreck; at this depth, it was not going to be possible to hunt for it. We would have neither the time nor the air for that.

And then, suddenly, my entire field of vision was filled with flat rusted metal.

I was staring at a vast wall of steel.

The wreck.

The size of it astonished me: it was far bigger than I had imagined. We were at the keel line, running along the bottom of the hull. We were at 160 feet. I started my stopwatch, and swam up to the side of the hull, at 140 feet. The metal surface of the hull was covered with beautiful sponges and wire corals. They made a wonderful pattern, but there wasn't much color this deep; we moved through a black-and-white world. We went over the side of the hull, and onto the deck of the ship, which was almost vertical, with the masts pointing down the incline. The geography was pretty crazy, but you got used to it. I took some pictures, we had a quick look around, and then our four minutes were up. We returned slowly to the surface.

When a diver breathes compressed air, nitrogen enters his bloodstream. Two things then happen. The first is that the nitrogen acts like an anesthetic, and causes an intoxication — nitrogen narcosis, the famous "rapture of the deep" — which becomes more pronounced the deeper you go. That narcosis was dangerous; intoxicated divers had died because they took out their mouthpieces to give air to the fish.

The other thing is that the nitrogen that enters the blood must be allowed to come out of the blood slowly as you return to the surface. If the diver surfaces too quickly, the nitrogen will bubble out of his blood like soda from a bottle when the cap is removed. These bubbles cause painful cramps in the joints; hence the name "bends." They also cause paralysis and death. The time needed to decompress is a function of how long the diver has been down, and how deep.

According to published dive tables, my sister and I were not required to decompress at all, but the need for decompression depends on such variables as temperature, the health of the diver that day, or whether part of his wet suit binds him and prevents the nitrogen from coming out of solution. It's so highly variable we decided to do double decompression stops — two minutes at twenty feet, six minutes at ten feet — just to be safe. We made our decompression stops, and swam back to the dock.

We were both exhilarated; we had dived the wreck, and hadn't died! And the wreck was remarkably beautiful.

We decided to dive there again, and explore it further. Given a four minute limit, we felt that we would have to make a separate dive to see the stern, and another to see the bow.

A few days later, we swam around the stern of the ship, about 180 feet deep. The dive went smoothly; we had a good look at the steel paddle wheels. We were starting to feel quite comfortable around this wreck. Our pleasure was considerable. We felt like kids who had broken the rules and were getting away with it, consistently. We were very pleased with ourselves. And we were getting used to the narcosis, too, accustomed to the way we felt drunk the minute we reached the wreck.

A few days after that, we made a third dive, and explored the bow. The bow was 210 feet down, and as we came around it, I felt the narcosis strongly. I gripped my instruments and kept checking my gauges, to be sure my air was all right. I was aware I was having trouble concentrating. We started each dive with 2,200 pounds of air, and I liked to head back with a thousand pounds remaining, since it took us nearly eleven minutes to reach the surface.

The wreck was incredibly beautiful; this was going to be our last dive on it; I had 1,200 pounds of air remaining, and we still had a little time left, so I decided to show my sister a tiny, delicate sea fan on one of the masts, 180 feet down. We swam out and had a look, and then it was time to go back. I checked my watch; the four minutes were gone, we were moving toward five minutes. I checked my air. I had six hundred pounds left.

I felt panic: six hundred pounds was not enough air for me to make it back. What had happened! I must have misread the gauges.

I looked again: five hundred pounds.

Now I was in trouble. I couldn't go up fast; that would only increase my risk of the bends. I couldn't hold my breath, either; an embolism would kill me for sure. Nor could I breathe less often; the whole point of blowing off the nitrogen was that you had to breathe it out.

I looked up toward the surface I could not see, 180 feet above me. I suddenly felt the weight of all this water over me, and my precariousness. I broke into a cold sweat, even though I was underwater. I didn't know such a thing was possible.

There was no point in wasting time; the deeper you are, the faster your air is consumed. We started up quickly.

The rule is, you ascend at sixty feet a minute, which meant it would take us three minutes to get to the surface. After one minute, at 120 feet, I had three hundred pounds of air left. After two minutes, at sixty feet, I had 190 pounds left. But still before me were the decompression stops.

I had never known such a predicament. Of course I could easily reach the surface — but that wouldn't do me any good. I had been under too long, and the surface was dangerous, possibly deadly, to me now. I had to stay away from the surface for as long as possible. But I couldn't stay down seven more minutes with only 190 pounds of air.

We stopped for the first decompression at twenty feet. My sister, who never consumed much air, showed me her gauge. She had a thousand pounds left. I was down to 150 pounds. She signaled: did I want to share her air?

This is something you practice in diving class. I had practiced it many times. But now I was panicked; I didn't think I could manage the procedure of taking my air out of my mouth, and passing her mouthpiece back and forth. I was much too frightened for that.

So much for diving class.

I shook my head, no.

We went up to ten feet, and hung in the water just below the surface, holding on to arms of staghorn coral. I tried to tell myself that the decompression stops were doubled, and not really necessary anyway. True, we had exceeded the no-decompression limits, but not by much. Maybe a minute. Maybe less.

I couldn't convince myself that I was fine — all I could think was how damned stupid I had been, to cut it so close, and to put myself in this danger. I thought of all my friends who had been bent, and how it had happened. The stories were always the same. Got a little sloppy one day, got a little careless, got a little lazy. Didn't pay attention.

Exactly my story.

I stared at my air gauge, watching the needle slowly go down. In my mind, the gauge was magnified, as big as a saucer. I saw every scratch, every imperfection. I saw the tiny fluctuations, the tiny pulses in the needle with each breath I took. The gauge was down to fifty pounds. Then thirty pounds. I had never had my air supply go so low. I noticed a tiny screw in the gauge, a stop-screw to keep the needle from going below zero. I continued to breathe, wiggling my arms to make sure nothing was binding. I completed the six minutes of decompression, just barely. The needle hit the stop-screw.

I had sucked the tank dry.

On the surface my sister asked me if I was all right, and I said I was. But I felt very jittery. I figured I was all right, but I wouldn't know for sure for a few hours. I went back to my room, and took a nap. In the afternoon I woke with a crawly sensation on my skin.

Uh-oh.

That was one of the signs of the bends. I lay in the bed and waited.

The tingly, crawly sensation got worse. It was first on my arms and legs, then my chest as well. I felt the tingling creep up my neck, taking over ... moving toward my face....

I couldn't stand it any more; I jumped out of bed and went into the bathroom. I didn't have any medicines, but I would do something, at least take an aspirin. Something.

I stared at myself in the mirror.

My body was covered with an odd pink rash. It was some sort of contact dermatitis.

I went back to bed and collapsed in a sleep. I never got the bends.

As best I could tell, the dermatitis was caused by the hotel soap.

In more than ten years of diving, I had never gotten into trouble. But during my vacation in Bonaire, I experienced serious trouble twice in two weeks.

At the time I just saw these incidents as accidents, bad luck. More than a year passed before I began to reflect on the pattern behind my own behavior, the fact that I had repeatedly taken ever-more-daring risks until I finally got myself into trouble. I was startled when I finally recognized what I was really doing. The conclusion was inescapable: on some level, for some reason, I was trying to kill myself.

Why would I want to kill myself? I could find no explanation in the events of my life at that time. My work was going well. I had ended an unhappy love affair, but that was months in the past, and no longer on my mind. All in all, I felt cheerful and optimistic.

And yet the pattern was there. I had engaged in repetitive, daredevil behavior without ever being consciously aware of the underlying pattern.

But was I really unaware? Because when I thought back, I remembered some odd and uncharacteristic worries during my stay in Bonaire. For a man on vacation, I had been unusually fretful. I worried that the dive shop would fill my tanks with bad air. I worried that the restaurants would give me food poisoning. I worried that I would have a fatal car accident on the road. Yet the roads were nearly deserted; the restaurants were spotless; the dive shop was scrupulously managed. At the time, I had commented to myself that these fears were particularly unfounded. Now I had to recognize that they were not fears at all, but disguised wishes.

In any case, I hadn't put the pieces all together during the time I was in Bonaire, and the entire episode left me with a renewed respect for the power of the unconscious mind. What I had demonstrated, to myself at least, was that my ordinary assumption that in some casual and automatic way I know what I am doing, and why, is simply wrong.

The acceptance of unconscious motivation obliged me to assess my behavior by methods other than ordinary introspective awareness, because what I think I am doing at the time is almost certainly not what I am doing. In some way, I had to get a perspective on myself.

One time-honored way is to listen to the perceptions of an outsider — a friend, associate, or therapist. There are also ways to get perspective by shifting consciousness, changing to what is sometimes called "the witness state." Those meditative states didn't interest me in those days. But I stumbled on another useful technique for entirely different reasons.

Starting around 1974, there was a lot of attention paid to so-called circadian rhythms, the daily rhythms of the human body and its hormones. It had been found that most human beings didn't follow a precise twenty-four-hour cycle, but that the usual cycle was slightly longer or shorter, which meant that we were sometimes in synchronization with the day, and sometimes not.

In addition, the psychological effects of the female menstrual cycle were receiving new consideration. In England, there were rumors of legal acceptance of a condition called PMS, premenstrual syndrome. And it was commonly accepted that many women experienced some monthly fluctuation in mood and behavior.

I began to wonder if there might be a male menstrual cycle as well. Or something equivalent. After all, there are physical analogues between the sexes — the male scrotum to the female labia, the testicles to the ovaries, the penis to the clitoris, and so on. It seemed to me unlikely that women would develop a complex monthly cycle of hormones and that there would be no trace of such a cycle in men.

That was a job for an endocrinologist, but I wasn't interested in the hormones. I was interested in seeing if there were patterns in my own moods that I wasn't aware of. How to keep track of this?

I asked my friend Arnold Mandell, a neurobiologist, how to keep an objective record of subjective mood. Because the danger, of course, is that you will inadvertently create a pattern in your own data. Arnold said the best way was each day to put a mark at the edge of an unmarked diary page, using the top of the page as the best mood, and the bottom as the worst mood. So I began to do this.

Since I was keeping a daily diary mark, I started to record little thoughts for the day, too. I had always thought keeping a diary was a belabored, Franklin-esque thing to do. But since I was doing it for another purpose, it was all right.

After a few weeks, I looked back over my notes with astonishment. Every day, I was so critical! One nasty comment after another, about something or somebody.

I didn't regard myself as particularly critical, but evidently I was. I began to observe my state more carefully during each day. It did indeed seem that I was frequently judgmental and snappish, even when I didn't mean to be. So I decided to watch for that behavior and modify it. It was surprisingly difficult to do.

I never was able to detect a monthly cycle of my own mood changes, though from time to time I tried again. In later years, I wrote a computer program to record my responses on a blank screen. I still suspect there is such a cycle, perhaps bimonthly, running seven or eight weeks. But I have never demonstrated it.

However, I demonstrated a great value to keeping a diary, and have kept one even since. I reread Franklin's *Autobiography*, and noted that he kept a record of himself, as I did, for exactly the same reasons. This most practical and observant of men had decided that careful record-keeping was the only way to find out what he was really doing.

SHARKS

"Have you dived in the pass yet?" the proprietor of the hotel asked the first evening, when we told him that we liked the diving.

"No," we said, "not yet."

"Ah," he said. "You must dive the pass. It is the most exciting dive on Rangiroa."

"Why is that?"

"The swiftness of the current, and also there are many fish."

"Sharks?" someone asked.

"Yes," he said, smiling, "usually some sharks."

I was in Tahiti for Christmas with my family — my brother and sister, and assorted husbands, wives, girlfriends, friends. We were visiting several islands, and we had begun with the most remote.

Rangiroa was more than an hour from Papeete, one of the Tuamotu chain of atolls. The highest point on Rangiroa was about ten feet above sea level. From the air, it looked like a pale, sandy ring in the middle of the ocean.

The Tuamotus were old islands; their volcanic peaks had been eroded until they finally disappeared, and nothing remained but the coral reef that had originally surrounded the island, but now merely enclosed a lagoon.

On Rangiroa, the lagoon was enormous — some twenty miles in diameter. There were only two breaks in the enclosing reef, through which the tides came and went twice a day. So much water, moving through just two passes, meant that tidal currents were strong indeed. It also meant that lots of fish were attracted to the pass, because of the great nutrient flow in the water.

"It is very exciting," the proprietor said. "You must do it."

We went to Michel, the divemaster, and said we wanted to dive the pass. He consulted a tide table, and said we would do it at ten the following morning. (You can only dive the pass when the tide is running into the lagoon. Otherwise you risk being swept out to sea.)

The next morning, with everyone out on the dock ready to go, my sister asked Michel, "Are there really sharks in the pass?" We were all experienced divers; she was the only one who hadn't seen sharks.

"Yes," Michel said. "You will see sharks."

"A lot?"

He smiled. "Sometimes many."

"How many?"

He saw she was getting nervous and said, "Sometimes you see none at all. Are we ready to leave?"

We got in the boat and set out. The pass was a quarter-mile-wide gap in the atoll. Inside was the calm lagoon, outside the swells of the ocean, which crashed continually against the outer reef. We took the boat to the outside, and Michel got out a float and a spool of thread. Then he gave us a lecture.

"You must stay together," he said. "Everyone get your equipment on, and everyone go into the water as close together as possible. Go right down; do not stay at the surface. When you are down, try to stay within sight of each other. I will be in front of you, with this float"— he gestured to the float in his hands — "so the boat can follow us. The current is very strong. Partway along the pass there is a valley where we can get out of the current for a rest; keep an eye out for that. From there we will continue, and we will be swept into the lagoon; you will feel the current slow; you can look around the coral at your leisure until you run out of air, and come up to the boat. In the pass, do not go below seventy feet. Okay!"

We got our equipment on, waited until everyone was ready, feeling the swells, the rocking of the boat. Finally everybody was ready, and we went over the side in a mass of back-ended flippered splashes.

In diving there is always an initial moment of adjusting, clearing the mask, feeling the temperature of the water, seeing the clarity, looking around, going down. The water here was clear, and I saw the side of the pass, an irregular rocky wall to my left, that went down from the surface to about seventy or eighty feet, where it became bluish sandy bottom.

We went down. It wasn't until we got near the bottom that I realized how fast we were moving. The current was really ripping. It was tremendously exciting — if you didn't mind being out of control.

It didn't matter whether you were facing forward, backward, or sideways: the current moved you at the same swift pace. You couldn't stop yourself, you couldn't hold on to anything. If you grabbed a piece of coral, you'd either rip it off or rip your arm off. You were just swept along by the current, in the grip of a force orders of magnitude greater than you could possibly fight. There was nothing to do but relax and enjoy it.

After the first few minutes, after getting used to seeing the others perpendicular to the current, or looking up, clearing their masks, or facing backward, but always carried along at the same pace, it became fun. It was a kind of amusement park ride, and our powerlessness became pleasant.

Then I saw the sharks.

At first they were moving at the limit of my vision, the way I am used to seeing sharks, gray shadows where the water turns deep blue-gray, far from you. Then, as I came closer, the shadows gained definition, I could see details, and I could see more sharks. Lots more.

The current was carrying us into the middle of a school of gray sharks, so numerous that it felt as if we were entering a cloud of animals. There were easily a hundred sharks circling in a large cluster.

I thought, *Oh my God.*

I didn't want to go right through the middle. I preferred to go to one side, but the current was uncontrollable and indifferent to my preferences.

We were going right through the middle of them. In an effort to control my panic, I decided to take a picture. I stared down at the exposure settings on the Nikonos around my neck, feeling slightly idiotic: *Here you are in the middle of a hundred sharks and you are worrying about whether the f-stop is f8 or f11. Who cares!* But it was one of those situations; there was nothing I could do about it, so I might as well think about something else, and I took a picture. (It came out very blurred.)

By now the sharks were all around us, above and below and to all sides. We were being swept along by the current, like passengers riding a train, but they did not seem affected by it; they swam easily, flicking their powerful bodies with that peculiar lateral twisting that makes their movements so reminiscent of snakes.

The sharks turned away, came back, spiraled around us, but I noticed that they never came close. And already we were moving clear of the cluster, swept onward by the current, drifting away from the compact cloud of sharks. And then gone.

My breathing had not returned to normal when Michel jerked his thumb, gestured to me that we were to go down into the crevasse he had mentioned. He was twenty yards ahead of me. I saw him swept across the bottom, and then he ducked down headfirst and disappeared into a trench. I saw a cloud of his bubbles rise as I was swept toward the trench. I also swung over, had a quick glimpse of a shallow little canyon perhaps ten feet deep, and twenty feet long.

I was much relieved to be out of the current, but unexpectedly found myself in a black cloud of surgeonfish. These plate-sized fish, moving in dense, impenetrable schools, seemed agitated. I presumed it was because of the arrival of divers into the trench.

Then the black cloud cleared, and I realized it was because of the sharks in the trench. A dozen gray sharks swam in the far end of the cul-de-sac. They were each about nine feet long, dull-snouted, beady-eyed. They swam irritably, within a couple of feet of me and Michel. I was vaguely aware of Michel, ever calm, looking at me to see how I was taking this. I was only looking at the sharks.

I had never been so close to so many sharks at one time, and a dozen impressions assailed me. The gritty texture of their gray skin (sharkskin).

The occasional injuries, white scars, and imperfections. The clean gill lines. The unblinking eye, menacing and stupid, like the eye of a thug. The eye was almost the most terrifying thing about a shark, that and the slashing curve of the mouth. And I saw the way one shark, hemmed in by us, arched his back in what I had recently read was typical gray-shark threat behavior that often presaged an attack —

The other divers came swinging over the lip, blowing bubbles.

The sharks fled. The last of them threaded his way between us as if we were pylons on an obstacle course. Or perhaps he was just showing off.

Now we all looked at one another. Behind the masks, lots of wide eyes. Michel let us wait in the trench for a few minutes; he checked everyone's air; we stared at the large surgeonfish and tried to get our bearings.

Pretty soon Michel gestured for us to go back over the lip, into the current. Again we felt it catch us, and we were swept forward into the lagoon. The current slackened and the water became murkier, the coral more scattered, separated in small heads by an expanse of brown muddy bottom. The coral heads were inhabited by small fish; they were familiar; the best part of the dive was over. We finished our air, and headed for the boat.

One measure of a good dive is the amount of adrenaline still pumping through you afterward, and how much you talk when you get back to the surface.

"Oh my God, *did you see that?*"

"I *thought* I was *going to die!*"

"Wasn't that *amazing?*"

"I was *terrified,* I really was. I *didn't* like it." My sister, seriously. But the conversation swirled past her.

"What a dive!"

"It was fan*tas*tic."

"Unbelievable! I admit it, *I* was scared."

"Scared! I saw you shaking."

"That was just cold."

"Yeah, right."

"What an *incredible* dive!"

Through all this, Michel just sat patiently, smiling and nodding, letting us burn off the tension, signaling to the boatman to wait a few moments, until we calmed down, before he started the engine and we ran back to the hotel.

At the hotel, we showered and changed and drifted to the bar. We could talk of nothing but the dive, our reactions, what we saw, how close the sharks came, how they looked to us, how we felt, whether the pictures would come out, whether the pictures would do the experience justice.

Implicitly, our attitude was that we had survived a brush with death. Deadly dangerous, but we survived. It was so dangerous we never would have done it if we had known what it would be like. We were lucky to have survived. Sure, it was fun, but it was also terrifying.

Then at dinner my brother said casually, "Anybody want to do it again?"

A silence fell over the table, because he was contradicting our implicit assumptions. If it was really so dangerous, we shouldn't do it again.

"I'm going to," he said.

One by one, we admitted that we *might* do it again.

By the following morning, we were irritable when Michel told us that the tides were not right and we would have to wait until tomorrow to dive in the pass. Wait until tomorrow! We were quite put out.

When we dived a second time, we saw hardly any sharks. Now we were *really* put out. What a waste of time: no sharks. So we were obliged to dive the pass a third time, when we at last saw lots of sharks, and had a delightfully frightening time.

I think the only true expression of one's beliefs lies in action. Like the way my family decided to dive the pass again. Whatever we said about sharks at dinner — then or later — we knew they weren't dangerous.

In 1973 I was shooting a movie that called for an actor to be struck by a rattlesnake. We needed shots of a snake crawling in the desert, then striking, then sinking its fangs into the actor, and so on.

To do this film work, particular rattlesnakes were cast as if they were actors. We had four "crawlers" to perform the crawling scenes, and six "strikers" to do the strikes. These snakes were brought to the location in big plywood boxes.

Immediately one of my first concerns about snakes was answered. Whenever I was in the woods, if I heard a rustling sound, I always wondered:

Is that a rattlesnake? I was always concerned that I would get bitten by something I had wrongly decided was a cricket.

When the snake wrangler pulled the plywood boxes out of the station wagon, everybody for a hundred yards snapped his head around at the sound. There was no question about the sound. You *knew.* That dry, hissing rattle could not be mistaken for anything else.

Then the wrangler pulled out the snakes. They were each six feet long and as big around as a human forearm, and hissing mean. The crew was impressed.

We set up for the first shot. The camera was placed on a tripod with a telephoto lens, about thirty feet from the snake. A blanket was hung to protect the solitary operator from the dreaded snake; the rest of the crew was even farther away. We all watched as the first mean six-foot rattlesnake was released to crawl menacingly toward the lens.

The snake took one look at all of us, turned around, and wriggled away toward the hills. The wrangler had to go catch him.

We set up again. And again. And again.

Each time the poor rattlesnake just tried to get away. Eventually we had to form two rows of people, standing just outside camera range, and herd the frightened snake between us toward the lens.

Once we had the crawling footage, we set up for the shot where the snake coils and strikes. For this we used our "strikers." They were supposedly mean and angry. The wrangler explained that they had not been milked, which would have made them passive.

For the next hour, we tried to get the strikers to strike. We had a variety of sticks, balloons, rubber hands, and cowboy hats, with which we waved, prodded, and generally irritated the snakes.

Occasionally one struck. But you could smack them around quite a lot before they would do so. It was easy to see why. A rattlesnake's strike is rather pitiful. A snake can strike only a fraction of its body length; these six-foot snakes couldn't lunge more than a foot and a half, or less.

What that means is that, at a dinner party, if the person sitting next to you had a big rattler on his plate, the snake probably couldn't strike you. In fact, it probably would have trouble striking the person whose plate it was on.

And the snakes weren't aggressive. After a strike, these big, ferocious rattlers would get their fangs tangled up in the equivalent of a snake's lower lip. They'd look silly, and they seemed to know it. In any case, they would generally back away rather than strike.

Between takes, the snakes were placed under a little yellow-polka-dotted parasol. As the day progressed and I didn't get the shots I wanted, I complained about this coddling of the snakes. Let them feel the sun! The wrangler protested, but I was adamant — and I nearly cooked one in a matter of minutes. The snake became extremely sluggish and had to be exchanged for a fresh one. These fearsome reptiles are unable to control their body temperature, and on exposed ground they will fry like eggs. Rattlesnakes are, in truth, rather frail creatures.

The outcome of all this was that, although we started out with blankets and telephoto lenses and a nervous operator by himself, by the middle of the day all the crew were standing within a few feet of these giant rattle-snakes, turning their backs to them, flicking cigarette ash on them, talking of other things. Nobody worried about snakes any more. We had quickly and unconsciously adjusted to the reality of what we had seen.

The rattlesnakes couldn't hurt us.

In most situations, wild animals are encountered so rarely that it's more appropriate to feel privileged than afraid.

Of course that depends on the situation, and the animal. White-tip sharks are relatively benign; other species of shark may not be. There's no point pretending that African lions are tame and therefore you can get out of the Land Cruiser and go over and say hello. But, by the same token, you should realize that if you did get out, and if there were no cubs around, the chances are that the lions would just move off.

For some reason it seems difficult for people to get an appropriate perspective on animals. In American national parks a certain number of people are killed or injured each year because they approach wild animals, such as bison, to get a better picture, or to feed them. For many urban dwellers it may be that the concept of "wild animals" is itself extinct; the only animals they encounter are pets or animals in zoos, so why not send your four-year-old daughter over to pose next to the buffalo in Yellowstone? It'll make a cute picture.

This kind of blind trust is the reverse of the blind fear that so many people feel. Sometimes I think that man needs to feel a special position within nature, and this leads him to believe that he is either specially hated by other animals or specially cherished.

Instead of the truth, which is that he's just another animal on the plain. A smart one, but just another animal.

I found it difficult to give up my fear of animals. I had to, because my experience was forcing me to stop seeing animals as fearsome; I couldn't pretend I wasn't seeing what I was seeing. But it was still difficult to give it up.

For one thing, a certain thrill is gone. We don't like to give up our thrills. I have told people about the fact that certain sharks and moray eels and barracuda are not dangerous and watched their faces fall, then tighten, grow pinched. They disagree with me. They tell me I am reporting special cases. They remind me of the limits of my own experience. Sharks not dangerous? Morays not dangerous? Snakes not dangerous? Please.

They don't like to hear it. Telling them facts and statistics only makes them more irritable. Yet the chances are almost vanishingly small that any Western person will have a dangerous encounter with an animal. In America, every year, sixty thousand people die of auto accidents, a possibility no one fears. Some seven people die of snakebite every year, and everyone is terrified of snakes.

Then, too, fear of animals is a part of popular culture, a theme of books and movies and TV. If you drop it, it gives you the same feeling of loss as not watching the latest hit TV show, or not knowing about this year's intellectual pinup, or not following professional sports. You lose something in common with other people.

The other thing that happens is that, since fear of animals is a part of popular culture, it reminds you that one of the deep, unquestioned beliefs of popular culture is wrong. This is a little unsettling, because you are obliged to wonder what else is wrong, too.

Fear of animals is also a pleasantly childish feeling, and to give it up is to exchange some of the magical feelings of childhood for some of the more practical feelings of adulthood. At first it's not comfortable. Later you wonder why everyone doesn't do it.

In the end, how does anyone benefit from being afraid? Maybe it's bolstering of the values of civilization, by making nature the bogeyman. Here I am sitting in this traffic jam, breathing carbon monoxide and pollutants, staring at a hideous manmade landscape, but I really am better off because, if all this were gone, lions and bears would attack and eat me.

If wild animals — and wild nature — were less frightening, perhaps civilization would be less palatable. But the truth is that civilization does not protect us from wild animals. It attempts, however imperfectly, to protect us from ourselves.

TIM CAHILL

From *Jaguars Ripped My Flesh*, 1987

THE UNDERWATER ZOMBIE

A zombie walks around all day in a rotten mood. Walking death does that to a guy. It's worse than bursitis. Most people don't enjoy the company of zombies. How many times have you heard some bigot say, "I'm not going to any restaurant that serves zombies," or "Marge, let's not go to Cleveland. The place is full of zombies." Zombies resent this sort of prejudice, and that's why they go around ripping up people like confetti.

These days, a new, bitter chapter is being written in the zombie saga. The walking dead, it appears, have taken to the sea. Probably not one diver in ten thousand knows what to do when confronted by an underwater zombie. Of course, these dead denizens of the deep are pretty rare, but a little preparation never hurt anyone. Expect them to walk on the bottom. They come strolling out of the deep, and they like to hold snorkelers down, and rip the regulators out of divers' mouths. They are extremely strong, impervious to pain, and no fun at parties.

I learned about the dread underwater zombie from a woman who lives in Cozumel and sometimes works as a shark handler for underwater films made in those waters. *"The Zombie* is a very successful Mexican horror film," she said. "In *The Zombie II,* he hangs out underwater a lot, and he mostly goes for girls who dive topless."

"I've never seen any woman dive topless around here," I pointed out.

"That's an instance where *The Zombie II* may not be entirely true to life. Anyway, they had this starlet who was diving topless, and the zombie came walking up."

"He wasn't a real zombie?"

"No, he was an actor playing a zombie. His shoes weighed fifteen pounds apiece, and they kept him down. He walked real slow. Just like a zombie. He'd take a breath, you know, buddy breathe with a support diver, then walk four or five steps with the camera rolling. Then they'd cut, and he'd take a few more breaths.

"All the local captains were in the water, watching this scene with the topless girl. Some of them, I know for a fact, hadn't been in the water for years."

"They were pretty curious about underwater zombies, I bet."

"No doubt. As it turns out, the thing to do with a zombie underwater is to hold up a piece of coral. Apparently they hate that. It's like vampires and crosses, I guess. Anyway, the girl held up the coral and zombie put his hands in front of his face and went 'arrggh' underwater and trudged back to the support diver. The girl surfaced, and every one of the gallant Mexican captains managed to give her a hand before she could get into her robe.

"That was the end of that scene. Now they were ready to film the grand finale to the movie: a fight between the underwater zombie and a shark. We had this nurse shark, six or seven feet long. We had six handlers: three of us holding the shark on one side, just out of camera range, and three waiting on the other side. The guy playing the zombie was in the middle, in front of the camera.

"My team pushed the shark over to the other team. They'd grab it, turn it around and push it back. I mean, this was a docile shark, and it just sort of drifted by the zombie guy. But they could cut the film so that it'd look like, you know, a series of darting attacks, what with the zombie waving his arms and everything."

"Can an underwater zombie take a shark?" I asked.

"No way. First the shark took off one of the zombie's arms. It was a fake arm, of course, and we had a pretty hard time getting the shark to take it. Then all this fake blood came out of the place where the arm used to be, and the zombie thrashed around for a while until the shark came along and dragged the zombie out to sea. The guy playing the zombie didn't much care for that last scene.

"You have to imagine it. He's got all this makeup on his face, and no mask, so he can hardly see. He's got a wire-cage deal hanging off his shoulder, and his real arm strapped to his body inside heavy clothes. He's wearing thirty pounds' worth of boots. And he's got one breath. The shark was supposed to bite the wire cage, and drag him away. We were supposed to catch the shark and get the regulator into the zombie's mouth.

"Well, the zombie wanted to talk to the director before this scene. They talked for quite a bit, and if I was the zombie, I would have asked for a hell of a lot more money for that scene. They talked for quite some time."

I could see the situation in my mind's eye. Half a dozen boats bobbing in the mild swell, blue sky, the sun blazing away, and here's a guy with a horribly distorted, rubber-looking face and one arm, arguing with some guy who's got a gold medallion hanging from his neck.

"The zombie must have gotten some assurances — probably he got some money — but anyway, he got back into the water and lumbered over to his spot. The shark took him. We got the shark and saved the zombie."

The lady shark handler and I had another drink. I had learned three almost important things. One: underwater zombies can be repelled with coral. Two: those who play underwater zombies in movies are pretty gutsy. Three: *The Zombie II* is another in a long series of Mexican horror films that I am going to force myself to miss.

JAMES HAMILTON-PATERSON

From *The View From Mount Dog*, short stories, 1986

COMPRESSOR

It is a strange moment when, whistling in a bare room, you chance to hit the precise note at which it resonates. For the duration of that note the room becomes live, it rings in sympathy; the very plaster declares its heart. A quarter-tone's deviation up or down and it at once falls silent, you become again a whistler in an empty room. Similarly there can come a moment, maybe only when you are past being quite young, when something happens which makes your lived past vibrate with a kind of accuracy likely to make you say, "Yes, that's me; that is how I have always been," but which also might make you much prefer to fall inwardly silent with that shame which is not guilt but years and years of wishing you were not so. Such a moment came, such a note was struck and such a recurrent fault was set trembling into inward audibility when you visited Tagud.

Thanks to Badoy, whose home village it was, Tagud had become a legendary place, a minor Mecca which, once you had heard its name, you were fatally destined to visit. For at Anilao you shared an exile: he from his birthplace, you from yours. And what brought you together in that dull coastal strip with its half-hearted fishing and its weary copra-making? What else but the sea, which, although it scarcely runs in your blood, does run beneath your character like an undertow, tugging and churning and — whenever you are close to it — unsettling the contours of your restless bed.

You did not become conscious of Badoy until several weeks of enforced exile had passed in Anilao. The government project — a feasibility study of the prospects of a dendro-thermal installation to generate electricity for the province with quick-growing timber — had stalled in the way in which such things do in that part of the world. Insinuations had come that the funds set aside for your salary had already bought the cement needed to build a house for the newly wed daughter of the manager of the electricity co-operative. Pending reassurances you stopped work. Many days passed, and in Anilao the days pass slowly. The mornings are blue and tropical; the afternoons are black and tropical, and the rains tramp in from the sea; the sunsets are resplendent until promptly the nights descend like swags of stifling black cloth shot with vast discharges of electricity. Not long, therefore, before your feet took you into the sea as others' take them into the room where the television is. And there you met Badoy.

You are hardly alone in your admiration for people with an elegant physical skill. It is pointless to deny there is always an erotic component, however well disguised, in such admiration since it is impossible to watch any body so closely without seeing your own. One day you were down among the corals in a mask, at least knowing enough so that the corals you sometimes held on to were not those which sting and leave the hands blazed with brown weals. In point of fact you were watching — for as long as each lungful of air lasted — the local species of bird wrasse with its long snout whose exact purpose seems not precisely known. It is a reasonable assumption that it picks its food out of deep crevices which other fish cannot reach; but this, as they say in scientific circles, remains unconfirmed. You had some idea that, as a casual amateur with time on his hands, it would be nice to confirm it one way or the other. They are not easy fish to observe, because unlike other species of small coralline fish they seem to be continually on the move, weaving rapidly from place to place rather than forever circling the same patch (for many species of fish recognise a territorial imperative).

On that particular occasion you had just gone down a fathom or two with freshly held breath when from behind a rock and not more than ten feet away there swam a fat parrot-fish, green and blue and scrunching away at the coral with its powerful beak-teeth. There was a sudden rushing sound, a *pok!* and the fish began flailing wildly. A shadow passed overhead and the parrot-fish rose, still struggling, hauled upwards with a long steel rod spitting it. You rose with it to the sunlight and there was Badoy sparkling and grinning in tiny home-made wooden goggles set with little olives of glass. He passed the struggling fish down along the spear and on to the length of green nylon cord which trailed in the water behind him.

"Did I surprise? But I thought, that's a delicious fish and you are down there without a spear-gun so why waste it?" He refitted the spear into the gun he was holding, a simple wooden stock shaped like a child's toy rifle with powerful heavy-gauge elastic tied to its short bamboo barrel: essentially an underwater catapult. You bobbed your head back beneath the surface. In front of you hung Badoy's legs, one foot wearing a flipper cut from marine plywood and held on by a piece of inner tubing tacked across it, and trailing downwards in the blue water like a thin tail from his spear-gun was the length of nylon which ended with perhaps two kilos of threaded fish, joined now by the still-flapping parrot-fish.

"How long did that take you?"

"Two hours, maybe more. It's not a good day. The water's too clear. Very easy for us to see the fish but very easy for the fish to see you. Also it is daytime. And anyway this is Anilao. Not like Tagud."

"Tagud?"

"Where I come from. Maybe forty kilometers down the coast." And Badoy pointed with the tip of his spear (which you now noticed was barbed with a nail bent and hinged ingeniously through a hole) to where the green of the palms disappeared in a succession of hazy headlands into the distance. "They are real fishermen there. Not like here in Anilao." He looked sardonically at the beach a few hundred yards away on which a handful of boats was drawn up but which was bare of activity except for the rootings of domestic animals.

"Is that thing very difficult to use?"

"No, not difficult to use. Difficult to *catch* things, yes. Ha, perhaps that is why not many people in Anilao go spear-fishing. They just use nets sometimes or look for small octopus in the rocks at low tide. They are very lazy here. Just drinking."

Of course you wondered why he was here if he seemed so contemptuous of Anilao and its inhabitants, and of course you were drawn to the only other person in the sea for what seemed like miles in any direction. Above all, you were filled with a great urge to *imitate*, to try spear-fishing perhaps for food (as you would have explained it sensibly to yourself) but more to become accomplished in a new skill, to have some of that nonchalant marine confidence and enter a new world with new companions and rise just as dazzlingly to the surface, teeth glittering with pleasure. But more still — although you did not at the time recognize it — because it promised fear and fresh confrontations with an old bugbear; for your submerged self sniffs out fear like truffles which your daily self shrinks from as poison.

Badoy's elegance underwater was complemented by his ingenious craftsmanship on land. He set about making a second spear-gun using the few tools he could lay hand on, hacking the stock out of a plank of coconut wood with a large knife. The spear was a metre of quarter-inch steel rod in which he gouged holes and slots and raised a jagged tooth at one end to catch wire loops attached to the stretched rubber thongs. And all the time you wondered why he was so eager. Was it because he had nothing to do? Or maybe because he wanted a companion in the water, even a tyro? Or because he was a natural didact anxious to pass on what he knew? A week or two had passed, the spear-gun long since finished and in daily use before you discovered that the much older woman who brooded discreetly in his house was Badoy's wife, evidently formidable enough in some undisclosed manner to insist on their living in her home village rather than in his. Her uncle, recently dead, had left enough money by local standards so that Badoy was not compelled to take regular paid work. What would he do but mooch and fish and, according to gossip, occasionally disappear for annihilating binges in the distant provincial capital?

Frightening as it all was eventually to become, you do remember those early days when you were learning the craft as ones of extreme happiness. Taking the spear-gun and spending three hours in the sea, often twice as long, sometimes with Badoy but more often alone, shooting and missing, stalking and missing, learning the habits of the different species. Exhausting at first: the continual swimming down to fifteen, twenty-five, forty feet in pursuit or merely on reconnaissance, then clawing back up for air, the process repeated for hours until a strange disorientation set in and you became in some sense unsure at any given moment which medium you were in. Learning to manage the long nylon line attached to the rear end of the spear was a slow essay in exasperation. The currents tangled it; the corals snarled it; your legs attracted it and snared themselves in it. One day you said "Enough" and cut the line off. It happened to be the day you got your first shot at a really decent-sized fish. The spear struck home satisfyingly and the fish made off with it at speed to vanish, heading downwards into the ocean deep.

Badoy merely grinned and unhesitatingly set about making a new one; but it took hours and he cut himself in the process and you felt contrite and sullied by incompetence. Thereafter you learned to use the line, holding the stop-knot on the end lodged between two knuckles until there was enough catch to weight it out of the way in the water.

Soon you began to return trailing small coral fish like paper cutouts on the tail of a kite. Most were familiar aquarium fish: angels, butterflies, Moorish Idols and the like, enough of which fried or toasted constituted a meal. Some days there were none; later there were a few but larger. And all the while Badoy hung around his dark house among the trees, whittling this and filing that or maybe sitting on the step morosely watching the eddies of hens around the pump where the maid did the washing and the sun never pierced the canopies of leaves. Behind him his wife moved somberly about the house. Your arrival — probably anybody's — would awaken both from their melancholy so that she smiled and Badoy sparkled. But when you left you could feel whatever strange and mutual reproach settle once more and no doubt remain until you next saw them: something which emasculated or unfeminised them into the gloomiest creatures.

Away from his house, though, Badoy was full of energy. Even when alone in the water you felt his presence over your shoulder explaining a diver's worst enemies or making you work the corals harder or pointing out that he always did most of his own impromptu repairs right there in the sea since he had nobody on shore to whom he could bring unraveled rubber bindings or broken wire loops. You were being urged along; steadily, certainly, you were being groomed but you still did not know exactly for what.

"You must come to my village," Badoy said one day. "Perhaps at the end of this month or next month we will visit Tagud. You would like to come? The spear-fishing there is very good. But first we must practice night diving."

"Night diving?"

"It's much better. The fish are asleep there in the corals. You go down and shine your flashlight and there they are. They don't move much. You can put the end of your spear this close" — he held his hands six inches apart — "and *pum!* Big fish, too; you'll see."

"Isn't it very — well — dark?"

"We will bring my cousin in a boat and borrow a pressure-lamp. It's not necessary, the lamp, but it makes it more easy for you the first time. Also we will have our flashlights. You have flashlight?"

"Just a cheap Chinese thing. It isn't waterproof, though."

"Of course. But we will make it."

Waterproofing torches by means of adding another, slightly larger diameter, lens and encasing it all in a length of motorcycle inner tube was merely one more of Badoy's skills. Two nights later you lowered yourself from a tiny boat into the black waters above what in daytime was a familiar reef. And there it was, pressing in all around you amid the fitful sparks of plankton gingered into momentary luminescence by tiny eddies and swirls. There it was, swimming upwards at you from those pitch depths. Certainly it had been preparing itself in instalments: the first time you saw a moray eel fix you with its blank and white-rimmed eye and bare its ragged teeth at you and at nothing else; the first time a sea-snake came swimming rapidly up in clear water to investigate you alone; the first time you speared but did not kill a stonefish whose poisoned spines could inflict agonising wounds and you were left on a tossing ocean trying to manoeuvre the twisting creature down the spear and back along the nylon line away from your naked feet. Pangs they were when in warm tropic seas a quick cold current ran over your body. But this black gulf which concealed all such things and no doubt many worse made for a fear which did not easily pass.

Then Badoy's torch flashed on and the pressure-lamp outlined his down-ward-swimming, purposeful body in sad green light like something which could not be followed but which you pursued anyway for your own safety, imagining always, imagining the very worst that could happen: the accident which sent your spear thudding into his body, the bent-nail fluke making it impossible to pull out and which would mean finding transport in the middle of the night (hardly likely in Anilao where the only vehicle was a battered motorcycle) to take a mortally stricken Badoy eighteen miles over atrocious tracks to the only hospital where, if rumour were to be believed, they often performed major surgery by candlelight with the aid only of dozens of ampoules of local anaesthetic since somebody had sold the nitrous oxide on the black market.

But here is Badoy's torch and then Badoy himself, alive and well, flashing his light briefly on the end of your line to see what you have caught and, doing likewise, you discover his own line already weighty with the big reef fish you dream of getting by day. And again you follow him down, but this time the excitement takes over when you flash your own torch unbelievingly into a hole and there not more than two feet away is a good solid half-kilo goatfish, one of the mullet family, its chin barbels twitching in the sudden light. Then your spear pocks through him and you have air enough left in your lungs to sweep him back along spear and line with a now practised gesture, trap your torch between your legs as you reload so as to see where to catch the stretched elastic, regain a lost few feet of depth and move on to the next hole, which contains nothing but a dark red slate-pencil urchin you have never seen by day. And so back up to the surface where the night now seems darker than the sea beneath you except for the single star of the pressure-lamp some way off and the air is almost cold in comparison with the water. You have suddenly shifted elements.

And the excitement never failed even though the fear lurched up before submerging again beneath sheer physical pleasure and interest. You always came back exhausted after three, four, and once five hours of working the reefs in darkness but never without some fresh knowledge of the sea and its creatures. Often you returned with handsome fish, many times with cuts and stabs and hydroid burns, various parts of your body embedded with the snapped-off tips of brittle black sea-urchin spines. ("Piss on them, that's the best," said Badoy the first time. "It dissolves them." "How can I possibly? They're *here*." "Forget them. They dissolve anyway in a couple of days".)

The moments of fear were almost always those when you allowed your imagination to intrude. The sudden confrontations with marine hazards were moments of extreme busyness, of co-ordinating spear and breathing; the fright only came later. You have never been phobic about the dark or of being alone, but there were times when both lightless boat and Badoy himself disappeared for upwards of an hour and you were quite alone in a black sea beneath a black sky sometimes not even knowing where the shore was since you were too far out for the breakers to be audible above the local slop of water. Then you felt — not fear, exactly, but a desolation, an abandonment such as prefigured a way of dying which might well turn out to be your very own, unlocatably small between a black space and a black deep. How, then, to explain that this doleful panic could turn, now and again, into the greatest exhilaration and send you plunging recklessly downwards with your torch switched off so that the twinkling of plankton beyond your mask were the stars in a downward firmament traversed by the brilliant comet of your spear-tip? And then, perhaps, far away at an unguessable distance off to one side a brief flash like the dimmest green lightning as Badoy's torch-beam outlined a range of coral like a bank of cloud.

All this time you knew how happy you were by the way the question "how long can it last?" re-posed itself in a variety of ways. Privately your hope was that the manager of the electricity co-operative had indeed embezzled your salary, maybe in so doing prolonging your stay indefinitely (for it costs next to nothing to live simply in a place like Anilao). But what of Badoy? He frequently referred to his plans for working abroad — in Saudi Arabia, in America, in Australia — anywhere overseas, really, where visa requirements and work-permit laws could be got round, fluffed over, or just plain flouted. Did you think his chances of getting a honeymoon visa and then overstaying and going to ground as an illegal immigrant were better in Australia or the US? was one of his ways of starting these conversations.

"But what about your wife, Badoy?"

"She stays here, of course."

"But surely you'll miss each other badly?" (Was this inquisitiveness or mischief?) "You may be gone a year. More," you added, thinking of gaol, "or less," thinking of deportation.

"Three maybe, perhaps five. Of course. But the money.... What else can we do? Without work there is no future for me here in Anilao. She will be happy because of the money."

"But what kind of work could you do in a place like Saudi Arabia?"

"Oh, anything. Construction, laboring, working in the restaurants for other foreigners like me. It doesn't matter."

"But it may be hundreds of miles from the sea. No more spear-fishing."

"Alas."

And finally in a gloomy outburst: "I don't want to live as a fisherman all my life. I want something better than this place. I want to see the world."

How uneasy were such conversations, which would recur practically verbatim and with your own lines beginning "But...." Even more uneasy were they when his wife was present, the looks of hopelessness she shot at him, at you. The atmosphere became heavy with the sense that there was a great inaccuracy somewhere, that you did not understand who was being reproached for what, if anyone were: he for longingly talking of desertion, he for battening inertly off his wife in Anilao, or you for treason in possibly aiding his going. Your own selfishness appalled you, the degree to which you wished to hold another person's life static to make a background against which you could do your plentiful discovering, your peregrinations. Struck then by the image of Badoy's marvellous talents and skills which he ironically so undervalued lying unused or even deteriorating in the blazing heat of an Arabian construction site, you were made sadder still. It became but a small step from raising practical objections concerning the difficulty of legally working abroad to finding yourself entertaining fantasies masquerading as plans to build a large fishing-boat of which Badoy could be the skipper while you — what? — held ropes and jumped over the side, dog-like, to retrieve lost paddles? It was absurd. Yet it was never quite enough to laugh at such plans, because self-mockery, too, has that quality of ringing as if round an empty room. The real self has opportunely just left, closing the door, and can be heard outside in the passage obtusely heading back towards the television room and fantasy.

II

And so in due time your probation ended and you finally reached Tagud. It turned out to be smaller even than Anilao, its greater dependence on the sea reflected by the purposeful way in which the bleached huts had their piles driven into the sand above high-tide mark and hugged the shore in a straggling line, scorning to spread inland among the sheltering palms. Behind the village rose a mountain whose steep sides were partly forested. A mile offshore was a tiny uninhabited island whose general shape and jungled cap were an aping in miniature of the mountain opposite. In between ran seas whose purples indicated their depth.

"Bad currents," said Badoy succinctly. "We will take a lot of rice and water and live on the island. You will like it there; very good corals."

The first two days there were a continuation of your Anilao spearfishing but now in paradisal guise. The corals were richer, steeper, the water clearer, the fish grander. Who has never hung above such reefs in the early light of morning, steeped in the bliss of altitude, has missed a vital fraction of the world's beauty. On one side the floor of the sea rises to become the rocks of shore; on the other it falls now shallowly through hillocks of coral — twenty-foot crags like model mountain ranges — now steeply in gorges and vertical cliffs slashed by crevasses into ever-purpler depths of invisibility. On the way down this magnificent descent are ledges of blond sand and creamy patches of coral fragments making irregularly spaced steps on a grand stairway down. Such now is your physical familiarity with what you lovingly see that you appraise each of these steps. "I could reach that…. I might just get down to that one…. I'd never make the bluish one, not at my age. Fifteen, sixteen fathoms and then straight back up, all right; but twenty-five fathoms, never." Yet, even if you will now never be able to get down much beyond a hundred feet without mechanical assistance, how beautiful it is as the light becomes stronger and higher; how bushy and furred those cliffs with multiform varieties of plant, how mysterious the brilliant fish moving isolate or in small flocks at all levels in this fluid mass like birds, how splendid the little sharks eighty feet beneath your soles and flexing like rubber daggers moving haft-foremost. This astounding medium sustains it all; it bears you up, in it you float, entranced by a paradigm of inwardness and depth.

But the fear was not long in returning. You could feel it coming each time you crossed back from the island to Tagud and met Badoy's family and the other fishermen of the community. They radiated a competence so great it immediately annulled your own pride at having acquired a small skill of your own. It soon became clear that this arose not from a disparity in your respective expertness with a spear-gun, superior though theirs was, but from their use of something which was evidently what Badoy had been leading you towards right from the beginning.

The compressor.

"When I come back home here to Tagud," Badoy said one morning, "I must seriously catch fish so I can sell them and bring the money to my wife in Anilao. I must work."

So playtime was declared over; there were livings to be earned. Either you went on dabbling on your own or else you followed Badoy on to the last stage.

"It's exciting," he urged. "It's the best. Far better than what we've been doing."

You felt a pang at this easy devaluation of weeks of pleasure.

"Far better?"

"Not *far* better; that's still very good," Badoy said encouragingly. "But you can get bigger catches of bigger fish because you can go so deep and stay down there for hours maybe."

"How deep?"

"Maybe 250, 350 feet sometimes."

Good God. "Is it very difficult?"

"Not so. With practice a week or less. We will try later today when the boat comes back."

Later that day you examined the compressor. The system was simplicity itself. The boat's propeller shaft could be disengaged and a fan-belt slipped over a pulley so that the engine now drove a small air-compressor from which led two thin polythene hoses each hundreds of feet long.

"That's all it is," said Badoy. "You control the air-flow by biting with your teeth, and when your mouth aches you squeeze a loop of the tube between your fingers like this. It needs a bit of practice to learn how to regulate it automatically."

"No valves or anything?"

"No."

"What about depth-gauges?"

"Do you have one?"

"Of course not."

"Neither do we. We learn to judge how deep we are from the pressure on the body and the colour of the water. We must also judge how long we have been down. Do you have a diver's watch? No? Did you know if you come up quickly from deep it hurts your joints like rheumatism? There is a man here in Tagud who was very drunk all night and he went down the next morning without sleep and still drunk and I think he comes up too quickly maybe. But he is now, what, paralysed from here... Did you know about this danger?"

Did you know? Good God, had you not heard about the bends when you were at school and since read the elaborate safety-codes for scuba diving? The carefully worked-out pauses for decompression at each depth, to be minutely timed on obligatory chunky watches? The depth-gauges and knives and nose-clips and wet-suits and cylinders and weighted belts and flippers and reduction valves and compasses and underwater flares and so on and so on: the expensive accoutrements of those who quite reasonably wished to take their pleasures safely.

"We will try now," said Badoy.

"Oh.... What happens if the engine fails? It's always running out of fuel."

"There's a reserve air-tank here. He pointed to a pitted and rust-corroded cylinder lashed to the side of the boat with nylon line.

"How long will that last?"

"Three minutes maybe?"

"So if you're at two hundred feet you've got *three minutes* to surface?"

"We won't go that deep. This is your first time. Easy practice only."

"What happens if that fan-belt breaks? It looks pretty frayed to me."

"Same thing. You will know. For a moment the air stops completely and then it comes again but less, so you will know it is reserve. Now, put the tube around your body twice and loop it over two times only to hold it and bite the end in your teeth."

With the engine running the compressor sent a huge draught of stink into your mouth, less air than the flavour under pressure of diesel oil and polythene tubing whose walls were infiltrated with colonies of yeasts. You retched.

"Don't worry. Up here the pressure is very great. Later when you have practice you will go down to sixty, seventy feet and the air comes just right. But when you go down to three hundred you must suck it in, the pressure is so few. Very tired, your lungs. Now, ready?"

And because you *weren't* ready you floundered about in the topmost yard of water like a beginner learning to swim. It was hard to remember to do so much at once: clench your teeth to breathe normally, equalise the pressure in your ears, ignore the stink and head down beneath the throbbing wooden hull of the boat. A moment's inattention and the air would burst into your stomach, your mouth open and sea flood into nose and mask; you would flail to the surface, choking and pouring and belching great gouts of diesel stench while the loose end of the tube whipped about in the water hissing and bubbling. And Badoy's colleagues, teenagers mostly, would peer down laughing.

That first session barely lasted ten minutes, but in that time you did get down about thirty feet and lay there for longer then you ever had when you relied on lungs alone, Badoy cavorting round you with his plastic umbilicus in his mouth, trailing bubbles and teasing little fish. Later that night, in the small hours, you went off with them in the boat for spear-fishing; but it wasn't the same for now you were left behind with your lungfuls of air while Badoy and colleague took the compressor's hoses between their teeth and you watched their flashlights going straight down and down and down, becoming green dots of luminescence before winking out behind coral outcrops as the polythene uncoiled on the deck above them. You could not yet join them at such depths, so disconsolately swam towards the black bulk of island to bring you to shallower inshore waters. And so that night you fished alone, spearing a bigger and better catch than ever before but surfacing companionlessly to listen for the faint diesel chug of the compressor out in the dark. Sometimes it moved when the boys on board paddled to keep pace with the long-vanished divers; at other times it disappeared altogether as the noise of the invisible surf nearby drowned out its sound.

Hours later and shivering with exhaustion you found the boat again, bringing with you about four kilos of fish on your line. You should have been overjoyed but you were tetchy, jilted, cold, and getting colder still as you sat on deck in the night air while the compressor chugged on and still Badoy didn't return. Then at last the green patches of light growing under the sea and flashing intermittently like electrical storms in tropical clouds seen from high-flying aircraft: the gladiators returning. And here they were, whooping on the surface in the dark, chattering excitedly, swapping stories while their abandoned air-hoses spurted and threshed in the water, then coming in over the side and needing help to pull in their nylon catch-lines with twenty kilos of fish threaded on each: rays, small sharks, groupers, cuttlefish, vast parrot-fish, surgeon fish, a middling octopus, the meat from a giant clam.

So it came to colour your days on the island. Enclosing the mere practice of swimming down and staying at sixty feet without a spear-gun but with your lungs overinflated with oily air, the jaws of that vice: *not to be left out* on the one hand and on the other *the compressor.* And always from somewhere afar off in the mind that ringing of an empty room, that fear which had reverberated for as long as you could bear to remember, reminding you that you were full of the wrong stuff. Sleep, snatched mostly during the days' intense heat, now became obsessionally haunted, shot through with descriptions and apprehensions:

It is just completely terrifying.

Two hundred and fifty feet overhead is brilliant sunshine. The sea is flat calm. Stray half-beaks and flying fish will be breaking the surface almost from sheer light-heartedness, flirting with that nebulous barricade between the two abysses.

But down here the pressure is like dark blue cement, transparent, unset, squeezing in from all sides against mask, hands, ears, genitals. You are in its grasp.

"Of the two kinds of eel the white one — you know, with the black spots? — that's the worst. The black one is bad but it does not attack so often. You must look for the separate lump of coral on the bottom, small like this room and maybe no more than two or three metres high, like an island? They like those for their nests. Sometimes there is the head of the eel sticking out and watching you. If he is about as thick as your leg *here*, he will be about two metres long and very strong. If his head is up like this — like a snake going to bite? — *ay*, he is dangerous. He will keep maybe his last half inside his house; with the rest he will attack. His teeth, they will take everything from your arm-bone, so you must remain to four feet of him and put your spear in the mouth *here*. That is his weakest, but you must be ready for a big fight. He is almost impossible to kill with one shot because the brain is very small and behind the eyes. Sometimes the tip of your spear goes up through the roof of his mouth and destroys the brain — *ay*, very lucky — but his body is stupid and doesn't know he is dead already. If you hit him in the head, he will always pull back into his house and he will take your spear with him. He's very hard to pull out then, and your spear will bend like plastic. But sometimes when we are swimming around we look for a coral like that and we look for a tail sticking out. When we see it we are happy because he is so easy then and we shoot to the tail, *pum!* because when the eel feels it he only wants to get away. He will not attack like that even if he is thick like my stomach *here*. He thinks only of the spear in the tail and leave his house to swim away from the pain. Always he swim away from the pain."

Away from the pain is straight up, away from this pressing liquid cell: up, up like a frail pink rocket trailing silver platters of diesel air which come wobbling up for half a minute after you first lie on the surface, feeling the sun on your face again, even now hardly believing in the world you have just escaped. But impossible: that exit route is blocked off by knowledge like a concrete lid over your head, knowledge of what happens to your body if you surface like that from an hour at forty fathoms. The images haunt: the agonising fizzing in the joints, perhaps the haemorrhaging in the skull, the crippling, the vegetable future. It is yet another vice *(down unbearable, up impossible)* each of whose jaws is dreadful. There is no room for panic down here. Better to discharge it all while you are asleep so it later lets you concentrate on the only thing that counts: that thin polythene tube wrapped twice around your body, the sighing end clamped between your aching jaws. The compressor.

Down there on the right where the sea-bed shelves steeply towards the violet drop which is the brink of a five hundred-fathom deep, towards the edge of that monstrous chasm the stink comes sluggishly through the tube. You're now at over three hundred feet, and the compressor can't cope. You drag the air into your lungs as through a miraculous chink in those dark blue walls. Afterwards, when you are on your way back up the shelf keeping a wary eye open for eels hidden in the myriad holes you peer into and slowly decompressing, the air-flow gradually increases. Until the first glimpse far above and some way off: that black lozenge with the twinkling outline which is the keel of the boat, home of the compressor, fount of all nourishment the taking of which makes your jaws ache around its stenching nipple. Right now, though, that mechanical breast is far away, and only from the thinly flowing taste do you know that it is still alive.

And how infinitely further that sunlit western world of safety and back-up systems and fail-safe. The scuba rules, the diving codes, the union regulations. Here they are not worth the drift of plankton and diatoms past the face-plate. Here there is nothing but a polythene tube in the mouth and a home-made catapult, nothing but the actuality of the moment pressing in with stray threads of scald from invisible stinging tendrils which drift through all tropical oceans as if from some single titanic and long-dismantled jellyfish, some toxic Kraken whose fibres still circulate the globe. Much later, if you are lucky (and because day has now magically elided into night) the banter round the driftwood fire, roasting your catch under a starry sky which still seems to draw you upwards hours after you have left the water:

"*Ay*, Badoy, I thought you couldn't manage him so I shot him in the gills here but it only made him madder." Blurts of laughter.

"And that hammerhead? I guess he was just shy. Big, though, wasn't he?"

The sharks. Some are not at all shy. You are there at 150 feet investigating a cavern beneath an overhanging mountain of coral, trying to spot something edible with all the time the knowledge that you yourself may be the most obviously edible thing for fathoms. There is something in there, too: a big grouper perhaps, like that monster a week or two ago. It was just such a cave, and you were similarly trying to screw up enough courage to go inside, when a bulk of shadow detached itself and suddenly a gigantic flat eye moved like a dinner plate slowly across the cave mouth followed by a wall of dark red scales with one or two parasites attached. If a pin could snare a wild boar, then maybe a metre of elastic-driven rod filched from the core of an electric power cable might have some effect on a creature that huge, but you were not about to try to see.

And amid such reflections the sense of shadow behind and, turning, you see the shark watching from about twenty feet away. Everything looks bigger underwater and this is a twelve-foot Tiger the size of a submarine. And instantly the word "requiem" flashes in the brain since the Tiger is one of the requiem family which in turn is one of the worst. The very word makes the liquid blue cement on all sides congeal and press coldly in, squeezing the upper arms involuntarily to your chest, squeezing the mind.

"They don't attack so often, sharks. Usually there is plenty of food for them down there, so they are not always hungry. But he is curious. He wants to know if you are worth attacking. He is attracted to light things, so we wear dark shirts and jogging pants when we dive, but sometimes he sees the soles of the feet in the distance. When he stays like that about twenty feet away, just watching, you must keep like him flat in the water, not upright. Because his mouth is underneath he needs to come at an angle when he attacks, so you must make it difficult for him by lying in the water with your head towards him. Always face him. Always watch his eyes: they look dead but they see everything. You keep your spear-gun pointed at him and you never take your eyes off him. If he moves round, you follow him round too, with the tip of your spear. He doesn't know what it is. He sees your goggles or mask and he sees your spear and he can't make his mind up if they will be dangerous to him if he attacks. Usually sharks just go away when they see you are so ready for them. But if he comes closer still maybe you will soon have to fire your spear. The only place is *here*, in the gills, because the rest of him is too hard and your spear will bounce off. If you hit him in the gills, he will go away; he doesn't like that. Also the end of his nose is sensitive, and he doesn't like to be hit there. If you get him in the gills slightly from behind, it'll go in. You'll lose your spear and your catch, but it is worth it. If you *miss* the gills? *Ay*, ha, I think you must not make a mistake. You are very alone down there."

Maybe you fire and maybe the shark does go away, but there you still are, 150 feet down without a spear and holding a useless length of wood like a child's toy with two impotently dangling strips of rubber, hyperventilating with a plastic hose stuck in your mouth and more or less at the mercy of whatever else turns up. You may have remembered to give three sharp tugs on the hose, and if by some extraordinary fluke someone in the boat was actually holding it at that moment and there was a spare air-line it might just have brought a colleague plunging down to your assistance. But what would he find? A pale figure in a wet cement cell holding a piece of wood. Then the slow, humiliating escorted swim back up the sloping coral shelf, pausing to decompress, waiting down there while your brain is still full of shark and everything inside is screaming at you to go, go, get *up*, get out of it, until at long last your head breaks the surface into the blinding lights and a ring of anxious faces. "What was it? What was the problem? You have lost your spear."

"Shark. A massive goddamned shark." Your voice is squeaky with air under pressure, your jaw aches so much from clenching the tube that you can't enunciate properly and your teeth no longer meet each other in the way they did, feeling lumpy and displaced to one side as after dentistry.

"Shark? Oh, what kind?"

And you know whatever species you say these boy gladiators in torn cotton will be immensely good-natured and agree it was high time to stop anyway because the compressor's getting low in fuel and we should maybe land and cook some fish. And always you wondered what it would have taken to make them just a little bit worried. Until that day you found out.

III

Well, night it was, to be accurate; for the choking practice-sessions and the worst of the haunted dreams were past and you had graduated to night-diving with the compressor. Much of the fear now could be held down by exhilaration: self-pleasure at doing things automatically so your body could take care of itself leaving your mind freer to speculate, enjoy, and attend to getting a good night's catch. For the fish down there were indeed bigger, though in that speckled darkness as docile as the little painted ones of the shallows when night came.

In point of fact the darker it was the better for spear-fishing, so sometimes you fished in the early part of the evening before the moon rose, coming back to the island at about midnight, the tarpaulin shelter stretched over sticks glinting in the starlight as one person set about making a fire and another began sorting and threading the catch for sale early next morning. At other times, though, the moon would rise as the sun set and you would all have to wait until it disappeared from the sky. On such occasions everybody slept when night fell at seven-thirty; everybody but you, of course, who would achieve an unreal doze at midnight, needing to be shaken awake at one-forty. And at that moment, as reality began to edge in to take the place of whatever dream, the very last thing you wanted was to get up, scramble through black surf into a boat, go out across a black sea beneath a black sky and go down and down with a torch and a spear-gun and a polythene tube in your mouth, the compressor overhead thudding the stink into you so that even next day you could taste it while belching after lunch.

Yet once out there in the dark off Badoy's village, balancing in the narrow boat while by flashes of torchlight masks and goggles are checked, spear-guns sorted, the coils of air-line kicked into more or less neat piles and the engine stopped so the boatman can disconnect the propeller shaft and slip the frayed fan-belt over the compressor's pulley, something changes. Amid those full black waters which so directly oppose the low ebb of your vitality and will the image crosses your mind of what people are doing at that moment in your own birthplace. It is nearly lunchtime there, and those dull shopping malls will be crowded, utterly safe with familiar names and products, utterly reassuring if you could ever suspend spleen and ennui. And the thought comes: what you are really doing is living *against* all that. The world is full of nest-builders and settlers-down but you will never be one of them. For you, only these present wrenches of pain and pure fear and glimpses of magnificent wildness will one day remind you that any of it was real; that it was not all fantasy and television, it was not all insulation; that the reefs beneath are there always. Do you crave a violent end? the mind runs on insistently in the darkness. But the compressor has started and Badoy is already in the water, his line hissing. Maybe; but not now, oh, not now this night....

You should remember every detail of that dive, but you don't. There were just the two of you working an unfamiliar stretch around the seaward side of the island. As you submerged there was a flash of distant lightning which lit the mountain on the mainland, partially obscured by the black bulk of the island in the foreground, then you headed down with Badoy, two abreast, into the dark. The sea-bed here revealed by your glancing torches was different: the same coral varieties but more mountainous and fissured in their formation. There were fewer slopes and inclines, more cliff-faces and crevasses. Badoy worked one side of a ridge, you the other. Often you caught sight of his torchlight although not the beam itself, fitful green lightnings on the far side of crags. The catch increased steadily. It was more difficult terrain but more rewarding. The steep gorges were silvery with hydroids, stinging ferns which waved in the currents; to get into them you had to swim on edge, and the back of the elbow holding the spear-gun was repeatedly wealed. Making your way about became more and more difficult as the drag on your catch-line increased. Adding a three-kilo grouper made it still harder.

And always the nerves alert, the quick flicker of glance for the least movement, for the white-rimmed eye moving in the eel's lair as a dot among all those undulating forests. The click of unseen crabs, the grunt of a creature disturbed, the directionless drumming on some thoracic air-sac. No longer can you hear the compressor's distant thump, and it seems like half an hour since you last saw Badoy's light or heard the far metallic ring of his spear-point on rock. You are investigating a black diagonal cleft little more than a foot wide. A yard inside and it turns to the right. There is nothing in this pocket other than small white pebbles on its floor, and it is precisely those white pebbles which should be telling you about the thick olive snake embedded among them which you mistake for — what? — the tail of a ray, perhaps. So automatic has become the sighting, the firing, the hauling-in of fresh trophies that you fire without thinking; then the thought, too late, catches up.

The spear is snatched from you so fast that its cocking lug and the first foot of nylon line take skin off your fingers. It lodges at the back of the cleft, quivering as whatever it is tries to drag it round the corner. Then amid the clouds of silt you glimpse what it has struck into and another, darker cloud comes billowing around the corner to engulf you. Octopus. The one creature of which Badoy has spoken with real fear.

"I don't like the feeling on your hand," he once said after winkling a tiny octopus from its hole with a steel prod at low tide. "They stick to you." He lifted up his hand with its dark parasite wrapped around it like a clot of leeches. "This one is too small; but even a little bit bigger — say, the head the size of half my fist? — and they will bite pieces out of you. That mouth, that beak you remove when you eat them, it's very strong and sharp. The big ones will always try to pull you towards the beak to tear you."

But even so you are already trying to get hold of the end of the spear, reaching right-handedly into the cleft to rescue that precious weapon, still perhaps not sure of the power and size of the creature you have engaged with and which still lies hidden around the corner. Only when you feel a second tentacle close over your forearm, wrapping it together with the spear and tugging you irresistibly forward, do you realise how truly awful is the mistake you have made and how likely it is to prove fatal. For there is a degree of strength which you know cannot be resisted for long. You know from so many encounters over the months with even insignificant-looking sea-creatures how powerful the small muscle of a clam is, how resistant to dying a little eel. And now you feel your arm being compressed, the skin being dragged forward towards the hand as if it were a long glove being pulled off and simultaneously your right shoulder catching half into the mouth of the cleft, your head desperately averted over it and wedging at an angle against the rock outside so that slowly the mask is being crushed sideways across your face and immediately the water spurts in to fill the face-plate and your nose.

Now, with your head bent back over right shoulder, left cheek ground flat against the coral, everything is dark. By some miracle your left hand still holds the torch, but it is pointing uselessly into the sepia-filled cave. The pulling stops for a moment but does not ease while both creatures

take stock of the damage and plan tactics for the immediate future. But
you have no tactics and very little future. A grain of reason makes you
bring your left hand as far away from the hole as possible and, reaching
back behind you, you fire a regular three dots of light in random directions.
Your heart-rate is way up and your respiration crazy, panting the rank air
out into your skewed mask in the hope that the pressure will empty it of
water again but it can only half-empty it: the seal between face and rubber
is too weak on one side to stop the in-flood of that liquid black cement.

An age passes; you are locked and entombed, your neck cannot be far
from breaking. Then something touches your hand holding the torch. You
flail it wildly, trying to shake loose this new tentacle. Badoy's light breaks
across your head and he comes round to peer in at your face-plate and, by
God, he's *grinning* as if to say: "*Ay,* now you're learning the trade." And
somewhere inside his lair the octopus senses reinforcements have arrived
and his pull increases again. Then suddenly your air stops. The tube is
pinched between you and the mouth of the hole, perhaps at the rim of
your mask, perhaps lower down your body. You wave desperately with
the torch, making confused gestures towards your head like someone
with an arm amputated at the wrist. Badoy, incredible Badoy, notices
straight away amid all else that your bubbles have stopped. He reaches
over and pulls your mask right off and the cement crashes into your eyes,
nose, mouth, then you feel a stabbing at your lips: another tube gushing
diesel stink. You grip it in your teeth and suck and choke and suck and
open your eyes. There in front of you is Badoy's face, slightly blurred now
that your mask has gone. He hangs there in his little olive-lensed goggles,
grinning and grinning until he reaches over and gently pulls the air-hose
from your mouth and puts it back in his own for a few breaths. Then he
makes a gesture you cannot understand because he, too, is holding his
torch in the hand that makes it and it stabs wildly. He thrusts the air-line
back in your mouth and disappears behind you. His light vanishes.

Now begins the octopus's attempt to pull its prey bodily into its lair. Its
grip no longer feels localised at your arm. Vaguely you know it must have
put out another tentacle to grip your body, but it surely cannot pull you in
like that: the cleft is too narrow to accommodate you and the tentacle; as
long as it goes on trying that way you are going to remain stuffed into the

entrance but not drawn in past it. And then that pressure, too, increases unimaginably and you realise that your reasoning did not include the inevitable collapse of your own ribcage. There must be some movement into the hole because your head twists round even further, making crackling sounds. It is now so far round it catches a glimpse of Badoy's torch pointing aimlessly upwards; you wonder why it should be until you sense it is your own, held behind your back in your left hand, now no longer a part of you. So where *is* Badoy, God damn him? Fiddling about somewhere below in the darkness....

Until his light, like a lark descending, strikes from above and there he is again. This time he tears the air-line from your mouth and pants great cavities into the water about you. His spear-gun is gone; in his hand he holds a knife. With this he retreats behind you after first pushing his air-hose back into your mouth. There are sensations of rending from your midriff; light flashes intermittently. Suddenly the appalling grip around your waist eases, your lower half is free to move a little away from the mouth of the hole and swivel to the right to relieve minutely your cracking neck. You are once again held only by the arm, which feels double its length. Badoy appears briefly, sucks air and disappears. This time there are no flashes of light: he is beneath you, wedging himself and his torch into the hole. There are confused feelings of tearing and pain from your arm, and without warning the rock floats away from the side of your head like feathers and a gentle cushion of water takes its place. Simultaneously there is a great roaring in one ear: Badoy is offering you your now-released air-line and takes back his own. For a moment you both drift, each sucking on your tube as somewhere in the night above the compressor chugs and chugs, blessed engine.

Badoy shines his light back towards the cleft, now ten feet away. A great cloud of ink floats about its mouth and a host of small nocturnal shrimp-like krill, attracted by the light, are prickling at hands and faces like flies on a summer's day. Then he propels you away and upwards in a slow journey that seems to take forever while pain begins gathering in your right hand and arm, the left side of your head, your neck and nearly everywhere else. The pressure of the air-jet increases as you rise, and you still go on breathing it even after your head breaks the surface, not quite sure that you have left one medium for another. Then you spit it out and it flails and gushes.

"Oy, Badoy! Badoy!" you shout in the darkness into the suddenly cold air. An answering cry comes from close at hand and now you can hear his own hose, discarded and bubbling. "Where the hell did you get the knife?"

"*Ayy!*" He gives a long exultant whoop. The compressor is close by; it chugs in the invisible boat, rising and falling. There are voices. "What did you say?"

"The knife. Where did you get it?"

"I went up for it."

"Jesus!" The implications. "But I had your air-hose."

"It wasn't so far. We were only down about seventy feet."

"But we'd been there a long time. Decompression..."

"No problem. I went up straight and down straight again. You can do that if you're quick."

"Why didn't we take bloody knives *with* us?" you heard your petulant rhetorical question go out into the night air. "So *stupid...*"

But what was this world to which you had returned? You still felt yourself travelling up and up into the sky as usual, but this time it was different. Something had changed; for the aftermath of fear is not relief and still less is it reassurance. The exact note had been struck, your whole life was ringing with that undeniable resonance, that messy echo of child-hood fear of fear, and hero-worship, and fear of cowardice, and longing for something or other to be over.

You got yourself into the boat, the compressor fell silent, the screw churned. There was not much talk and no banter even from those who had spent the night safely aboard. You slumped, the deck slippery with your blood and the mucus which had come from the octopus and coated everything. In the dark you discovered your arm was burst and a thick muscle now lay exposed; you turned your torch on it in loathing but merely found a foot or so of severed tentacle still stuck there.

"Ah," said Badoy, "that was good, bringing a bit of the octopus. Better than none at all. We'll cook it by and by."

You smiled in the dark at this. "What was your own catch like before all that?"

"OK. Not bad, not good. Not a very good night for fish. About like you."

"Damn. Of course, my own catch is still down there."

"No, it's here. I cut off the nylon before we came up." He flashed his light on to a jumble of fish bodies in the bilges. He had also brought up your mask.

"You're quite unbelievable."

You returned to the island where you examined your wounds. Nothing desperate. The round sucker-weals stood out in scarlet over right arm and waist, each pinpricked with livid blood-spots. The side of your face and head was gouged and scratched but it was all superficial. There was a single deep cut on the inside of your forearm where Badoy's knife had sliced through the tentacle. "Sorry," said Badoy.

Dawn was coming. The air turned grey. You all packed up and crossed back to Tagud. The story was told and retold, but only because there was nothing else to do with it. There is no way outside the gruff fiction of derring-do to thank someone for saving your life; it is far too complex a matter to merit simple thanks. Must you not have *wanted* to die, just a little bit? Must there not have been that desire tucked down in your unconscious to entomb your conscious as well in those dark gulfs, even as your betrayed body tried to escape them? How else could you have ignored so many danger signals, have been so cavalier? And Badoy, too, had he ever had any real option? What were the psychic rewards for being a hero? Or for failing? How, knowing all this and suspecting still more, could you possibly say anything as banally inappropriate as "thank you"?

For the rest of that day and, it seemed, for weeks afterwards the stench of the compressor came back up from inside.

On the way back to Anilao, Badoy said once again, and not at all apropos of the incident (which you really believed he had half-forgotten): "I don't want to be a fisherman all my life. Are there jobs in television in your country? I would like that, I think."

For a short time you resumed your leisurely life in Anilao, although it took time to muster the courage to go spear-fishing again, particularly at night. As if to urge you through this bad patch Badoy made you an even better spear-gun to replace the other, with a redesigned trigger of whose mechanism he was extremely proud. Then one night he said: "To be a fisherman you need to be brave." It was the first time he had ever alluded to questions of fear and courage. You were surprised.

"Of course," he went on, "of course you are scared down there. Plenty of people there at Tagud will not go down at night like you, like us. They do not want to use the compressor. We're all scared; it's a bit dangerous sometimes."

You knew then that right from the beginning it had been a plot. For reasons of his own Badoy had wanted you to feel fear, had needed to set up that howling echo just as much as your submerged self; had led you inexorably to the compressor so you could suck in great draughts of it. The reasons — oh, they were lost in the workings of his psyche maybe; or perhaps they were his direct way of counteracting an impression of impotence he hated giving. For might not a foreigner like yourself so richly endowed with nonchalant mobility, such passports and visas and letters of credit, who moved so fluently in the clear waters above a sullen Third World labour pool — might not such a foreigner be badly in need of a lesson in respect? To make light of two great obsessions of the affluent West, technology and physical security, even as he dreamed of clawing his way into that world — might that not have been Badoy's real elegance, his deadliest accuracy? And if you had not been ruffled by this suggestion of war would you not have allowed a burst of affection for the way it had been declared?

"There's one thing," you said magnanimously. "If that night we'd been wearing pukka scuba gear, I'd most likely be dead. You couldn't just have given me your air-hose while you went up to fetch the knife."

"Perhaps," he agreed. "You see? Simple things are best."

On the other hand, of course, you would almost certainly have been wearing a knife....

You did fish again but it was not the same. Your dreams were full of aggression aimed at Badoy, the lucklessly innocent repository of your fantasies. Nobody is as put out as a jilted fantasist, and the fantasist who thinks to perceive an actuality in what he is doing is the most put out of all. You became tired of his voice, his "*ay!*," his wife moving dolefully about their dark house while radiating some tough resolve. You hoped he would soon get a job abroad. One day word reached you that the dendro-thermal project was shelved and with it your feasibility study, but that if you went back to the capital and bullied the right civil servant you could get your accrued salary.

Your leavetaking from Badoy was friendly, offhand, as if in six months or so you might well fetch up back in Anilao and find him still mooching and dreaming of emigration. Then he would dig out your old spear-gun and you would both slip back into the water as if no time had passed. But on the battered once-a-day bus which took you away up the coast you sat on the landward side, ignoring the blue waters creaming over the reefs on your left, staring fixedly into the palm-groves and the forest above them pouring skyward through ravines and gullies to the peaks of the central massif. And what were you thinking? That even if you never did return to that particular place wouldn't the sea always be in waiting? And wouldn't there be other Badoys and other involuntary opportunities to hear that lone whistler with his private note set ringing a bare inner room? For you cannot help yourself.

As even now the distant thud, the compressor's stench rise from inside.

WILLIAM MATTHEWS

From *Rising and Falling*, 1979

SKIN DIVING

The snorkel is the easiest woodwind.
Two notes in the chalumeau:
rising and falling.
Here is the skin of sleep,
the skin of reading, surfaces

inseparable from depths.
How far does the light go down?
Wouldn't we like to know.
I love this exact and calm
suspense, the way the spirit is said

to hover above a deathbed,
curious and tender as it is
detached, a cloud on the water,
a cloud in the sky,
as if desire were already

memory. Just as a diction
predicts what we might say
next, an emotion loves its chums.
But here, in poise and in hard thought,
I look down to find myself happy.

NURSE SHARKS

Since most sharks have no flotation bladders and must swim
to keep from sinking, they like to sleep in underwater caves,
wedged between reef-ledges, or in water so shallow
that their dorsal fins cut up from the surf.
Once I woke a nurse shark (so named because it was
thought to protect its young by taking them
into its mouth). It shied from the bubbles I gave up
but sniffed the glint the murky light made on my regulator.

My first shark at last. I clenched
every pore I could. A shark's sense of smell
is so acute and indiscriminate that a shark crossing
the path of its own wound is rapt.
Once a shark got caught, ripped open by the hook.
The fisherman threw it back after it flopped
fifteen minutes on deck, then caught it again
on a hook baited with its own guts.

Except for the rapacious great white
who often bites first, sharks usually nudge
what they might eat. They're scavengers and like
food to be dead or dying. Move to show you're alive
but not so much as to cause panic: that's what the books
advise. The nurse shark nibbled at my regulator
once, a florid angelfish swam by, the shark
veered off as if it were bored. Its nubbled skin
scraped my kneecap, no blood
but the rasped kneecap pink for a week.

Another year I swam past a wallow of nurse sharks asleep
in three feet of water, their wedge-shaped heads lax
on each other's backs. One of them slowly thrashed
its tail as if it were keeping its balance in the thicket
of sharks sleeping like pick-up-sticks. Its tail sent
a small current over me, a wet wind.
I swirled around a stand of coral and swam
fast to shore, startling the sharks to a waking frenzy:
moil, water opaque with churned-up sand,
grey flames burning out to sea. Last time I go diving
alone, I promised myself, though I lied.

STEPHEN HARRIGAN

From *Water and Light,* 1992

HARMONIUM POINT

There were always parrotfish on the flats. You would hear them gnawing on the coral, breaking off chunks with their huge front teeth. The teeth reminded me of chisels, or of the overgrown incisors of cartoon donkeys. The parrotfish swallowed the pieces of coral and processed them through the pharyngeal jaws in their throats. I imagined these jaws as a mighty grinding machine, its cutting edges as hard as diamonds, that pulverized the coral in powdery explosions as it came down the conveyor belt of the fish's throat. The process liberated the filigree of nutritious algae that grew on the coral. This was what the parrotfish ate. Everything else became dust, and all over the reef you could see little downward drifts of sand, the grains sometimes sparkling when the light caught them, as the parrotfish evacuated it from their brilliant bodies.

That first week on the reef I found the water still murky from the passage of tropical storm Emily, and it was laced with upwelling cold currents. But compared to the silty Texas lakes I was used to diving in, the reef was ravishing. I could see perhaps fifty feet. We would moor the boat just above the abyss of the wall and descend thirty or forty feet to the sand flats on the landward side. The sand was as pure as a snowfield, and when the sun was high there was a mild glare. Seaward the sand disappeared beneath a solid hedge of reef crowned with sea fans and other soft corals that waved in the surge like windblown plants. On the other side of the hedge was the wall.

Usually I saved the wall for the second half of the dive, not wanting to approach it too suddenly, not wanting the sensation of soaring out over its lip to become too common. I preferred to sink to the sand beneath the shadow of the boat and spend a few meditative moments savoring the knowledge of where I was. I felt the way I had felt the one time I went to Paris: never able to trust that I was there, to convince myself that I had actually crossed the Atlantic and that the great sights before me — Notre-Dame, the Arc de Triomphe, the Winged Victory in the Louvre — were not hallucinations but things that I truly beheld, and that in some odd way beheld me in turn. It was as strange as Paris here on the reef, as strange and as magnificent. When I first slipped off the diving boat and sank to the sand I was seized with a puritan insight: it seemed to me that the surface of the island was somehow being punished with drabness for the profligate beauty it displayed beneath the surface.

The flats stretched out before me like a miniature Sahara, the sand laced with snail tracks that looked from on high like the tracks of desert caravans. Coral oases loomed in the distance with the hazy, teasing presence of a mirage. Some coral heads were no larger than floral arrangements, others were massive entities, worlds unto themselves across whose orbits speeding fish traveled in meteoric swipes. The coral heads themselves were full of crevices and overhangs through which other sorts of fish wriggled in and out, back and forth, searching for food or refuge. I knew the names, at least, of most of them: bluehead wrasses, rock hinds, blue tang, groupers, a dozen different kinds of gobies darting about in their start-and-stop fashion above the fissures and buds of the coral surfaces. Doctorfish, trunkfish, cowfish, boxfish, butterflyfish, lizardfish, hogfish, squirrelfish, parrotfish — their names reinforced the perception that always took hold of me underwater, that I was in a kind of counterworld, where every feature and principle of surface life had its alien obverse. Including me, the manfish.

But it was the parrotfish that fascinated me the most, perhaps because they were so hard to miss as they swarmed over the coral, rasping and biting and grinding it to dust. There were eight or ten different species. Some were small and as dull in their coloring as bass. Others — the rainbow parrotfish, the midnight, the stoplight, the blue — were so glorious that each scale covering their skin was like a panel in a stained glass window, the color always ebbing or flaring as the light changed sixty feet above.

Parrotfish are sequential hermaphrodites. As they grow older, they sometimes change sex. A fish that begins as a female may end life as not just a male but a supermale, a massive, radiant creature that is soon to die but seems triumphant in its terminal masculinity.

I saw supermale parrotfish often on the flats. The blues were the hardest to miss. They were three feet long, broad and weighty, with a royal blue coloring that the light brought out in ever more intoxicating, ever more complex hues. When they were younger, their heads had sloped to a wedge, but as supermales they had the bulbous foreheads of sperm whales. They moved slowly over the sand, not in a hurry, their every move announcing power and experience. Unlike the more junior parrotfish, which swarmed over the reef by the hundreds but were essentially solitary, the supermales usually traveled in groups of three or four. I watched as a group hovered above the sand, seeming to confer and deliberate among themselves until one of them trimmed his fins and sunk to the bottom like a submarine taking on ballast, plucking some calcareous morsel from the sand with his teeth.

I would watch the supermales until they dissolved into the haze, and then I might turn my attention to the garden eels that sprouted from the bare sand like a sparse, swaying mat of grass. Sometimes there would be what seemed like an acre of them, a great field of miniature eels protruding halfway out of their burrows, heads turned toward the current and bodies moving with rhythmic undulations that put me in mind of a thousand cobras rearing from a thousand baskets. I could get within five or six feet of them, but then the eels closest to me would begin to disappear as if some invisible scythe were preceding me and cutting them down. They popped back underground with startling speed, and the sand closed over the holes of their burrows, leaving no evidence that they had ever been there.

When I was feeling patient I would sink to the bottom and creep up to them inch by inch, exhaling quietly and steadily until I was close enough to see the silvery glint of their eyes, the only feature I could discern on those waving stalks. In the next moment, as I advanced weightlessly on the tips of my fingers, they would be gone. The way they withheld themselves from my sight pestered me and struck me as slightly malevolent. They made me think of a television program I had watched when I was very young, a puppet show called "Time for Beany," about a little boy and a sea monster. The monster's name was Cecil, and the viewer saw only his top half. I was too young to understand that he was a puppet, that his bottom half was only a hand inserted into a sock. *Something* — the rest of Cecil — was below the edge of the screen, and it aggravated me that I could not see it. Standing in front of the television, I would set my eyes against the glass at the top of the screen and peer down, hoping through this angle of sight to catch a glimpse of Cecil's mysterious extremities.

The garden eels had that same disturbing, unrevealed quality. In my fish book back at the Island Reef was a cross-section diagram of an eel in its burrow, looking like a wood screw embedded deep in a two by four. The burrows are reinforced by the mucus the eels secrete from their skin. Though the creatures have the ability to swim, and the males sometimes venture out in search of better mating opportunities, in general they are as rooted to their spots in the sand as if they were potted plants. They mate by twining around each other and releasing eggs and sperm, the ends of their bodies still touching base in their burrows.

Usually I lingered behind the other divers, respirating on the bottom with the eels while the rest of the group headed straight for the wall. I had hooked up with a group called Blue Water Divers, which at that time was one of the two diving operations on the island. Blue Water's sole significant asset was a twenty-three-foot hydrofoil boat with a sixty-five-horsepower outboard that could zip out to the reef in only a few minutes. Underwater, I was always aware of the boat hovering above us like a protective cloud and of Mitch Rolling swimming watchfully along on his back, his arms folded across his chest in an attitude of meditation.

Mitch was one of the two owners of Blue Water. In the time I was on Grand Turk I never met his partner, who had gone back to the States on urgent family business and lingered. He and Mitch came from Ames, Iowa (the parent company of Blue Water was called Iowa Undersea Adventures). Upon graduating from high school eight years earlier, they had lit out without hesitation for the tropics.

"We had this dream ever since we were sophomores," Mitch told me. "We were going to go to an island. For the last two years of high school we researched where to go. We wrote a letter to the Tahiti immigration office, but when they sent us back an application in French we blew it off. There was this pilot in Iowa, though. He'd done a little charter work in the Bahamas, and he asked us if we'd ever heard of the Turks and Caicos. We hadn't, of course, but we went to the travel agent the next day in Ames and she looked it up. She found out that Air Florida flew there from Miami for 250 dollars round trip. That was the key right there."

Mitch had originally come to the island with the intention of finding a congenial place to play his guitar, and over the years he had emerged as Grand Turk's only musical celebrity. My second night on the island, I had gone to see him in the thatch-roofed bar of the Salt Raker Inn, where the tables were strewn with laminated fish charts and back issues of *Skin Diver*. He sang standards by Jimmy Buffet and Kenny Loggins and, upon request, the theme from "Gilligan's Island."

Mitch lived and worked in a house just north of the center of town, thirty yards from the sea wall. The mummified head of a jewfish, as big as a boulder, sat on the front porch. Its jaws hung open, and in the middle of its head was a hole where it had been speared by the man Mitch and his partner bought the dive business from. The living room of the house resembled the cabin of a ship, with dark wooden beams and white walls covered with nautical charts. In a brick-and-board bookcase sat a dusty set of Great Books, and above them a collection of antique bottles, shells, barracuda skulls, and the armored headplates of spiny lobsters. From the ceiling, running the length of the room, hung a life-size great white shark, sculpted in papier-mâché.

I would ride up to Mitch's house every day at eight o'clock on my rented scooter, my mesh bag of dive gear balanced on my lap. Mitch would be in the compressor shed behind the house, filling the day's tanks, singing "Island Girl" or some other song I recognized from the cassette he offered for sale on the Manta Ray label. The tanks were aluminum, taller and lighter than steel but still heavy when filled with compressed air. I carried them two at a time across the street, holding them awkwardly by the valves, picking my way across the rocky ground in my flip-flops. When I had lined them up on the sea wall, ready for loading onto the boat, they made a pretty sight, a row of bright yellow cylinders against the glorious blue of the ocean.

Usually five or six divers had signed up for the trip. They might be solitary accountants or civil servants who had come down to Grand Turk on business, or honeymooning couples who had come over for the day from the Club Med on Providenciales. Or they might be serious divers, touring the Turks and Caicos for three or four weeks at a time, carrying their gear in 300-dollar backpacks. The appeal for them, and for me, was the unspoiled bounty of the reef — the lush coral, the swooping columns of fish. Grand Turk had not yet been "dove out." The place was calm and undiscovered, lacking any amenities except the reef itself. This was not yet a major dive resort, where the cattle boats disgorged forty or fifty underwater tourists at a time; where the coral was broken and bruised by the careless swatting of fins; and where the fish, ruined by handouts, swam up to the divers expecting an aerosol burst from a can of Cheez-Whiz. "Yeah, this is pretty great," a paper salesman from Seattle told me one day as we headed in from a dive. "Come back in ten years, it'll break your heart."

Mitch had made more than a thousand dives on the Grand Turk wall, and in that first week he took me to all of the main sites, some of which he had named. A few of the names were evocative: the Black Forest, for a spot beneath the overhang of the wall where fronds of black coral grew sheltered from the brunt of the sun; the Amphitheater, for a site distinguished by a vast sloping bowl of sand. Other names were flatly informational, simple declarations of underwater landmarks: the Anchor, the Canyons, the Tunnels. During my months on Grand Turk I developed an intimate acquaintance with most of these places, but on those first few dives I could scarcely tell them apart. At the beginning I saw only the repetitive textures of coral and sand, the patterns in an endless bolt of fabric that seemed to unspool below me as I drifted along. And the essential experience was constant: the loitering in the sand flats, the lazy saunter upcurrent along the top of the wall, and the trip back along its face with our bodies hanging over the abyss — an enchanted dispensation from the laws of gravity.

At some sites the wall was a sheer vertical drop into the darkness, at others the descent was interrupted by a staggered series of terraces. But there was always the feel of deep ocean beneath, a sensation like no other on earth: hanging unsupported along the face of a precipice with miles of blue nothingness ahead and the black ocean pit below. I felt like Wile E. Coyote in the "Road Runner" cartoons, when he inadvertently runs past the lip of a cliff and stands there in midair, looking sheepish as he awaits the plummet.

But the plummet never came, and that was the magic. Instead I would let myself drop, descending at my own pace, following the wall for fifty, sixty, seventy feet as the color bled away and the hard, expansive corals gave way to softer things, to deep-water lace and the looping coils of sea whips that grew straight out from the wall. It was a region of colorless filigree, of waving, pliant forms that gave no resistance to the crushing weight of the water. I would punch the inflater button on my buoyancy vest as the sea's increasing density threatened to draw me deeper, into what I imagined as a region of ghastly bioluminescent fish and steaming ocean vents. A part of me wanted to go there, but I hovered instead at a sensible depth, looking out and not down, out toward the trackless blue water beyond the reef, water that was like a magician's cloak from which anything could materialize.

One site in particular kept drawing me back. It was named the Library in honor of the shoreline landmark — a pink stucco library, formerly a church — that was visible two hundred yards away on Front Street. In one area here the wall was cut through with two deep canyons, creating a promontory that looked out commandingly over the empty ocean. Some places have a kind of power, a provocative allure, simply by virtue of the way they inhabit space, the way they sit there, as if sentient and alert to their existence. This promontory at the Library drew my eye and focused my vision along its narrowing platform until I saw what it wanted me to see: a triangular shelf of coral rock, vectoring out into the blue.

At the very edge of the shelf stood a barrel-shaped growth of cavernous star coral—*Montastrea cavernosa.* (I had been teaching myself the Latin names since the common names for coral species differ from book to book.) It was an elegant specimen — three feet high, slightly squarish, colored a muted shade of forest green that made the coral boulder look as worn and soft as an upholstered ottoman. The polyps in their bulbous cups were bunched up on the surface like biscuits in a baking tin.

The perfect location of the coral upon the promontory, its deeply satisfying presence and symmetry, made me think of Wallace Stevens, whose poems I had been reading back at the Island Reef in between entries of *The Encyclopedia of Aquatic Life.* I remembered one poem in particular from high school, "The Anecdote of the Jar." It was one of those perfect, embalmed poems that are most likely to be preached in school, and I had always held it in secret contempt. Now, however, forty feet underwater, I heard it again. It was no longer a finicky verbal still life but something authentic and urgent, a poem so precisely constructed that the logic of the universe seemed to sluice through it like the water of a diverted stream. "I placed a jar in Tennessee," it began,

And round it was, upon a hill.
It made the slovenly wilderness
Surround that hill.

The wilderness rose up to it,
And sprawled around, no longer wild.
The jar was round upon the ground
And tall and of a port in air.

It took dominion everywhere.
The jar was gray and bare.
It did not give of bird or bush,
Like nothing else in Tennessee.

Though this part of the wall was called the Library, the promontory itself had no name. Like most features of the underwater landscape, it was anonymous. But this was a spot I knew I would return to again and again, so I borrowed a word from the title of one of Wallace Stevens's books and named it Harmonium Point.

I swam out to its farthest edge, hovered for a moment over the abyss and then, as if gravity were a threat, back-pedaled with my fins until the solid coral rock was beneath me. Then I positioned myself vertically, set my hands on my hips, and let my heels touch down harmlessly on a patch of sand at the edge of the point. A small spotted moray eel rippled across the terrain in front of me, and near my foot was a sea anemone whose stout tentacles looked like a multitude of miniature elephant trunks waving in unison. From the abyss, like a thought slowly forming, an eagle ray swam into sight. Its hide was speckled, and at first I saw only white spots, a dense, drifting constellation against the deep blue of the ocean. Then the rest of the creature slowly disengaged from the background.

Rays were common on the reef. I had already seen many stingrays wandering in the sand flats or skimming low over the coral surfaces. Stingrays are bottom feeders. They tend to snuggle into the sand and, when alarmed, take off in short, contour-hugging flights. But this was the first eagle ray I had seen, and an eagle ray is to a stingray as a Frisbee is to a cast-iron skillet.

Gliding and banking in front of Harmonium Point, the animal took on the power of an apparition. Its snout was elegantly tapered; its wingbeats were powerful and far more fluid than a bird's. Watching it, I felt my heart beat faster and felt a serene chill creep up my wetsuited spine. I thought that if I hovered here long enough, other such creatures would come to me: giant sunfish, sea turtles, basking sharks, humpback whales. My pressure gauge showed I was running low on air. A prudent diver surfaces with six hundred pounds per square inch in his tank. I was a prudent diver, but I stayed on, sucking another few hundred psi and trying to sort out what I was feeling, what I wanted here. And it came to me that I simply wanted to be included, to be inside the frame for once. I wondered if that were possible, or if, as an alien visitor to the reef, I would always be like Wallace Stevens's jar in Tennessee, helplessly taking dominion everywhere.

STEPHEN HARRIGAN

From *Water and Light*, 1992

FACELESS

When I first came to Grand Turk, I had a problem with fish. I didn't like them much, didn't respond to them, didn't understand what they were supposed to be about. Fly fishermen are always chattering on about the nobility and mysterious cunning of trout, and the dedicated aquarium keepers I know seem to regard their fish tanks as an almost spiritual locus. But when I used to hunt for redfish and sea trout in the waters of Laguna Madre I regarded my prey with cold disinterest. Looking back, I suspect that this was only a boy's way of demystifying the creatures he has sworn to kill. Denying my fascination with them was my way of distancing myself from the guilt and emotional trauma of destroying them. I willfully embraced the popular notion that fish do not feel pain, and when I watched them expiring on the deck, their gills flapping and their mouths puckering in silent agony, I convinced myself that these were mere mechanical spasms, no more "felt" than the shuddering of a dying engine. I had heard somewhere that slipping an ice cube into a fish's mouth would kill it instantly, and I tried this over and over without success, determined to believe in this magic shut-off valve.

Like most people, I usually encountered fish when they were dead or dying — trussed up on ice in a fish market or hanging limply from a stringer off the side of a boat or pier. In their sameness, their helplessness, their mute acceptance, they struck me as pathetic. There was no recognizable warmth or passion in them — no purpose. And the exotic living specimens I saw displayed in the aquarium tanks of zoos and oceanariums were simply animate baubles, to be admired for their pretty colors but never considered as sentient beings. I was drawn to moist-eyed mammals or to forthrightly repellent reptiles. The only fish that interested me were the fish I had some overt reason to fear — sharks or electric eels or grotesque poisonous stonefish.

When I began diving in the ocean I should have seen at once how puny my imaginative responses to fish had been, but for years I squandered my opportunities to observe them in their rightful context. I watched them dart across the reef, full of their urgent business, and I learned most of their names, but my attention was arid and dutiful. My imagination refused to reach out to them.

This was my state of mind during my first few weeks of diving at Grand Turk. I would float at the promontory of Harmonium Point and list the passing fish on my slate as if I were recording the details of some exotic procession. Here was a queen angel, a rock beauty, a hogfish, an immature bluehead wrasse. Duly noted. But I kept straining my eyes past them, hoping to see some creature I recognized as belonging, in some unknown way, to my own kind. I wanted to locate a brute mammal — a manatee, a humpback whale — calling to me from across the void.

Then one day a school of creole wrasses swam by, following the lip of the wall. There were so many of them that they filtered out the sunlight, and the water grew darker as they passed. Wrasses — whose many species include the hogfish, the bluehead, the yellowhead, the clown wrasse, the puddingwife, and the slippery dick — make up one of the most common families of fish on the reef. They tend to have colorful and rather blunt bodies, with a frilly ridge of fin along their backs. Creole wrasses are larger than most of their wrasse cousins, and stockier. They are usually blue, with a black nosecone marking covering their forehead from their eyes to their upper lip.

Something about this school swimming by attracted me, and I joined them, rising from the promontory and coasting along in a flow of eight-inch fish. They swam in perfect unison and perfect order, moving forward with sweeping motions of their pectoral fins, each one with a focused and unquestioning will. I was as exhilarated as if I had flown up into the sky and joined a flock of migrating geese. Soaring along with these wrasses, I felt myself warming to the idea of what a fish might be. Every member of the school had the same dour and determined look, the same lifeless eyes, but for the first time this sameness struck me not as threatening but as beautiful. I saw that the fish were not so much individuals as particles, the spangly elements of a mysterious scattering layer that seemed to be constantly shifting in quest of one ultimate coherent shape. The school moved like a dense current, with small groups breaking off here and there to form swirling eddies that eventually found their way back to the main channel. Swimming along with the wrasses were smaller fish, blue and brown chromis, and on the flanks of the school carnivorous jacks and barracuda kept watch like malevolent shepherds, waiting for their chance to attack.

Beside me, inhabiting the same plane, swam a Spanish mackerel, its black dorsal fin tipped with white.

I dropped down deep into the center of the school and followed the wrasses as they trailed between twin pinnacles of coral. When they passed through the pinnacles they swam upward and then down again, moving across the reef in an undulating wave. Swimming with them, borne along on this tide of fish, I felt eerily happy. Unbidden, the theme from *Gone With the Wind* kept playing over and over in my head as I swooped through the reef formations with the wrasses. When the fish in front of me suddenly swerved in another direction, and the light hit their scales from a sharp new angle, it was as if they had been struck with a magic wand. They lit up in a sparkling explosion of blue.

The school moved forward as if it had a destination. Creole wrasses are plankton feeders that tend to patrol the midrange waters of the reef in the brightness of day, sinking down at night to burrow into the sand and fall asleep. I assumed they were feeding now, plucking jellyfish and copepods out of the water, but I could not get myself to focus on one fish long enough to be able to tell. And this is probably the primary reason why fish congregate in schools — to frustrate predators, to hopelessly splinter a potential attacker's visual cues. I remember once diving through a tunnel in Grand Cayman that was filled with a school of small, glistening fish known as silversides. They appeared to be not just a congregation of individual creatures but a solid mass, and as I stroked through the tunnel I could see nothing else, just a glistening silver curtain that kept parting endlessly in front of me. If I made a sudden gesture, if I tried to reach out and touch a specific fish, the school exploded in a blinding starburst in which my target fish was endlessly refracted.

Threatened with attack, a school of fish becomes something like an optical illusion, a mirage hovering continually out of reach. These creole wrasses were not as spectacular in their schooling behavior as the silversides I'd seen in that tunnel, but they clearly subscribed to the notion of safety in numbers. Here on the seaward margin of the reef, where the big predators were on the prowl, they could search for food in relative peace of mind, able to instantly congeal into a pointillistic whole and whoosh out of an attacker's way like a matador's cape.

No one knows exactly how schooling fish communicate danger with such precision and alacrity. Every fish in the school appears to receive the message at the same time, as if wired into some central power source. It is known that fish have rich sensory lives. They are able to hear, and they communicate with one another by all sorts of chirps, grunts, and grinding sounds. Their eyesight is good, and most species see in color. The lenses of their unblinking eyes are thick and bulbous to bend light waves traveling through the dense water and direct them onto the retina. Some fish have excellent binocular vision; others — those whose eyes face outward from the sides of the head — apparently perceive the world as two more or less distinct lobes of sight. (Creole wrasses belong in that category. Their eyes can move independently of each other — one eye locked on a floating morsel of food, the other scanning the opposite horizon for danger.) Fish have taste buds not only on their rigid tongues but often in the probing barbels that hang down from their mouths, and in some cases taste buds are scattered all over their bodies. Some species of catfish, for instance, can taste with their tails.

Fish, by and large, are prodigious smellers. As with humans and other vertebrates, the neurons that convey a fish's sense of smell report directly to the complex areas of the brain that govern emotion and behavior. Living in the water a fish is steeped in dissolved smells. For many, the sense of smell is what provokes them the most, spurs them to "higher" responses like sexual desire or fear. In laboratory experiments, male gobies have gone into courtship displays when the water in which a breeding female had been swimming was poured into their tank.

Smell helps lead fish such as salmon back to the rivers and streams of their birth. Smell helps fish find food and perceive danger, and it probably is a factor in the impulse that gathers them into schools. But other sense organs are important in schooling as well, particularly the lateral line.

Generally, fish perceive the world in a way that we can understand. Like us, they hear, see, taste, smell, and have at least a dull sense of touch. And we can speculate, at least, on a fish's mental awareness — a brain full of sudden decrees and impulses that do not linger long enough to be considered thoughts. But we are unequipped to grasp the sensations that come to them through the lateral line. This is a sensory canal that runs along each of the fish's flanks. It is studded with sensitive motion detectors, which constantly monitor low-frequency vibrations. The lateral line allows fish to "hear" changes in water pressure, to gather information about other creatures by the way their movements disturb the water. Because of the lateral line, fish in a school are able to swim at an unvarying distance from one another, and to view the ocean space between them and their neighbors as a tingling web of perception.

The school of creole wrasses, the more I swam with it, struck me as a lovely work of architecture, a solid thing created by the dynamic tension of swarming molecules. But the individual fish still filled me with a vague anxiety, and I realized that my lifelong disenchantment with these creatures might have been based on the fact that they have no faces. Fish do have certain fixed looks that can strike us as familiar or even endearing. A French angelfish has a soft and expressive visage. An African pompano, I have observed more than once, bears a direct resemblance to J. Edgar Hoover. And if you look at the pale undersides of certain species of rays and skates you will see what looks unnervingly like the face of a human baby. But these are masks. Fish have no facial muscles, no way to vary their frozen expressions. They can look permanently startled, quizzical, wrathful, serene, but their countenances are accidents of evolution, of ages of hydrodynamic trial and error, no more reflective of the fish's interior state than its fins or scales. That was why, as a boy, I was able to convince myself that they did not feel pain — because they did not seem to *care*. But this lack of caring, this pokerfaced nonchalance, frightened me more than it comforted me. I think I worried that it was contagious. I had a horror of being faceless myself, of being numb and indistinguishable and marching with hypnotized unconcern into some dreadful trap. Fish to me were the brainwashed legions, the living dead.

Now, watching them underwater, I began to understand that fish were as fervent about their lives as I was about mine. I peeled off from the school of creole wrasses and saw them disappear into the enveloping distance like a haunted caravan. As I headed back toward the boat, I was interrupted by the attack of a damselfish about six inches long.

The damselfish didn't bite, but would have if I had persisted in trespassing on its tiny patch of algae, which it was cultivating on a tableland of dead star coral. More than likely the damselfish had helped kill the coral, nibbling away at the polyps until they were gone, like a farmer ridding his pasture of tree stumps. Many species of damselfish are precisely that: farmers. They grow algae and they eat it. Their fields are usually minute tufts of green, which the fish patrols frenetically. At the approach of any stranger, no matter how large, the damselfish attacks. Damselfish are everywhere, and if you swim low over the reef, you are constantly rousing them to action. They make heedless lightning charges, and they will not be repulsed. I backed off just outside of this damselfish's boundaries and studied its fretful possessiveness. When a big parrotfish swam by, the damsel took after it with the ferocity of a water buffalo, and the parrotfish veered off without hesitation. Why it would be intimidated by such a slight adversary I had no idea, but the confrontation had the air of ritual, of a dance whose movements were so deeply encoded in both fish that it transcended my understanding of natural logic.

More parrotfish streamed by, potential claim jumpers that gave the embattled farmer no rest. It was a bright afternoon, and fish were everywhere in schools or loose federations. I counted the species within a three-yard radius of where I was swimming: trumpetfish, black durgons, creole wrasses, striped parrotfish, stoplight parrotfish, blue chromis, barracks, yellowtail snappers, goatfish, banded butterflyfish, bluehead wrasses, fairy basslets, assorted gobies and blennies, trunkfish, cowfish... I gave up. It was suddenly astonishing to me how visible it all was. What if the terrestrial world were like this! What would it be like to take a stroll in the forest and find, within an arm's-length radius, a similarly teeming display of woodland creatures: beavers, robins, woodpeckers, deer, squirrels, chipmunks, rabbits, foxes... ?

A coral reef may be the most industrious, pulsating, *driven* environment on earth. Something was always going on here, most of the time right in front of my face, yet the action was so cryptic and so furious that I could not track it, and much of what I happened to see I could not comprehend. But the reef in its vibrancy appeared to have nothing to hide. Many of the fish I routinely encountered — like the various parrotfish and several iridescent species of gobies — were turned out in what Konrad Lorenz called *plakatfarben*, "poster colors." And even fish that I thought of at first as drab had, on close inspection, a radiant undercoat that shone through their scaly hides like some deeply woven design rising from the fabric of a carpet.

I followed a black durgon for a while, attracted by the breezy, rippling motions of the dorsal and anal fins that framed its flat, high-beamed body. At first glance a black durgon is not a colorful fish — it is black. But now I noticed the color lines highlighting the base of each fin, two silky blue stripes as rich as the lining of a tuxedo. And the more I looked at the durgon's black background, the more I saw a shimmering play of colors — a spectral blush beneath the skin, as unexpected as the rainbows that sometimes form in roadside oil slicks.

On the reef you cannot get away from the color, from the infinitely varied play of water and light upon shining surfaces. Sometimes the display is lurid, sometimes so subtle you see it only as a wavering illusion. For fish, color often functions as camouflage. Like the octopus, many species of fish can alter the pigment cells in their skin to match their background. Cruising above the sand flats, I learned to spot motionless peacock flounders by the oval patterns they made in the sand; the fish themselves were almost invisible, their tan skin accessorized with faint blue rings that imparted a suggestion of flickering surface light. Flounders, like octopuses, are among the supreme masters of camouflage. (In one laboratory experiment, a flounder managed to produce a crude imitation of the checkerboard background on which it had been placed.) Just as impressive in their covert survival strategies are all the warty bottom dwellers like frogfish, toadfish, stonefish, and scorpionfish. These tend to be creatures with cavernous mouths, sometimes with fleshy lures attached. They look like slimy hunks of coral or encrusted rocks. When a prey fish swims close enough, drawn by the wormlike lure, it is inhaled with breathtaking speed, sucked into the bony, hollow darkness of its ambusher's mouth.

The most notorious such animal is the Australian stonefish, which lingers in shallow waters, indistinguishable from the coral rubble. It has thirteen venomous spines along its back to fend off, among other things, the human foot. I grew up believing that if you so much as touched a stonefish you would experience three to five minutes of unimaginable pain followed by a certain and merciful death. This is nine-tenths folklore. It's true that people occasionally die from stonefish encounters, but while the venom is consistently agonizing, it is not often fatal.

Here in the Caribbean, the local variant of the stonefish is the scorpionfish. The neurotoxic venom of a scorpionfish is not as powerful as that of its Australian counterpart — in a laboratory experiment, the venom of eight scorpionfish was required to deliver a fatal dose to a guinea pig — but it is definitely to be avoided. On the reef I became adept at spotting scorpionfish after Mitch showed me a few. When he first pointed one out I had no idea what he was calling to my attention. He kept pointing at a nondescript piece of spongy looking coral, reddish in color and covered with all the usual growths and protuberances. It took me a long time to realize it was alive. Finally I saw one of its eyes, a blank, glassy disk. The fish was wedged at an angle against the rock, supported on its stubby pectoral fins. Mitch took off his snorkel and poked it, and the scorpionfish threw off a cloud of silt, swam a foot or so away, and settled down again, unconcerned and undetectable.

Scorpionfish and flounders use color to conceal themselves on the bottom. Many other creatures use it to tone down their visibility in open water. Dolphins, rays, sharks, sea turtles, jacks, tuna — all are counter shaded, dark on top and pale below. Seen from above, their blue or brown dorsal surfaces blend in with the ocean depths. When viewed from below, their undersides are hard to distinguish from the white light of the sun pouring through the water.

For the bright reef fish in their *plakatfarben*, however, color is a way of standing out. For French angelfish, with their sparkling yellow spots, or for golden hamlets or heliotrope basslets, camouflage is not a central issue. Unlike the naturally sluggish scorpionfish, they do not survive by being inconspicuous but by being fast and maneuverable enough to dart into a coral hole at the approach of danger. And in any case, the fish that prey on them in the muffled crepuscular light of early morning and late afternoon tend to be colorblind.

The brilliant colors seem to be for the benefit of other members of the species, a way to flash sexual enticements or territorial warnings across the gloomy ocean distances. Many of the brightest-colored species, like the parrotfish, are programmed to change sex from time to time, and each new phase is broadcast by a variation in color that alerts the rest of the breeding population to the individual's new gender.

I passed over a cluster of tube sponges swarming with tiny blue gobies. To my eye — always restlessly in search of leviathans — these fish were usually about as interesting as gnats. But today I was arrested by their shining colors, and I sank down onto the sand and watched them for a moment, trying hopelessly to look through their eyes. What did they see, what were they watching for? I tried to imagine the intensity of those color messages and of all those other mysterious stimuli — sound, smell, lateral line excitations — that formed the known universe of a goby's perceptions. Would a zooming yellow stripe, glimpsed across the chasm of the sponge opening, provoke a goby to an intolerable sexual pitch? Would the head-on approach of a territorial rival, its ventral fins whirring, its wide mouth moving up and down in percussive gulps, send a charge through its body that I would recognize as fear? I wondered, too, how gobies regard the ocean itself. They are dense, low-slung fish, lacking the swim bladders that allow other fish to adjust their specific gravities and move up and down at will through the varying density of the water column. To a goby, perched on a sponge or a piece of coral or a bed of sand, its face and eyes permanently canted upward, the ocean overhead must appear as an unreachable vault, the way the heavens do to us.

I looked down at these darting fish, two or three inches long. My eyes crossed as I tried to keep track of their comings and goings, and my imagination wore itself out trying to conjure up some authentic sense of the tenor of their existence. I knew that many gobies are monogamous, that the male and female excavate a nesting burrow together in the sand, and that in some species the male slips into the burrow to stay with the eggs while his mate closes off the entrance with sand, releasing him a few days later to swim around a bit before sealing him up again. But what does this mean? How does it feel? Could the reflexive pair bonding of gobies loom as dramatic to them, as essential, as human love does to us? I didn't know. I felt sheepish in even speculating about it. Gobies in love! And yet, *why not?* We dismiss animals as instinctive beings, and we think of instinct itself as an unfeeling mechanical urge, an electrical command fired from a witless brain. But we only know what we observe; we see only the motions. The acts of fish may be in fact nothing more than instinctive impulses, but we can never know the specific timbre of those impulses or the way a fish feels when it is impelled by them.

I became attached to a certain blenny. It lived on the coral precipice of Harmonium Point, forty feet below the surface. I first noticed it when I was idling through a deep sand channel with my faceplate inches away from the silty coral rock. Only the blenny's head was visible. It peered out from its burrow, a horizontal hole in the coral which the fish fit as perfectly as if it had been machined into place. When I looked it up later in a field guide, I saw that it was a secretary blenny. I guessed its length at about an inch and a half, though only its head — with its down-turned mouth and bristly appendages known as cirri — was visible to me. Two yellow rings neatly encircled its eyes like the war paint on a Comanche pony. Inside its burrow the blenny waggled its head from side to side, joyless and rhythmic.

Blennies are closely related to gobies. They are, on the whole, a little frillier, a little stouter. Like the gobies, they have no swim bladders, so they tend to stay on the bottom. They swim the way a seal walks, awkwardly, with their tails lower than their heads. But some blennies are able to travel across dry land, hopping like frogs from one tide pool to another. Blennies are generally carnivorous, and a few species are aggressive, but when I put my finger in front of this one it did not snap; it merely withdrew into its burrow.

The secretary blenny merited only two lines in my field guide and was not mentioned at all in the other books I consulted, so its life ways remained a mystery to me. But time after time, day and night, I dove down to Harmonium Point to check on this particular fish. It was always there, lodged in its burrow, moving its head from side to side. I was drawn to it because of its deadpan expression, its reliable location, its mysterious *lack* of behavior. As far as I could detect, it never did anything. Its world was limited pretty much to this minute hole in the coral rock, in one of the thousands of nameless canyons and sand channels cutting through the Grand Turk wall.

That little blenny became a touchstone. Once I dreamed about it. In the dream, I swam down as usual to the fish's burrow but found it empty. The blenny was gone. Only its yellow eye circles remained, vivid against the darkness of the burrow, sweeping back and forth with a ghostly vigilance. But even when I was wide awake the blenny struck me as vaguely unreal, stranger than all the other strange things on the reef. Its flush position in its burrow and its woeful expression reminded me of some other imprisoned face that, for a long time, I could not call to mind. Then, after weeks of perplexed pondering, it dawned on me: Señor Wences! Señor Wences was a puppet that used to appear, decades ago, on various TV variety shows. He was nothing more than a surly face trapped inside a box, whose lid would open now and then to allow him to make some acerbic, rapid-fire observation.

When I remembered Señor Wences, I felt a momentary triumph: I had the blenny pegged at last. I had managed to assign it a role, an identity. In my mind it was already a character to put beside the damselfish's embattled farmer, or the barracuda's sinister outrider. After a while I found that without consciously meaning to do so, I had peopled the reef with my own creations. One by one, I had given each fish a personality, and the stronger that illusory personality was, the more the fish interested me. When a fish did not remind me of anything or anyone, when it did not express itself in a way that captured my attention, I ignored it.

This was, of course, rank anthropomorphism, but I could not stop it, any more than I could get the theme from *Gone With the Wind* to quit playing inside my head. Though categorizing creatures in this way is a simple human tendency, harmless and ineradicable, I became impatient with myself for trying to reduce all this alien grandeur to something comprehendible and comfortable. I longed for my pedestrian imagination to fall away, because finally it was what barred me from truly perceiving the reef.

MICHAEL CADNUM

From *Voices from the Deep*, 1988

UNDERWATER

A blanket of Creole wrasse
spins and parts

around the body that has always
hated itself but now

soars
in gentle thunder

climbing breath.

PHILIPPE DIOLÉ

From *The Undersea Adventure*, 1953

YOUR MINGLED ATOMS

I have no particular "stories" to tell.

Breaking the surface of the sea, roaming about in the deep waters of the ocean, going down slowly, eyes open, watching the flicker of mullet and the dance of castagnoles, chestnut substitutes in these liquid skies for butterflies — all this does not constitute a "story."

But if I do not know any stories, I have perhaps lived a miracle, one which I want to talk about: I have traveled to another world in which "action is sister to the dream." I have swept away in the heart of the sea, at a depth of several fathoms, all my anxieties as a man. Worries of the moment, scientific curiosity, metaphysical doubts, have all been hurled into the sea and I do not regret it.

Like many others, I do not feel in perfect harmony with our age and the solitude of diving lulls and stays a deep-rooted dissatisfaction. Down below, where dream and action move silently forward, side by side, through the dense waters, man feels for a moment in tune with life.

Whether that is telling a story or not, I don't know. It is always possible to write an account of journeys on land. I have been from one end of

Europe to the other and made almost a complete tour of Africa. Every country I have visited can be described: it is simply a question of landscape, people, distances. But for three years my life has been entangled in the life of the sea. The only period of my existence worth anything in all this time has been spent far from other men, beyond a curtain of crystal, with fish or underwater animals more foreign in appearance and habits than anything one might come across if one traveled to the ends of the earth. It was an adventure without incident, and it is not yet over. Probably it will end only with my death, for those who have once listened to the siren songs of the ocean bed never return to land.

In fact one does not go straight into the sea. Between the air and the water, a steel blade quivers. What people call the surface is also a ceiling: a mirror from above, watered silk from beneath. Nothing is torn on the way through. Only a few bubbles mark the diver's channel and behind him the frontier soon closes. But once the threshold is crossed, one can turn back slowly and look up: that dazzling screen is the border between two worlds, as clear to one as to the other. Behind the looking glass the sky is made of water.

Is this light spilling out in all directions, this pure and deep substance, really water? So much brilliance and clarity do not seem to belong to the green, frothing surface, the sticky and resilient element through which the swimmer has to strike his path. Once he has broken the surface, the diver who is properly ballasted has no more weight, no more resistance: an aerial softness transports him where he wills. Here the world is sweetness. There is not a place in his body, from head to foot, which is not relaxed. It is a pleasure to stretch out, to lie on one's back and to feel the perfect fluency of one's muscles. Dreams float very slowly up from the sea. Walled in silence and completely alone, the diver begins an interior monologue in the cell of his undreamed-of content.

At a depth of two or three fathoms all swell subsides. Not a weed moves. A carpet of sand gleams faintly in the cleft of a rock some yards farther down. A mysterious continent traces itself below me. I swim between the huge pages of an illuminated manuscript. Now I am dazzled by the purity of the light, the luminous beauty of the deep. A crystalline quality of light gives everything the purity of glass. The opened pages end in a maze of rocks, beyond which a flow of blue water narrows out of sight and then widens. Over them is stretched a thick sky on which I glide until I reach shapes that turn into submarine peaks, or cathedrals rising from the plains on summer mornings. Inspecting these summits, feeling the hard rock under their soft exterior of weed, gives one a respite before the final slide towards an invisible bottom. I swim around a sapphire steeple. Everything in front of me is blue, but if I look down, a whole purple universe seems to swing out of the depths. Shall I go down to the foot of this tower or forget about it? At twenty fathoms, everything is forbidding, congealed, and cold, and the sudden iciness stabs me. I don't know whether it freezes or paralyzes me: I feel it in me like a living thing, a disease. What have I come here for? To explore the sea? I already know all that can be seen in it. I have come down in pursuit of a mirage. I have yielded to the dizzy madness of tearing open this blue canvas and making for the very heart of the dream. The rock cod, motionless in the shadow of their holes, gaze at the passer-by without stirring. Gorgonia spread their huge fans, quite still in the breathless water. Who has spoken of jungles? Not a single evasive flurry, not a moving shadow, brings this palace without walls to life. Were blood to flow, for example, it would not stain the crystal purity, for it would look blue. What is this vague terror as from a chamber of horrors? The slightest touch makes me tremble. I have even forgotten what the sky looks like, the real sky in which men can breathe without equipment.

One day, in a little cave near Toulon, Captain Philippe Tailliez sent me down with some flasks of compressed air on my back and made me bite the rubber tube. I breathed my first draughts of air. The sea opened. I crossed through the looking glass, no longer the ghastly, pallid body with the jerky movements that fish and divers observe with some disgust splashing on the shore.

This underwater baptism, in the freshness of the spring sea, not only crowned me with riches from a kingdom that nobody could ever take away, but provided me with keys to unlock certain parts of myself. Drunk with the discovery of a new continent, I began at first to learn more about myself than about it.

Valery has written a line in *Charmes*, in which, with the foresight of true genius, he expresses the very essence of what I felt. *Heureux vos corps fondus, Eaux planes et profondes!* (Happy your mingled atoms, O waters smooth and deep.) I was this "corps fondus" — mingled atoms — the idealized but lively image of myself, and I moved in a landscape of dazzling reflections. The reverse side of the looking glass was inhabited: fish, seaweed, now at eye level, offered me the extension of a reality for which I was not prepared. I felt one by one, like twinges of arthritis, my ties with land. The mind was still less at home than the body. Freed of all anxieties about breathing, I moved about in the forbidden world. I was at least as much of a man in the water as I was on land: a man who could observe with discretion and no longer a wretch tortured by asphyxiation, blinded by splashes, going down a fathom or two only at the expense of great physical effort. The air was obedient to the call of my lungs. Everything became as simple as in a dream and this air which I breathed out climbed to the surface in great expanding bubbles, the supreme proofs of the miracle.

Lest anyone should misunderstand this story, let me repeat: I was a novice, a complete beginner. I have revisited the place of my first exploits. The depth of the cave is childish, but no act of great daring could today ever give me so great a feeling of discovery, of the joy of wandering alone through a virginal forest, the sun rays piercing the sea, revealing my own golden goblet.

On the rocks that day a family from Toulon was having lunch. It was a Sunday. I remember their loud voices, their amusement on the water's edge that anyone should bother to explore its depths. Were they aware, these Sunday revelers, that I was fulfilling all my promises to the sea and, thanks to this second baptism, renewing between man and the sea a contract broken for two thousand years? Did I even know it myself?

Philippe Tailliez smiled at my enthusiasm. He didn't tell me that I had seen nothing yet and that I still had everything to learn. I discovered that for myself at my next dive. Then began a slow apprenticeship. To lose one's head over diving is only the beginning; the next step is knowing how to get the most benefit, once the sea has closed over one, out of the state of being a live, drowned man. One has to learn to be worthy of one's position as a "melted body." So a new life begins, with more exacting pleasures.

The weight of our heredity, our whole past, dissuades us from accepting this sumptuous gift that the twentieth century offers us. Our ancestors who lived in forests have bequeathed us eyes that deceive us under water. Hunters have left us ears which are bad for diving and a sense of hearing which is useless in the sea. Accustomed for thousands of years to being warned and thus able to avoid danger, by trusting to our eyes, our smell, our hearing, we are suddenly disarmed in an element where our horizon is limited to a few yards and where silence reigns. A fear born of ignorance keeps us company for a long time in this country where we do not know how to distinguish dangerous from friendly creatures, plants from animals. We need this proof to be reminded of our ancient heritage, like those royal palaces one wishes to transform into museums, but which set the architect appalling problems. How many walls to knock down before we see the daylight, how many habits that we had taken to be the very marks of human intelligence to renounce — our idea of space, the hierarchy of our senses, and the way to interpret their signals. Our disconcerted brain asks to be reassured by a gradual and careful approach to these new truths of the sea. And these new marine truths are in the process of becoming new human truths, for in future this apprenticeship to the deep will interest the masses. A large public, more numerous each year, tries to learn about the sea, about conditions that scholars scarcely understand. Biology, the study of marine plants, hydrography, all still the preserve of specialists, are becoming subjects of holiday discussion. Office workers and housewives, as soon as summer comes, put on goggles to gaze into the waters and to sample an enchantment which ten years ago was reserved for initiates. For children, the magic of the sea is as commonplace as television and radar. I am not one of those who deplore it. So immediate an intimacy suggests that the underwater world is less impenetrable than it seems. New discoveries open before us, future activities are planned: all has not yet been said about the evolution of human life.

One has to resist the urge, in the sea as much as on land, to try to see everything at top speed and do nothing leisurely. This disturbing fever, which burns in the veins of generations of tourists, unfortunately upsets some of our diver friends.

An underwater site, even of poor quality, has many secrets to yield and probably one never discovers them all. It takes more than one visit to explore it carefully. Not only because its passages, its crevasses and other challenges are not easy to explore, but because a slight difference in time, in the season, can completely change the lighting effects, the animation, the algae. Marine life cannot be studied at the rate of a conducted tour of Versailles.

In this rich shrubbery of a world where animals and plants, so closely related to each other, shy from man's gaze, life is not so haphazardly ordered as it seems. To a diver's eyes, sea creatures do not mill about like passers-by in a street. Life under water could, without exaggeration, be called static, congealed in its luxuriant surroundings and secret retreats. Nor is it only coral, gorgonia, mollusks, sea anemones, starfish, and actinia who can be called the permanent residents of a particular site. Day after day, and from dive to dive, the same rock cod and lamprey can be seen at the same hole, the same octopus lying in wait by its rocky hollow, the same group of minnows exercising in the same patch of sea.

Seaweeds and plants seem to the beginner like a confused mass in which he can scarcely distinguish shapes and colors. There are not only varying kinds of foliage, but all sorts of things embedded in them. The plant world is at its most exciting under water: here there are draperies and hangings lining the rocks, rather than the "carpets" dear to botanists. Their texture is so closely woven that the diver, grazing this woolly cloak, notices only the soft uniform surface of a field of grass or corn.

Discovery of this kind of universe can be made only by degrees. The pace of underwater hunters in search of prey is too fast for anyone really wanting to get to know the sea. Many divers protest that they see nothing because they are always on the move. The most exciting discoveries are reserved for those who can stay in one place for some time, compiling facts about all likely rocks and crevices. Pleasure in the submarine world is usually the reward for attention to detail.

The very technique of diving requires leisure. In an element eight times heavier than air, exertion is tiring and nervousness extravagant. And if one gets out of breath, one uses up a lot of air.

A restless temperament does not get the most out of miracles and life under water is composed of small miracles: the miracle of going down to lie on a bed of sand warmed, through the sea's density, by the heat of the sun; the miracle of going inch by inch over a sheer wall crammed with seaweeds, with the sea depths spread out like a blue sheet underneath; the miracle of coming unexpectedly on a narrow opening, a window cutting out to seaward a turquoise disk bejeweled with red plants.

It is here that the diver has a great advantage over the underwater fisherman. The latter flies over a universe which he only enters now and then for quick glimpses. But the diver reaches slowly down to the heart of the waters. He has time to dream. There is, surely, a world of difference between looking down over a street from the fifth floor and sauntering on the pavement. The diver has the whole mansion of the sea at his disposal: with a flick of his feet he can cruise around it from the outside, go down to the basement, and then up to the first floor, like a deep sea loafer.

A leaden sky slowly thickens about me. I move with small strokes in this atmosphere, threatened by submarine night. I continue to go down, slipping over rays of sunlight half strangled by shadow. A silky silence broken by the rhythm of my breathing, a comic gurgling, like pipe bubbles, accompanies my exploration of this endless blue silk.

I roll over on my side for the pleasure of lying on a bed made of water. At the same time I bask in my loneliness: the sea surface seems far away, no longer watered silk but a dazzle of stars behind a sash of mist. Someone overhead is throwing pearls into the sea. No, I am wrong; these pearls are born of my breath. Rainbow-colored bubbles climb at steep angles and break on the sky; there are fragments of gold everywhere. My own pattern of bubbles bears witness that I am still alive, that I have not foundered on the sea bed.

But can I convince others that I am alive? Am I sure of it myself? With the help of two steel bottles filled with air an idea keeps going in the heart of the sea, but how hazardously!

"We commit his body to the deep." The ritual phrase pronounced on board English ships when a corpse is thrown into the sea. I too am committed to the deep and similarly ballasted. Intoxication and dream cradle me. Reason still controls me, but, enticed by every kind of treachery, it is poised for mad flight to the sky, attracted by the slumbering phantoms of the deep. I am the sleeper of the sea, the drowned but conscious man drawn by the wires of dream into a dangerous monologue.

Now comes the worst stage: the liquid sky over me is blotted out and I know that it is no longer any use my looking for it. I recognize this grisaille in which every color is diluted: I am in the body of the sea. But the sea bed cannot be far off. I shall find land again, a false land rubbed away by water, but firm, almost reassuring. Points of brilliance dance in front of my eyes: phosphene. Oppressive majesty of the solitude in which I move, dazzled and blind. No more familiar fish, or rocky labyrinths. I have never gone down so far before. Perhaps I have overestimated my resources and agony is lying in wait among these shadows writhing below. A sky of terrifying storm has taken possession of the sea. I remember an evening when we were flying toward the African coast and found it guarded by black columns. We twisted between the pillars of tornadoes, into open corridors like so many snares. The snare is here, in this crevice which I am now going to explore.

Why do I think of Saint-Exupery? Because of the storm, the black sky, or because of the trap? The pilot of *Night Flight* also discovered the trap in an opening between cyclones, and he entered it as I am going to do, in spite of the distaste of that "I" who keeps watch, uneasy.

In my liquid sky I understand at last this fulfillment in insecurity that was Saint-Exupery's constant fulfillment. It was studiously hidden from the eyes of land dwellers and only showed itself in his writing. He made it the excuse for his art. In public he only built card houses with his strong and supple hands.

Land of men. Sky of men. Now, sea of men. Slow conquests. These metal constructions, which are called ships, airplanes, or diving suits, are worth less than the flesh which inhabits them. Man alone is interesting: it is he who dares the tempest, the cyclone in which Fabien perished, the abyss into which I am thrusting.

One must try to give a name to those confused reflections. But perhaps the human weight, the feeling of one's body that comes from submarine adventure and which machines take away, is the greatest sensation that the sea affords. Strange human weakness: a new world opens and man seeks an intercessor, the intervention of some enchanter to soothe the low reaches of his soul and persuade him to acts of daring. The low or the highest? That is a question for eternal debate. I am a lonely man who hesitates on the edge of the abyss and it is less with the abyss that I deliberate than with myself.

The further man explores the world of water, the deeper does he become involved in human problems. That, at any rate, has been my experience. The sea has met my demands with incalculable generosity. Whether it was a question of searching for the remains of ancient Mediterranean civilizations, turning over in the sea the problems of life, or nursing those non-Cartesian sides to the soul which claim their own portion of happiness, it has never failed me.

Perhaps there is, in fact, more to be got out of the sea than food reserves and increased scientific knowledge; an element of reassurance, giving us back confidence and balance, a reminder of true values, a biological wisdom. "I think," Robert Gruss has written, "that diving in self-contained equipment has created a new race: Men of the Sea. They view it in its totality, they bear its weight, and try to learn its secrets. I have never considered diving as an ordinary distraction, or even as a sport. The moment the sea closes over me I feel some great thing is happening. I feel a kind of awe, without really knowing why." Unless it is because the ocean depths give us the chance of a new humanism. Yet I think that we have not quite reached that stage; I'm not very happy about the word. Is it really a humanism, this slow impregnation, this gentle and pervasive enlightenment, prerogative of the "men of the sea"?

Anyway, the name doesn't matter. It is the assurance we get from our life under water that counts. Just as there is no part of the diver's body which remains unexercised or unsoothed in the sea, so there is no part of his mind not brought into play. What possibilities lie ahead!

CONTRIBUTORS

Writer and naturalist **DIANE ACKERMAN** is author of the bestseller, *A Natural History of the Senses*, and hosted the PBS television series based on the book. Her most recent book is *Cultivating Delight: A Natural History of My Garden*. Her other works of nonfiction include *The Rarest of the Rare, A Slender Thread,* and *Deep Play*. Her poetry has been collected in six books, including *Wife of Light, Jaguar of Sweet Laughter,* and *I Praise My Destroyer*.

JOHN BARR's sixth book of poems, *Grace*, was published by Story Line Press in 1999. A Wall Street investment banker by profession, he has also served as president of the Poetry Society of America and chairman of the board of Bennington College. In the company of his sons he has dived the Caribbean, Tonga and the Great Barrier Reef while his wife and daughter snorkled above.

DAVE BARRY has written a number of "short but harmful books," including *Babies and Other Hazards of Sex, Dave Barry's Complete Guide to Guys,* and *Dave Barry Is Not Taking This Sitting Down*. His column in the *Miami Herald* is syndicated in several hundred newspapers. He received the Pulitzer Prize for commentary in 1988, "pending a recount."

WILLIAM BEEBE was director of the New York Zoological Society's department of tropical research from 1899 until his death in 1962. In 1934 he made a record-breaking descent to 3,028 feet into the ocean in a bathysphere, which he wrote about in *Half Mile Down*. Among his other widely read books are *Jungle Peace, Galapagos,* and *The Arcturus Adventure*.

PETER BENCHLEY is the author of *Jaws*, the most successful first novel in literary history. Subsequent novels include *The Deep, The Island, The Girl of the Sea of Cortez*, and *Beast*. An ardent conservationist, Benchley's nonfiction work includes *Ocean Planet*.

NEAL BOWERS is Distinguished Professor of Liberal Arts and Sciences at Iowa State University. His books include three collections of poems (most recently, *Night Vision*), the novel *Loose Ends*, and a nonfiction account of being the victim of a chronic plagiarist (*Words for the Taking*). He has received a National Endowment for the Arts fellowship and the Frederick Bock Prize from *Poetry* magazine.

MICHAEL CADNUM has published more than a dozen novels, most recently *Redhanded, Rundown*, and *Raven of the Waves*. He also has published several books of poetry, including *Foreign Springs*, and illustrated books for children, including *The Lost and Found House* and *The Book of the Lion*.

TIM CAHILL's adventures have been chronicled in many magazine articles and books, including *A Wolverine Is Eating My Leg* and *Pecked to Death by Ducks*. A founding editor of *Outside* magazine, he writes regularly for *Rolling Stone, Esquire,* and *National Geographic,* among other publications. Co-author of the documentary films *Everest* and *The Living Sea*, he also is the author of *Dolphins*, published in 2000.

With his Aqua-Lung, his words and his images, **JACQUES COUSTEAU** opened the ocean to millions. He produced more than 100 films, winning the Academy Award and the Cannes Film Festival. He authored or co-authored more than fifty books, including *The Silent World*. His television documentary series, including *The Undersea World of Jacques Cousteau*, earned more than 40 Emmy nominations. The foremost environmentalist of his time, he was awarded France's Legion of Honor and the U.S. Presidential Medal of Freedom. In an interview shortly berfore his death at age 87 in 1997, he said: "The reason why I love the sea I cannot explain. It's physical. When you dive, you begin to feel like you're an angel."

Author, director, and producer **MICHAEL CRICHTON** began writing fiction while attending Harvard Medical School. His bestselling novels, many of which have been made into highly successful films, include *The Andromeda Strain, The Terminal Man, Congo, Jurassic Park, The Lost World, Airframe* and *Disclosure*. He has directed several films, including *Coma* and *The Great Train Robbery*. Crichton also is creator of the award-winning television drama, *ER*.

Journalist, archeologist, and diver **PHILIPPE DIOLÉ** wrote *Underwater Exploration* and *4,000 Years Under the Sea*. He also co-authored several books with Jacques Cousteau, including *Diving for Sunken Treasure, Life and Death in a Coral Sea,* and *The Whale: Mighty Monarch of the Sea*. Diole died in 1977.

JACK DRISCOLL's novel, *Lucky Man, Lucky Woman,* was published in 1998 and won the Pushcart Press Annual Editors Book Award. He also has written four books of poems and an award-winning collection of short stories *Wanting Only To Be Heard*. He has received the PEN/Nelson Algren Short Fiction Award and a National Endowment for the Arts Creative Writing Fellowship. His most recent novel is *Stardog*.

SUSAN FAWCETT is a textbook writer, poet, and environmentalist. A former English professor at Bronx Community College, CUNY, she is the author of *Evergreen: A Guide to Writing* and three other texts for under-prepared college writers. She has published a poetry chapbook, *Abandoned House*. Her poems and articles have appeared in *Poetry, The Nation, Ms. Magazine,* and many other publications.

In 1912, at the age of sixteen, **GUY GILPATRIC** set a world airplane altitude record of 4,665 feet. He went on to serve as a pilot in World War I, after which he became vice president of a major advertising agency in New York. Later, Gilpatric moved to the French Riviera, where he learned to spearfish and wrote the successful *Inchcliffe Castle* stories featuring merchant mariner and "disreputable roisterer" Mr. Glencannon. Gilpatric died in 1950.

Fictionalized as *Dolphin Adventure*, the incident described by **WAYNE GROVER** in "Dolphins" became a best-selling children's book. Four years later, the same dolphin, now an adult, saved Grover after he was lost at sea. This led to a second book, *Dolphin Treasure*, also a best seller. A third book, *Dolphin Freedom*, was published in 1999. Grover still sees his adopted dolphin during dives off the Florida coast.

A Newdigate prizewinner at Oxford, **JAMES HAMILTON-PATERSON's** newest novel, *Loving Monsters*, will be published in 2002. He has published two books of short stories, including *The Music;* several works of nonfiction, including *Playing with Water, A Very Personal War,* and *Three Miles Down;* books of poetry, and works of fiction for children. He lives in Italy and the Philippines.

STEPHEN HARRIGAN's bestselling novel, *The Gates of the Alamo*, was published in 2000. He also has written two other novels, *Aransas* and *Jacob's Well;* two collections of essays, *A Natural State* and *Comanche Midnight,* and many screenplays. His work also has appeared in *Texas Monthly, Esquire, New Yorker,* and *Outside*, among other periodicals. *Water and Light* was re-issued by the University of Texas Press in 1999.

A native of Austria, **HANS HASS** is a true diving pioneer. At age eighteen, he learned spearfishing from Guy Gilpatric on the French Riviera. At age nineteen, he took his first underwater photographs. At age twenty, he published his first book, *Hunting Underwater.* He went on to write more than twenty-five books, including *Diving to Adventure* and *Men and Sharks.* He also produced more than one hundred films and won an Academy Award. His most recent book is *From the Pioneering Days of Diving.* In 1972, Dr. Hass advocated a ban on spearguns.

JAMES JONES's first novel, *From Here to Eternity*, won the National Book Award in 1951 and sold more than four million copies. Based on his World War II experiences in the Army, where he won the Purple Heart and the Bronze Star, it also became an Academy Award-winning film. Later novels include *Some Came Running* and *The Thin Red Line.* Jones died in 1977.

LAURENCE LIEBERMAN is professor of English at the University of Illinois and poetry editor for the University of Illinois Press. He has published three books of criticism and 12 books of poetry, most recently *Flight from the Mother Stone* and *The Regatta in the Skies: Selected Long Poems*. His poems have appeared in *The Atlantic Monthly, New Republic, Sewanee Review* and *Southern Review*, among other publications.

CLARE BOOTHE LUCE was the author of several successful Broadway plays in the 1930s, including *The Women* and *Kiss the Boys Goodbye*. She also was an editor and correspondent for national magazines, a two-term Congresswoman from Connecticut and U.S. ambassador to Italy from 1953 to 1957. Married to Time, Inc. founder Henry Luce, she reportedly suggested the idea for *Life* magazine. She died in 1987.

WILLIAM MATTHEWS authored more than a dozen books of poetry, including *Ruining the New Road, Sleek for the Long Flight,* and *Time and Money*, which won the National Book Critics Circle Award for poetry. Matthews served as president of the Poetry Society of America and received the Ruth Lilly Award of the Modern Poetry Association. He died in 1997, and a posthumous collection, *After All: Last Poems*, was published in 1998.

BUCKY McMAHON writes about the outdoors and other topics for many national magazines, including *Esquire, Men's Journal, Outside* and *National Geographic Adventure*. A former field editor of *Rodale's Scuba Diving*, he lives near Tallahassee, Florida.

A diver and sailor, **DAVID POYER** graduated in 1971 from the United States Naval Academy, where his work is now required reading in the Literature of the Sea course. He has written more than a dozen novels, including *The Med, China Sea* and *Fire on the Waters*. Previous Tiller Galloway novels include *Hatteras Blue, Bahamas Blue,* and *Louisiana Blue*.

ADRIENNE RICH's first volume of poetry was chosen by W.H. Auden for the Yale Series of Younger Poets in 1951. Her poetry includes *The Dream of a Common Language, Time's Power,* and *Dark Fields of the Republic*.

Prose works include *On Lies, Secrets and Silence* and *Arts of the Possible*. She has received the Ruth Lilly Prize and a MacArthur Fellowship, among other honors.

DENNIS RYAN is an associate professor of English at Buena Vista University in Storm Lake, Iowa. His specialty is modern American literature. *Bahamas: In A White Coming On* was part of the *Contemporary Poets of Dorrance* series.

ROBERT STONE received the National Book Award in 1975 for his novel *Dog Soldiers*. Other novels include *Hall of Mirrors* and *Outerbridge Reach*. Stone has received a Guggenheim fellowship, an award from the American Academy and Institute of Arts and Letters, and a National Endowment for the Arts fellowship, among other honors. His most recent novel is *Damascus Gate*.

CARSTEN STROUD has written two award-winning crime novels, *Lizardskin* and *Sniper's Moon*. He also is the author of the bestselling *Close Pursuit: A Week in the Life of an NYPD Homicide Cop*. His latest novel, *Black Water Transit*, was published in 2001.

ANDREW TODHUNTER is the author of *Fall of the Phantom Lord* and *Dangerous Games*. A freelance writer and filmmaker, he writes for numerous national magazines on subjects ranging from rock climbing to nautical archaeology, including an ongoing series of articles for *The Atlantic Monthly*. Todhunter lives in Northern California with his wife and two children.

ACKNOWLEDGMENTS

First and foremost, we express our sincere gratitude to all the authors, agents and publishers who graciously granted their permission to reprint. Many not only shared their work; they provided suggestions and encouragement as well. Stephen Harrigan — whose book *Water and Light* should be read by every diver — deserves special thanks for generously offering his aid and insight many times over. It made the difference.

Thanks also to Cathy Stone, and to the staff of the Glenview (Illinois) Public Library, for their invaluable aid in research. David Cubbin not only shot the cover photograph, he supported our efforts from the beginning. Others who offered help and suggestions include Jean-Michel Cousteau, Carol Hastings, Steven Krolak, Jay Papasan, Alison and Mark Gaynor, Dr. Tracy Kittrell, Dr. Barb Endel, Char Miller, Frank Dineen, Dan Orr, Stan Waterman, Dee MacKenzie, Alice Bumgarner, Mark Suchomel and the staff at IPG. Jan Reid and David McCormick at Look Away Books believed in the project and provided expert guidance. This is their book, too.

Finally, our thanks go to Kristine; to Andrew, the best buddy a diver ever had; and to Jeannie — as always, for everything.

CREDITS

William Beebe, "Brothering Fish" from *Beneath Tropic Seas* (G.P. Putnam's Sons, 1928.) Copyright © 1928 by William Beebe.

Guy Gilpatric, "Merou the Bonehead" from *The Compleat Goggler* (Dodd, Mead & Company, Inc., 1957.) Copyright © 1938 by Guy Gilpatric. Reprinted by permission of John Rexford.

Jacques Cousteau, "A State of Transport," from *The Silent World* (Harper & Row, 1953.) Copyright © 1953 by Jacques Cousteau. Reprinted by permission of HarperCollins Publishers, Inc.

Clare Boothe Luce, "The Reef and Its Treasure" reprinted courtesy of *Sports Illustrated*, September 16, 1957. Copyright © 1957, Time Inc. All rights reserved.

Peter Benchley, "I Know What I'm Doing Here, I Think" from *Holiday* magazine, August 1969. Copyright © 1969 by Peter Benchley. Reprinted by permission of International Creative Management, Inc.

James Jones, "His Capital M Manhood" from *Go To The Widow-Maker*. Copyright © 1967 by James Jones. Used by permission of Dell Books, a division of Bantam Doubleday Dell Publishing Group, Inc. and the Tessa Sayle Agency.

Dave Barry, "Blub Story: A Very Deep Experience" from *Tropic* magazine, February 19, 1989. Copyright © 1989 by Dave Barry. Reprinted by permission of the author.

Wayne Grover, "Dolphins" from *Sea Frontiers* magazine, January/February 1989. Copyright © 1989 by Wayne Grover. Reprinted by permission of the author and *Sea Frontiers* magazine.

Carsten Stroud, "The Dolphin and the Shark" from *Reader's Digest* magazine, November 1979. Copyright © 1979 by Carsten Stroud. Reprinted by permission of the author.